THE LEFT SIDE OF HISTORY

Kristen Ghodsee

THE LEFT SIDE
OF HISTORY

WORLD WAR II and the UNFULFILLED PROMISE
of COMMUNISM in EASTERN EUROPE

Duke University Press   Durham and London   2015

© 2015 Duke University Press
All rights reserved
Printed in the United States of America on acid-free paper ∞
Designed by Heather Hensley
Typeset in Minion Pro by Tseng Information Systems, Inc.

Library of Congress Cataloging-in-Publication Data
Ghodsee, Kristen Rogheh, 1970–
The left side of history : World War II and the
unfulfilled promise of communism in Eastern Europe /
Kristen Ghodsee.
pages cm
Includes bibliographical references and index.
ISBN 978-0-8223-5823-7 (cloth : alk. paper)
ISBN 978-0-8223-5835-0 (pbk. : alk. paper)
1. Communism—Bulgaria—History. 2. Anti-fascist
movements—Bulgaria—History. 3. Post-communism—
Bulgaria. I. Title.
HX363.G48 2015
940.53′499—dc23   2014022131

Cover (from left): Frank Thompson in 1939;
Elena Lagadinova in 1945

FOR MY DAUGHTER—
may she always have heroes

CONTENTS

MAPS AND ILLUSTRATIONS

How do you write a book by mistake? I am still trying to sort this one out. In 2010, I began research for a different project on the activities of a communist-era women's committee in Bulgaria. This was going to be my fourth book on this small, southeast European country, but it would be my first about life before 1989. Spending time in the archives in the capital city of Sofia was a nice change of pace from the rural fieldwork I had done before. As I lost myself in the boxes and folders of documents, I became obsessed with the past. For me this past had a specific face — that of Major Frank Thompson, a twenty-three-year-old British officer sent to Bulgaria to help support a local partisan resistance force against the country's pro-German monarchy in 1944. But this interest in World War II guerrillas was tangential to my project. I never intended to write a book about it.

The beginning of this new archival research, however, coincided with the start of the Greek anti-austerity riots. While I tried to lose myself in historical records, the ongoing political chaos in Bulgaria's southern neighbor kept distracting me. In April 2012, a seventy-seven-year-old retired pharmacist committed suicide in Athens. Dimitris Christoulas shot himself in the head in the middle of Syntagma Square just across from the Greek parliament. Civil unrest in Greece intensified as the ex-pharmacist became another martyr of the Eurozone crisis. In his suicide note, Christoulas compared the current Greek government with the Greek leaders who had collaborated with the Nazis during World War II.

The political chaos spread from Greece to Bulgaria in February 2013. Massive demonstrations against foreign-owned electricity distribution monopolies forced the Bulgarian government to resign after violent clashes between police and protestors. Bulgarians, like their Greek neighbors, were fed up with the corruption of their political elites. Bulgaria was the poorest country in the European Union, and many citizens lived in crushing poverty that no democratically elected government had been able to reverse. A caretaker cabinet took power and scheduled snap elections for May 2013, but there was growing doubt that another round of voting would be enough to solve Bulgaria's deeper economic problems. In towns and villages across the country, ordinary men and women gave up hope.

One day in March, I left the archives to grab a snack. There was a foul stench in the air, but I was not able to figure out what it was. I was back at my desk about an hour later when I learned that a fifty-one-year-old man had dumped a can of kerosene over his head and set himself alight in front of the Bulgarian presidency, only a block away from the archives. This self-immolation was the sixth in the span of about a month. From the notes some of the victims left behind, it was clear that these were political acts, born of extreme frustration and despair.

I tried to continue with my original research project, but grew more distracted by current events in Europe. Across the Continent, it was easy to see how the crushing social effects of austerity had fatigued and radicalized populations. Protests were taking place in other countries besides Greece and Bulgaria. In Spain, the *indignados* (the outraged ones) had continued their massive, anti-austerity protests for more than four years. Protests spread in Italy as well. In September 2013, thousands of Poles took to the streets of Warsaw demanding the resignation of the government. Marching under the banner of "Solidarity," Poles demonstrated against their worsening economy.

The anti-austerity indignation fueled popular support for relatively new political parties on the far right. Since the beginning of the Greek anti-austerity riots, a neo-Nazi party called Golden Dawn had been gaining popularity among those Greeks frustrated by the economic situation and aggravated by European Union pressure and intervention. Black-shirted, torch-bearing rioters had massed in Athens shouting, "Greece is only for the Greeks." Golden Dawn began setting up Greek-only food banks and doing Greek-only blood drives.

Golden Dawn gangs (with the implicit support of the Greek police) started by targeting Muslims and immigrants from North Africa and the Middle East, but then turned their attentions to Greeks with leftist political sympathies. In September 2013, fifty Golden Dawn activists carrying crowbars and bats attacked a group of fellow Greeks who were distributing literature in a working-class, immigrant neighborhood in Athens. Nine victims of this attack were sent to the hospital with serious injuries. A few days later, a Golden Dawn activist stabbed to death a left-wing hip-hop artist, sparking new riots. The streets of Greece's capital were filled with teargas as Greeks protested against both the economic conditions and their fascist spawn.

The far right was making a comeback in Bulgaria as well. The snap elections in May 2013 brought to power a new government, which took office with the support of a nationalist party called Ataka (Attack), characterized in no small part by its harshly negative attitude toward Bulgarians of Turkish or Roma descent. The leader of Ataka threatened peaceful antigovernment protesters with "civil war" and had seized upon the political frustration of poor ethnic Bulgarians outside of Sofia. Ataka's popular support paved the way for other far-right parties, offering similar anti-Turkish and anti-Roma rhetoric.

Watching the situation in Europe, and especially in Bulgaria and Greece, I could not help but think that this had all happened before: a massive economic recession followed by the rise of xenophobic right-wing parties using the language of nationalism to mobilize popular support for projects of ethnic purification. The irony here was that this time it was primarily the Germans who were leading the EU into imposing austerity on countries like Greece. Of all nations, it seemed to me that Germany should be the first to realize that severe belt-tightening imposed by foreign powers can lead to the democratic election of less-than-desirable political parties.

Given the widespread dissatisfaction with global capitalism and the politics of austerity, the resurgence of right-wing, nationalistic discourse was perhaps no surprise. Men and women across Europe were looking for alternatives to globalization and its promotion of outsourcing and immigration as tools to control labor costs. Like the Occupy Wall Street movement in the United States, the anti-austerity protests in Europe started out as a movement against the global financial crisis, but not in favor of any particular alternative. The far right had merely seized upon preexisting popular outrage and twisted it to its own purposes.

In the wake of the economic crisis that began in 2008, neoliberal capitalism, particularly as practiced in the poorest parts of Europe, was clearly

"Death to Capitalism" with a hammer and sickle and a red star

having its problems. People were suffering; people were angry; people were looking for viable political alternatives. As I watched the rise of right-wing parties with trepidation, I found myself reflecting more and more on the local history of World War II, specifically about Frank Thompson and the Bulgarian partisans he had been sent to assist. They had openly called themselves "communists," and they believed in the transnational solidarity of all working people. They struggled against the Nazis and their allies on the far right. Thompson and the Bulgarian partisans fought on what one might call the left side of history, a left that has been deemed out of bounds in mainstream political discourse for decades.

But now I started noticing new graffiti around Sofia. Slogans like "Oligarchy = Capitalism" and "No Poor" began to appear in red spray paint on the sides of buildings, always accompanied by a red star and a hammer and sickle. On a bus stop, I saw the acronym CCCP, the Cyrillic version of USSR. On Boulevard Bulgaria, I stumbled upon a series of slogans spray painted in red where they would be visible to thousands of motorists as they inched their way through the center of Sofia during the morning and evening rush hours. Walking farther toward the National Palace of Culture, I saw the slogan "Death to Capitalism!" A bit farther down someone had simply written the word Комунизм. Communism.

"Have you noticed all the communist graffiti around Sofia?" I asked one of my closest Bulgarian friends.

He nodded. "Yes," he said. "And anarchist, too."

"I've never seen so much of it before," I said.

"There has never been so much." He exhaled a lungful of smoke from a Marlboro Red.

"Do you think it is just a couple of kids?" I said.

My friend shrugged. "I think it is frustration. A lot of people are tired of democracy. It's not working."

Like my friend, most Bulgarians do not make a semantic distinction between the words "democracy" and "capitalism." For them, the capitalist ideal of the profit motive and unrestrained free markets goes hand in hand with so-called free elections, which all too often seem controlled by the economic elite who can afford the most advertising. For many Bulgarians, everyday life was much worse after the collapse of communism in 1989 and the introduction of "free" elections and "free" markets.[1] As I returned to take pictures of the pro-communist graffiti with my camera phone a week later, I wondered if the political future of Bulgaria could literally be discerned from the writing on the wall.

On August 20, 2013, in a situation much like what had occurred in Bulgaria earlier that year, the Czech parliament voted to dissolve itself, paving the way for snap elections.[2] Many observers at the time suggested that the new Czech elections would mean a return to power for the Communist Party of Bohemia and Moravia (referred to by the acronym KSČM). Although the Social Democrats would most likely win the plurality, in order to rule it would be necessary to form a coalition with the KSČM. The Social Democrats had already stated publicly that they were willing to do this. After more than two decades out of power, the Communist Party was poised to make a stunning comeback due to the lingering effects of the global financial crisis.[3]

In both Bulgaria and the Czech Republic, however, many made concerted efforts to smash any possibility of communism's return, even in the face of a less-than-savory right-wing alternative. At the prospect of the return of Czech communists to parliament, former Czech president Vaclav Klaus flew into an apoplectic fit. The conservative Klaus argued that leftist radicals wanted to destroy Czech democracy. He issued a manifesto urging the "Democrats of Europe" to wake up to the resurgence of leftist parties and their promotion of "human-rightism, environmentalism, Europeanism, NGOism and homosexualism."[4]

Klaus's tirade was just one voice in a sea of detractors. In the quarter of a century since 1989, the complexities of ordinary people's attitudes toward the communist past have been bulldozed by both the official history and the popular imagination of this past. This "official" history is dominated by a wide coalition of scholars, activists, and politicians like Klaus operating on both sides of the former Iron Curtain. Books, articles, memory projects, museum exhibitions, and so forth have combined to paint a picture of communism as an irredeemable evil.[5]

At the exact moment when ordinary people are searching for political alternatives, many official historical institutes are supported (often with funds from the West) to discredit communism. For instance, in Bulgaria, one finds an official Institute for Studies of the Recent Past (ISRP), and in neighboring Romania an Institute for the Investigation of Communist Crimes and the Memory of the Romanian Exile (IICCMRE).[6] The majority of the scholarship emerging from these institutes focuses on the crimes of the communist era: the secret police, the wide network of informers collaborating with the state, and the testimonies of people sent to labor camps.

Such strident anticommunist rhetoric demonizes anyone who once called himself or herself a "communist" or who believed in the communist ideal. After 1989, in towns and villages across Bulgaria, statues of local heroes who lost their lives fighting against the Nazi-allied Bulgarian government during World War II were defaced and torn down because the people in question had been members of the Communist Party. The thousands of Bulgarian partisans are today remembered as "red scum."

In her provocative book *The Communist Horizon* (2012), Jodi Dean offers a diagnosis of the widespread anticommunist rhetoric.[7] As Dean notes, when we think of capitalism, we do not think only of its worst excesses, for example, slavery, price-gouging monopolies, rampant unemployment, or wild inequalities in wealth. The history of capitalism is allowed to be dynamic and nuanced. By contrast, if one utters the word "communism" in academic circles, an automatic chain of nefarious word association usually follows. First, Dean argues that communism is equated with the Soviet Union. Communist experiments in Poland, Hungary, Yugoslavia, Mongolia, China, Vietnam, Cuba, Zambia, Yemen, India, Angola, Mozambique, and so forth are ignored. Second, the entire seventy-year history of the USSR is reduced to include only the twenty-six years of Joseph Stalin's rule, so that his worst crimes come to exemplify the so-called true nature of communism. The ultimate collapse of the Soviet Union is seen as the inevitable result of Stalinism and the economic stagnation and consumer shortages that plagued the planned economy. The experience of the Soviet Union, its violent authori-

An anticommunist sign from the protests in Sofia in the summer of 2013

tarianism and its economic inefficiencies, becomes the "proof" that communism is an ideal that can never work in practice. In the popular imagination, communism, therefore, becomes a static, fixed point, one that will *always* end with purges and the gulag.

An excellent example of the way that American conservatives automatically reduce all leftist politics to Stalinism occurred in the days following the death of the legendary folk singer Pete Seeger in January 2014. Those who opposed Seeger's long and varied history of left activism immediately seized upon his early refusal to recognize Stalin as anything but a "hard driver." Headlines like "Seeger Was a Useful Idiot for Stalin," "Pete Seeger, Stalin and God," "The Death of 'Stalin's Songbird,'" and "Obama Praises Stalinist and Folk Singer Pete Seeger" spread across the Internet. An image accompanying the article "Pete 'Potemkin' Seeger: Stalin's Little Minstrel" on the website www.renewamerica.com featured an elderly Seeger singing to a rainbow-haloed image of Stalin superimposed into the frame. Writing for the *Daily Beast*, Michael Moynihan asserted, "Pete Seeger's love of Stalinist ideals endured through the nightmare of pogroms and purge trials in the Soviet Union. His totalitarian sympathies should not be whitewashed."[8] It did not matter that Seeger openly renounced Stalin in his book *Where Have All the Flowers Gone* (1993),[9] or that he actually left the Communist Party of the United States in 1949. For conservative journalists and historians, the mere fact that Seeger identified with communist ideals meant that his entire political ideology was Stalinist. As the economist Paul Krugman observed in an astute op-ed in the *New York Times*, "If you so much as mention income inequality, you'll be denounced as the second coming of Joseph Stalin."[10]

Jodi Dean's analysis rang true to me as I contemplated the lives of Frank Thompson, the young Englishman who was murdered in Bulgaria in 1944, and the Bulgarian partisans who fought alongside him. These people were communists, but they were also idealists who fought and sometimes died for those ideals. As a boy in England, Frank Thompson loved poetry and philology. Before his death, he would learn to speak ten languages because he believed that a new world was coming, one in which the peoples of all countries would live together in peace. He was eighteen years old when he joined the Communist Party of Great Britain. Frank Thompson was only nineteen when he volunteered for military service two days before the official British declaration of war against Adolf Hitler. At twenty-three he parachuted into Bulgarian-occupied Serbia to help supply the underground partisan resistance movement.

As I learned more about World War II in Bulgaria, I discovered a family of guerrilla fighters: a father, three brothers, and a young sister. This family, the Lagadinovs, also loved poetry. The father had founded a branch of the Bulgarian Communist Party in his hometown in the 1920s. The eldest son, Kostadin, became politically active as a teenager. For his part in distributing communist newspapers and pamphlets, Kostadin was persecuted and forced to flee to the Soviet Union when he was nineteen. There he spent years in exile before returning to Bulgaria to help lead the partisan resistance in 1941.

The middle and younger brothers of this Bulgarian family, Assen and Boris, also leftist activists, spent their childhoods in and out of trouble for spreading "dangerous" ideas. Their sister, the youngest member of the family, was the only female in the house (her mother had died when she was four). Little Elena began actively supporting her brothers when she was eleven years old. She was fourteen when the Bulgarian police burned down her natal home. She fled into the mountains to take up arms and join the resistance. The Lagadinovs huddled around their small fires reciting from memory the verses of the great Bulgarian poet Hristo Botev. In poetry, they found inspiration.

It was hard for me to think of these people simply as "red scum." It seems that we need to go back and revisit the stories of people like Frank Thompson and the Lagadinovs. Communism may be making a bit of a comeback in Europe, but it is also the case that some political elites are working harder than ever to stop it by blackwashing its history. Who will win this struggle? It is impossible to say. Anyone can see that there is massive frustration with global capitalism today, a deep yearning for some sort of alternative. If the very idea of a communist ideal is obliterated, tarred over with the black brush of Stalinism, then the remaining alternative to unfettered neoliberalism will be the hate-filled, scapegoating, nationalist rhetoric of the far right. I find this terrifying.

The pages that follow tell the tales of a handful of men and women who lived through some of the most tumultuous events of the twentieth century: World War II, the Cold War, and the collapse of communism in Eastern Europe. We need to understand people like Frank Thompson and the Lagadinovs. We should try to comprehend the cause they were fighting for, without the preconception of communism as one homogenous and undifferentiated evil. To be sure, we need to understand how their ideas could, and sometimes did, go wrong in practice. But we must also be open to the possibility that communism had beneficial effects in terms of industrialization, mass education, literacy, and women's rights. Most importantly, we should endeavor to understand how a political ideal, openly referred to as communist, could inspire both a privileged English gentleman and a poor peasant girl to take up arms and risk their lives.

Finally, I do not come to these stories as an objective bystander attempting to answer broad theoretical questions. I write these words as someone who is trying to make sense of an uncertain future. Although I have been studying the region for the better part of two decades, this book is not a conventional history or a traditional ethnography. There is too much present in the past, and too much past in the present to be able to draw neat disciplinary boundaries. The complexity of the politics of cultural memory in Eastern Europe today transcends the bounds of any one scholarly field.[11]

Nor am I trying to produce any kind of comprehensive or "revisionist" account of World War II in the Balkans. There are many books cited in the bibliography that provide a more thorough analysis of events. Rather than focus on the broad sweep of political or diplomatic history, I concentrate on the stories of a few men and women who lived this history. As an ethnographer, my goal is to share this little window onto the past, and how this window helped me to see that past in a new way. So I suppose this book is part memoir as well—a journey through my own discoveries and digressions. As an American, I grew up with a lot of stereotypes about communists, and especially communist leaders. While I wrote this book, I learned that there were men and women who struggled to make communism a better reality than it came to be in the end. There were dreamers among those whom I had been taught to view as self-serving hypocrites. I could not see this before I started digging in the archives and interviewing the handful of remaining survivors.

Sometime in the late 1980s, Stanford University invited E. P. Thompson to give a series of lectures. He focused these talks on the contested history of his older brother, Frank. E. P. explained that:

> [It is we,] in the present, who must always give meaning to that inert and finished past. For history is forever unresolved, it remains as a field of unfinished possibilities, it lies behind us with all its contradictions of motives and cancelled intentions and we — acting in the present — reach back, refuse some possibilities and select and further others.[12]

In the pages that follow, I am reaching back to an unfinished past to rescue this small handful of clobbered idealists from the dustbin of memory. Social history teaches us to appreciate how ordinary people experienced significant events, and ethnography allows us to understand how individuals find meaning in their everyday lives. Small histories can reveal grand narratives, and grand narratives can inspire new ideas. Some prefer to start with the ideas. I think it's better to start with the stories.

Transliterating the Bulgarian Cyrillic alphabet into Latin letters presents particular challenges, as there are many different accepted traditions and much inconsistency regarding usage. The most tricky characters are the Bulgaria ф (which can be transliterated as "ff" or "v"), the ъ (which can be written as an "a" or "u" or "ŭ"), and the ц (which is either "tz" or "ts"). Throughout the book, when doing my own transliterations from the Bulgarian, I have chosen to use a "v" for ф, a "ts" for ц, and the character "a" for ъ. I also transliterate the "ж" as "zh," and the "я" as "ya." However, in the case of previously published materials and names already transliterated into Latin letters by the authors, I have reproduced the words in their published transliterated form. I have also retained the English spellings of well-known geographical names such as Sofia and Bulgaria (rather than Sofiya and Balgariya). As a result, there will inevitably be some inconsistencies in the text.

Bulgaria (post–World War II borders). Map courtesy of D-Maps.com, with editing by
Hayden Sartoris and Christine Riggio.

PART I | THE WAY WE REMEMBER THE PAST DETERMINES OUR DREAMS FOR THE FUTURE

Тоз, който падне в бой за свобода,
той не умира: него жалеят
земя и небо, звяр и природа
и певци песни за него пеят . . .

(He who falls in the fight for freedom
He does not die: he is mourned
By land and sky, beast and nature
And troubadours sing for him their songs . . .)

—"HADZHI DIMITAR," HRISTO BOTEV (1848–1876)

1 | THE MYSTERIOUS MAJOR FRANK THOMPSON

I rarely pay attention to street names unless I am lost. Although I learned the Cyrillic alphabet early on, I tended to navigate my way around Sofia, the capital city of Bulgaria, by landmark. I must have walked up and down Major Thompson Street a hundred times because it was in the neighborhood where my in-laws lived. I assumed this Thompson was not a Bulgarian, but it never occurred to me to ask who he was. Not until a decade later, in a conversation with an octogenarian British physicist in Princeton, New Jersey, would I learn the identity of the mysterious major. This revelation would more or less consume the next six years of my life.

In 2007, Freeman Dyson was eighty-two years old, forty-five years my senior. He was an emeritus professor in the School of Natural Sciences at the Institute for Advanced Study in Princeton, New Jersey. I was a junior professor, a member in the School of Social Sciences for the academic year 2006–2007. I often saw Professor Dyson at the three o'clock tea held each day in Fuld Hall. I was too shy to approach him, for he was the academic equivalent of a rock star, a lead singer for the global scientific community. He was also a known contrarian and had recently outraged his colleagues by saying that the problem of global warming had been grossly exaggerated. In addition to his scholarly fame, Dyson enjoyed the adulation of the wider *Star Trek* geekiverse for the inclusion of a "Dyson sphere" in the 130th episode of *The Next Generation*.[1] He seemed to me a god among mortals.

After six months of crippling intimidation, I found myself right behind him in the lunch line at the institute cafeteria. He seemed so unassuming as he considered the choice between the blackened haddock and the baked acorn squash stuffed with quinoa.

"Uh . . . Professor Dyson?" I said.

"Yes," he said, looking back.

I hesitated. He kept his eyes fixed on me.

"It is an honor to meet you," I said. "My name is Kristen Ghodsee. I'm a member here this year. In social sciences."

"I see," he said. "Are you an economist?"

I shook my head. "No, I am an ethnographer. I work in Bulgaria. I'm writing a book about Bulgaria."

"Bulgaria?" His eyes widened. "Are you Bulgarian?"

I told him I wasn't.

"Do you speak Bulgarian?" he said.

"Yes," I said. "I've been doing fieldwork there for the last ten years."

"Well, then," he said. "You must come and see me. I have a dear friend who died in Bulgaria many years ago. Maybe you can help me with something."

"I'd love to," I said, my heart thudding. It was perhaps the first time in the United States that I told someone that I worked on Bulgaria and received genuine interest in return.

I made my appointment with Professor Dyson's assistant. I met him in his office on the second floor of Bloomberg Hall. I was very nervous. Our conversation was casual and friendly; he slowly put me at ease by regaling me with stories of his early days at the institute, the one thing we had in common. He had first come to Princeton in 1953 when Robert Oppenheimer was the director and Albert Einstein was still in residence.

"I don't remember much about Einstein, but I do remember seeing T. S. Eliot in Fuld Hall. I was too shy to speak with him," he said.

"Yes," I said. "I can imagine."

We spoke for a while about science and science fiction, a genre of which we were both great fans. Our conversation flowed to Charles Simonyi, the president of the institute's board of trustees. He had just returned from a two-week trip to the International Space Station. For the mere sum of $25 million, Simonyi had become the world's fifth space tourist.

"So what do you think of space tourism?" I said. "Is this where we'll all be spending our holidays in the future?"

"I have the feeling that this sort of extravagant space exploring by private

Freeman Dyson in 2007

citizens does have a future," Dyson said. "But, of course, I was brought up as a socialist and the idea of extravagant wealth is evil in itself."

I looked around his spacious office. Along the walls stood floor-to-ceiling bookshelves, crammed full of volumes on physics, biology, mathematics, philosophy, history, and literature. The surface of his desk was piled high with papers, files, and books that he was going to review for the *New York Review of Books*.

"Where I work in Bulgaria," I said, "there are still a lot of people who think that extravagant private wealth is evil."

Professor Dyson tilted his head. He smiled at me. It seemed to me a conspiratorial smile, as if we were now going to share secrets. I was amazed at how comfortable I felt in his office. He was so soft-spoken and modest, and I could not believe how intimidated I was by him just one week earlier. Perhaps he knew that. Perhaps he told me that story about T. S. Eliot on purpose.

"Yes, we see that in Germany very strongly," he said, leaning back in his chair. "I don't know whether you are familiar with Germany, because my wife is German, and we still have family there. And, of course, the Easterners and Westerners are still very different. She is an Easterner. I used to visit the village where her family lived. And in those times, during the communist times, it was actually a happy place. The system worked. The Germans were very proud of it. And they said, 'After all, we invented communism. The Russians messed it up, but we can actually make it work.'"

I was surprised to learn that Professor Dyson knew so much about Eastern Europe. Many of the scientists of my generation are a narrowly focused lot. There are geniuses to be sure, but not always the sort of genius that extended beyond their subject area. Dyson was of a generation that still cultivated the idea of the Renaissance man: a scholar who was widely read and conversant in many disciplines. I also knew that Dyson had served in the British Bomber Command during World War II. Though his mind was dedicated to mathematics, his life had been bound up with politics.

"And they did make it work in a sense," Dyson said. "That society was a very humane society, unless you wanted to be a politician. Of course they were brutal if you got involved in any sort of political activity. But for the people in the villages, it actually worked. The village was prosperous. It was growing stuff it sold to the Russians for fixed prices. It was a fixed economy and everybody had a job. Everybody had security. And the village actually had a zoo, which was their pride and joy. The school children took care of the animals. It was run by the local Communist Party. They actually ran it well. There was a professional veterinarian in charge. It was a great asset to the village."

He paused. He looked away from me and glanced at the screen of his computer. I guessed that an e-mail had arrived. He was adjudicating its relative importance.

"But, of course, as soon as the reunification happened it was destroyed," he said, turning back to me. "It then had to pay for itself, and there was no way you could sustain a zoo in a village like that. So that was just one of the many things that was destroyed. I don't know what the villagers would say today. Of course, the village is transformed totally now. Most of the people who lived there were out of work and had to move into the cities. They have been replaced by stockbrokers and business people who have country cottages there. The village has now been gentrified. They don't do much farming there anymore. But it is just as beautiful as it ever was."

Dyson leaned forward over his wide desk. "We had cousins in Leipzig who joined the march when they began marching against the communist government," he said. "They were trying to reform the communist government. They marched at the same time the Solidarity people were marching in Poland. It was part of the same movement for reform. But one thing they were not marching for was to be swallowed by the West. They did not have that in mind at all. What they wanted was to have a government of their own that was more responsive. And that would sort of be like Austria, an independent country. But what happened was totally opposite. They were immediately swallowed by the West, and all of their institutions were upset and destroyed. And there is still a lot of bitterness, of course."

"Yes," I said. "There is a lot of bitterness in Bulgaria, too. Democracy is not what they expected it to be."

I knew that East Germans had only narrowly voted to adopt the West German constitution. Some GDR citizens would have preferred to reform their brand of socialism rather than embrace capitalism. For many East Germans reunification felt more like a territorial grab by the West, something the Social Democratic politician Matthias Platzeck would refer to as an *Anschluss*, making reference to Hitler's annexation of Austria in 1938.[2] In Bulgaria, many were reluctant to see their whole system dismantled and voted their own "reformed" Communist Party right back into power in the first free democratic elections after 1989. Like the East Germans, Bulgarians wanted change, but they wanted to be in control of that change.

In the popular memory, the peaceful revolutions of 1989 were a triumph of democracy over despotism. East European men and women rose up to throw off the yoke of communism and rushed headlong into the open arms of the West (or at the very least into the Western department stores). But even from those earliest years, many were wary of the promises of liberal democracy and free markets and the economic inequality and social hardships they might bring.[3]

I told Professor Dyson that a lot of Bulgarians were also nostalgic about the past.

"Bulgaria," Professor Dyson said. "Yes, of course. You work in Bulgaria. I had almost forgotten about Frank. Will you be going to Bulgaria any time soon?"

"In a month," I said.

"Good," he said, staring back at his computer screen.

"I'd be happy to help in any way I can," I said.

"There was a young man, a classmate of mine, who died fighting with the partisans in Bulgaria," he said. His eyes turned back toward me. "We were at school together at Winchester in 1937. I was twelve and he was fifteen. Do you know E. P. Thompson?"

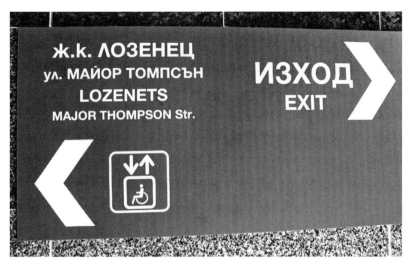
A sign for Major Thompson Street in Sofia

"The historian?" I said.

"Yes," Professor Dyson said. "Frank Thompson was his older brother. Frank was my friend before the war. Before he went to Oxford, fell in love with Iris Murdoch, and joined the Communist Party. There is a train station in Bulgaria named after him, did you know that?" Dyson said.

"No," I said. "I didn't. But I think there is a street named after him in Sofia. Near where my ex-in-laws live. It's called Major Thompson."

"Yes, that's him," Professor Dyson said, smiling. "I've been collecting information on Frank for many years. The circumstances surrounding his death in Bulgaria are a bit suspicious. There are documents about Frank that should be in the British archives, but are missing. It's a mysterious business. I think there are some books written about Frank in Bulgarian. I'd very much appreciate it if you could bring one or two of them back for me if you happen to come across them while you are there."

"I will," I said. "I can find them in the National Library."

"Good," he said. "That would be very good."

A month later, in the National Library in Sofia, it was easy enough to finger through the old card catalog for the subject: Thompson, Frank. I immediately found an eponymous book published in Bulgarian in 1980. I wrote the bibliographic information down in my notebook. That afternoon I walked

Frank Thompson
with his pipe

from Sofia University to Slaveikov Square where the booksellers crowd together in an outdoor market. Just up from the square on Solunska Street, one finds antiquarian booksellers. If I wanted to buy a book published before 1989, it was here I had to look. The booksellers were middle-aged men who spent most of the day smoking, chatting, and playing backgammon as they waited for customers.

"I'm looking for a book about Frank Thompson," I said to the first vendor in Bulgarian. "From 1980."

"Frank Thompson? The Englishman?"

"Yes," I said. "The authors are Gyurova and Transki."

"Thompson," the man said. "A great hero."

"Do you have the book?" I said.

"No," he said. "There isn't quite the market for *those* kinds of books anymore."

"What kind of books?" I said.

"Books about heroes," he said. "You can try one of my colleagues."

I walked up the street to the next vendor. "I'm looking for a book about Frank Thompson."

"The English communist?" he said, peering at me through squinted eyes. He looked a bit drunk.

Dyson had told me that Thompson had joined the Communist Party at Oxford. That technically made him a communist. "Yes," I said. "Frank Thompson, the Englishman. He died in Bulgaria."

"Filthy communists," the man said, waving me away. "I don't sell books about filthy communists."

I walked on to the next stall.

"I am trying to find a book published in 1980. It is called *Frank Thompson*. The authors are Gyurova and Transki." I tried to keep my voice librarian neutral. I wanted to buy a book. I did not want to get in a political debate.

"Maybe," the man said.

He stared down at his boxes. I watched him for a few moments as he walked his fingers across the spines of his books. I thought maybe I should just return to the National Library and xerox their copy. But I had hoped to bring Professor Dyson the actual book. After several moments, the bookseller pulled a thin paperback out of the third box and showed it to me. The cover featured the face of a young man smoking a pipe. He was looking, with a furrowed brow, off to the left of the page. It was a handsome face, and the young man seemed lost in thought. Was this Professor Dyson's childhood friend? The title read *Франк Томпсън*. I had found it.

2 | A COMMUNIST BY ANY OTHER NAME . . .

Professor Dyson was quite pleased with the book I brought back for him in June. He could read Cyrillic and a bit of Russian, and said that he had a Bulgarian friend who could translate for him if necessary.

"It will be interesting to read the Bulgarian side of the story," he said.

"I think there may be another book or two," I said. "I'll be going back in December. I'll keep an eye out for them."

"Yes," he said. "Please do."

"So was Frank really a communist?" I said.

"He always had a great admiration for communism, and he became a member of the Communist Party of Great Britain," Professor Dyson said. "Of course, it all meant something different back then."

"Because of the war?" I asked.

"Because of the world," Dyson said.

Europe in the 1930s was indeed a very different world. The stock market crash of 1929 had plunged the United States and much of western Europe into the Great Depression. Market speculation caused the suffering of millions of men, women, and children. Europe was still struggling to recover from World War I, and the Germans had been forced to pay crippling reparations after its military defeat. The desperate poverty of the Continent gave rise to new nationalist parties based on racism and xenophobia. As fascism spread, working-class political movements were mercilessly crushed by the likes of Francisco Franco, Benito Mussolini, and Hitler. Those who called themselves "communists," "socialists," or even "social democrats" were vilified and persecuted. Hitler filled the first concentration camps with German communists who challenged Nazi rule, forcing them to wear the inverted red triangle.[1] In many countries it was an act of great courage to openly call oneself a "communist."

I left Princeton that August, but professional obligations would bring me back at least twice a year. Between 2007 and 2013, I often met and had lunch with Professor Dyson when I visited the institute. We developed a kind of friendship around "Frank" and would talk about contemporary political developments in Bulgaria. Dyson had bright, inquisitive eyes and always seemed keen to hear about my latest research projects. He took the time to read two of the books I had written about everyday life in communist and postcommunist Bulgaria. It was as if Professor Dyson felt closer to Frank Thompson by learning about the country in which he fought and died.

At Firestone Library, I tracked down the first article that Freeman Dyson wrote about Frank Thompson. It was a piece published in the *New Yorker* in 1979 called "Disturbing the Universe," a sort of autobiographical essay about the scientific life in the twentieth century. Dyson and Thompson had been schoolmates at Winchester, a grand old boarding school dating from the Middle Ages where boys were called "scholars" and had uniforms that included black flowing robes and tall top hats. The boarders slept in large shared rooms, regardless of age. Dyson had been assigned to the same room as Thompson. Professor Dyson recalled: "The buildings [at Winchester] were 550 years old and we lived in them as our fourteenth-century predecessors had lived, in a constant and cheerful uproar. Coming into this bedlam as a shrimpy twelve year old with a treble voice, I crept into a corner, wondered and watched and listened. . . . Among the boys in our room, Frank was the largest, the loudest, the most uninhibited and the most brilliant. So it happened that I came to know Frank very well, and learned from him more than I learned from anybody else at that school."[2]

Freeman Dyson admired Frank Thompson's remarkable ability with languages, and Dyson even joined a specially arranged course in Russian so that he could share "one of Frank's enthusiasms." Thompson had also started an obscure languages club, inspiring all of the boys in his room to learn insults in foreign tongues. His ravenous acquisition of languages (he learned six of

Freeman Dyson in 1937 in his Winchester robes

them at Winchester) was only second to his budding political engagement. Frank Thompson cared about politics, his poet's soul moved by the struggling and suffering that characterized the 1930s. Professor Dyson wrote:

> [Frank] was more deeply concerned than the rest of us with the big world outside: with the civil war then raging in Spain, with the world war he saw coming. From him I caught my first inkling of the great moral questions of war and peace which were to dominate the lives of all of us ever afterward. Listening to him talk, I learned that there is no way to rightly grasp these great questions except through poetry. For him, poetry was no mere intellectual amusement. Poetry was man's best effort down the ages to distill some wisdom from the inarticulate depths of his soul. Frank could no more live without poetry than I could live without mathematics.[3]

Frank Thompson left Winchester for Oxford in 1938. England declared war on Germany on September 3, 1939. Dyson spent his time in the war trying to convince the higher-ups in Bomber Command to make the British bombing campaigns more efficient. He saw firsthand the ongoing waste of young men's lives due to military bureaucracy and incompetence. He was also dismayed at the British fire bombings of German civilian targets; the war was making monsters of everyone. Only Frank Thompson seemed committed to fighting the right kind of fight to build a better, more just world. Dyson was crushed when he learned that Thompson had died fighting with the partisan rebels in Bulgaria in the summer of 1944.

In his article from 1979, Professor Dyson quoted extensively from an account published in the *News Chronicle* a year after Thompson's demise. The source for the *News Chronicle* article was a Bulgarian delegate to the World Trade Union Congress in London. She had supposedly been an eyewitness to the mock trial where Frank Thompson had been sentenced to death. The eyewitness reported that the trial hall had been filled with onlookers. Thompson apparently faced his captors calmly, smoking his pipe, and answering their questions in colloquial Bulgarian, much to the amazement of those in attendance. The Bulgarian eyewitness reported the following conversation: "'By what right do you, an Englishman, enter our country and wage war against us?' he was asked. Major Thompson answered, 'I came because this war is something very much deeper than a struggle of nation against nation. The greatest thing in the world now is the struggle of Anti-Fascism against Fascism.' 'Do you not know that we shoot men who hold your opinions?' 'I am ready to die for freedom. And I am proud to die with Bulgarian patriots as companions.'"[4]

At this point, it was reported that Major Thompson led the condemned men away from the hall, raising a clenched fist and shouting to the assembled Bulgarians, "I give you the salute of freedom." Thompson and the other prisoners all died raising their fists in this salute, and the eyewitness declared that "the scene was one of the most moving in all Bulgarian history, and that the men's amazing courage was the work of the English officer who carried their spirits as well as his own."[5] This moving account of the final moments of Frank Thompson's life made a deep impression on Freeman Dyson, who only questioned one detail of the account. In his article from 1979, he wrote: "Everything in this account rings true except one word. The word 'Anti-Fascism' is, I suspect, a euphemism supplied by the Bulgarian trade union delegate. Frank always called a spade a spade. I am almost sure that he really said, 'The greatest thing in the world now is the struggle of Communism against Fascism.' He was, after all, a Communist. His Bulgarian comrades were Communists. They did not live long enough to discover that Communism and freedom are not always synonymous."[6]

Professor Dyson understood quite well that the word "communist" was dangerous sounding to men like Winston Churchill whose alliance with the Soviet Union had only been born out of desperate necessity. But Dyson was convinced that his friend had died for an ideal; Frank Thompson was fighting *for* something as much as he was fighting *against* fascism. By 1979, Professor Dyson still admired this about his friend and soberly compared Thompson's heroic sacrifice in Bulgaria to his own time spent at British Bomber Command. During the war, Dyson questioned the morality of trying to demoralize the Germans by bombing civilian targets. He was horrified by the use of the atom bomb on Japan. He wrote:

> A good cause can become bad if we fight for it with means that are indiscriminately murderous. A bad cause can become good if enough people fight for it in a spirit of comradeship and self-sacrifice. In the end it is how you fight, as much as why you fight, that makes your cause good or bad. And the more technological the war becomes, the more disastrously a bad choice of means will change a good cause into evil. I learned this lesson from my years at Bomber Command, and from the example of Frank's life and death. Unfortunately, many of my generation who were on the winning side of World War II did not learn this lesson. If they had learned it, they would not have led us to disaster twenty years later in Vietnam. I had the advantage, when the American bombers began bombing in Vietnam, of knowing that our cause was hopeless, because I knew that Frank's spirit was out there in the jungle fighting for Ho Chi Minh.[7]

Like Frank Thompson, Dyson had a gift for words and I often found myself wondering about Frank's spirit and where it might be today.

In May 2012, I visited Professor Dyson at the institute once again. I had recently returned from Bulgaria where I was conducting interviews with women who lived during the communist era. The more I learned about Bulgarian communism, the more fascinated I became with Frank Thompson. He had been the same age as my undergraduate students at Bowdoin College when he signed up to fight against the fascists. Thompson had been full of energy and political passion, writing poetry throughout his short life. My own students seemed numb to the world: lost in a haze of electronic stimulation, self-absorbed, and apathetic. Most would not know a social injustice if it hit them on the head.

A confident
Frank Thompson

"I think I would like to write something about Frank," I said to Professor Dyson at lunch. "About how he and the Bulgarian partisans are remembered in Bulgaria today."

"That could be very interesting," Dyson said.

I had already started doing some preliminary research on the partisan movement and had discovered some information about a whole family of partisans called the Lagadinovs. A father, three brothers, and their younger sister had been members of the first partisan brigade formed in Bulgaria during World War II, and I wondered if they had ever worked with Frank Thompson or one of the British Special Operations Executive missions.

"I have your article, and E. P. Thompson's two books.[8] I have the Bulgarian book and I can access the Bulgarian archives," I said. "But all of Thompson's papers have been stored away with his brother's at the Bodleian Library. Sealed until 2043."

Freeman Dyson in his office at the Institute for Advanced Study

When E. P. Thompson died in 1993, his papers were donated to Oxford and sealed for fifty years.

"I have some materials that I have collected over the years," Professor Dyson said. "If you would like, I can have them copied for you."

"That would be wonderful," I said.

It was in Professor Dyson's personal papers that I found a series of letters between E. P. Thompson and Professor Dyson. Frank Thompson's younger brother first wrote to Dyson following the publication of the *New Yorker* article. By the late 1970s, Edward Palmer Thompson was perhaps one of the most famous living historians in the world. In 1963, he had published one of the foundational works in the field of labor history: *The Making of the English Working Class*. E. P. Thompson had, like his brother before him, been a member of the Communist Party of Great Britain. Unlike Frank, he had lived long enough to see the horrors of Stalinism and the brutal realities of

East European totalitarianism. E. P. Thompson and many of the left intellectuals of his milieu formally broke their ties with the Communist Party after the Soviet invasion of Hungary in 1956.[9] E. P. Thompson abandoned the word "communist," preferring instead to call himself a "socialist humanist" and a member of the "New Left."[10]

In his first letter to Dyson, E. P. Thompson wrote that he was "very much moved" to read the "Reflections" article in the *New Yorker*. In this letter, E. P. Thompson lamented the recent publication of a book called *Agents Extraordinary* by the journalist Stowers Johnson. Since the British wartime archives related to Frank's mission in Bulgaria were still sealed, the book was little more than a series of fabrications based on scraps of rumor and myth, portraying Thompson as a reckless ideologue who exceeded his orders so that he could foment a peasant rebellion. The Bulgarian Communist government had also produced both a film and a book about Frank Thompson in 1978 and 1979, canonizing him as a great communist hero. E. P. Thompson and his wife had been persuaded to visit Bulgaria as tourists in the 1970s, "only to be kidnapped into a huge official operation." E. P. Thompson was unhappy with the way his brother's memory was being skewed for different political purposes. Frank Thompson and his comrades among the Bulgarian partisans were being strategically celebrated to bolster the legitimacy of the current Bulgarian government. E. P. contrasted his trip to Bulgaria with his visit to Yugoslavia, where he had been able to visit the Serbian mountains where Major Thompson had been based in the winter of 1944. E. P. had the chance to speak freely with some of his brother's former partisan companions.

"The whole matter is far too complex for me to put it down in this letter," E. P. wrote to Dyson. "But it seems I shall have to write something sorting out facts and myths which I will do soon." E. P. Thompson asked if he could quote a bit about Frank from Dyson's recollections of him at Winchester. E. P. Thompson regretted that the memoir published in 1947 that he had compiled with their mother, *There Is a Spirit in Europe*, had excluded the voices of so many of Frank's friends.

"There was only one point in your piece which I thought incorrect," E. P. wrote to Dyson:

> [And] that is your comment that Frank would have more probably said the struggle between Communism and Fascism. It is not of great importance, but on repeated questioning in both Serbia and Bulgaria, veterans all agreed that at the time they had no notion that Frank was a communist:

he behaved correctly as a British Liaison Officer, although (by sharing the partisan hardships, and also their songs, dances and speech-making) they knew him to be warmly sympathetic and . . . a strong anti-fascist. Since the "Fatherland Front" was an anti-fascist alliance, I think it likely that Frank would have spoken as reported. Moreover, and this is a more speculative point, there are indications in many of his late letters that (a) he was becoming wise to many aspects of Stalinism, and (b) had come to elevate the anti-fascist popular front <u>above</u> the communist part of it.[11]

E. P. Thompson's letter then continues on to explain that the question of Frank's communism is an important one. Frank's membership in the Communist Party of Great Britain had fueled rumors (such as those promoted by Stowers Johnson) that Frank was responsible for the failure of his mission. These assertions could not be refuted because there was almost no information about Frank's mission made available by the British government. The complete silence surrounding Frank's mission by British "officialdom" infuriated E. P. Thompson. His letter also tried to enlist Dyson's aid in a campaign to open the relevant archives. Thompson wanted to force the British government to give access to documents that should have been made public in 1973 (according to an official thirty-year rule). He was convinced that they were hiding something.

The carefully typewritten letter was dated August 22, 1979, and was followed by several handwritten responses to Dyson's replies. Reading these letters in 2012, I felt that there was something very personal in E. P. Thompson's insistence that his brother's commitment to antifascism was stronger than his commitment to communism. In the late 1970s, after the Soviet invasions of Hungary and Czechoslovakia, the word "communist" had become inextricably conflated with Soviet imperialism. E. P. Thompson might well have been worried that the nobility of his brother's cause and the selflessness of his death would be undermined by his self-identification as a communist. Moreover, "bloody British officialdom" was suspiciously circumspect about the case of Frank Thompson. He had been a uniformed British officer, and under the terms of the Geneva Convention the Bulgarians should have kept him as a prisoner of war. Frank Thompson's execution was a blatant violation of the convention. His younger brother believed that there was more to his brother's story than the British were willing to reveal. E. P. Thompson, with the finely attuned nose of a professional historian, smelled a rat.

The correspondence between Dyson and E. P. Thompson made me start thinking about the nature of heroism. Is it true that all brave and selfless acts are intrinsically heroic? Was the value of Frank Thompson's short life and death so dependent on later political assessments of the ideals he was fighting for? Or does heroism require brave and selfless acts in the service of a great cause? Dyson had argued the reverse—that a good cause could be tainted if it was fought for using ignoble and "indiscriminately murderous" means. From where I was sitting in 2012, it certainly seemed that the widespread cultural derision toward the communist ideal could obliterate the honor of fighting and dying for a cause one truly believed in.

I had recently been reading the work of the moral philosopher Susan Neiman.[12] She argues that the contemporary world is too besotted with victims and that competitive victimhood has become the defining characteristic of twenty-first-century political engagement. Neiman claims that we need to embark upon a new era of heroism; our apathy and hipster irony have us all feeling empty and unsatisfied. Rather than solely focusing on things as they are, we should also focus on things as they should be. Humans are moral creatures; we are only shadows of our true selves without some sort of larger ideal to believe in. It is much harder to be a hero than it is to be a victim. In order to be a hero, you have to do something. But if you do something, you risk doing something wrong.

As I held E. P. Thompson's letter from 1979 between my fingers, I wondered if he believed that being a hero was worth the risk. If all acts of heroism are ultimately weighed and judged by subsequent generations of historians (like E. P. himself) with their own political agendas, why be brave? Why take a stand? How can you ever be sure that you are fighting for the right thing?

It was these questions that fueled my obsession with the stories of Frank Thompson and the Bulgarian partisans he befriended after being dropped from the sky one night in January 1944.

3 | "I SIMPLY WANT TO FIGHT"

Frank Thompson was born in India in 1920, the son of Edward John Thompson, an English Methodist missionary, and Theodosia Jessup, born in Syria to an American Presbyterian missionary family. Thompson's parents returned to England when he was three years old and settled in Oxford. His father wrote many books on India and was a widely recognized expert on Indian affairs. Young Frank grew up in an intellectual household infused with politics; Robert Graves and Sir Arthur Evans were their neighbors, and the Thompsons counted Jawaharlal Nehru and Mahatma Gandhi among their houseguests.

Edward Palmer (E. P.) Thompson was born in 1924, and the two brothers shared a close bond. They overlapped for a year at their primary school where the young Edward believed himself the "family duffer" compared to the intellectually precocious Frank. Edward, however, excelled at sports while Frank was clumsy and lumbering. Speaking at Stanford University in the late 1980s, E. P. described the fundamental contradiction in his relationship with his older brother:

> Admiring my older brother as I did, yet I felt that he needed protection in all practical matters, and that I was his protector. He had been ill in infancy in India, and from that time until perhaps his 22nd year he never quite seemed to catch up on his own

Frank Thompson
as a child

strength. As a schoolboy he was tall and thin, his head a little too large for
due proportions, his limbs not exactly responsive to his control. He was
notorious, until his very last year or two, for his accident-prone passage
through the world—breaking things, knocking things off tables, collaps-
ing chairs. . . . At that robust, brutal and nasty preparatory school he was
the kind of boy who became the butt of bullies and I, too little to protect
him, would intervene with flailing fists and tears. He bore his own clum-
siness philosophically and often turned it into comedy, but I, his younger
brother, could not be philosophical at all.[1]

E. P. would no longer have the chance to protect his elder brother after the
latter won an open classical scholarship to study at Winchester. Frank left his
family behind to become a boarder at the school where just three years later
he would meet a young Freeman Dyson. Frank Thompson blossomed at
Winchester; his natural intellect was nurtured and encouraged. He was truly

exceptional with languages. E. P. would later claim that all of the linguistic genes in their family "descended in superabundance upon my brother."[2] At Winchester, Frank Thompson studied Latin, Greek, Russian, German, and French. He also taught himself Italian by working on a collective translation of Dante with his fellow students.

In his first year at Winchester, Frank Thompson was apparently intrigued by the trial of the Bulgarian communist Georgi Dimitrov.[3] The Nazis had charged Dimitrov with the arson of the Reichstag in 1933, and he famously chose to represent himself at the trial. Excerpts of Dimitrov's closing speech were reprinted in newspapers across the world, and it was perhaps in reading about the trial that the young Frank had his first full exposure to communist ideals. Standing accused before the German court, Georgi Dimitrov gave a moving account of why he felt compelled to refuse counsel and speak in his own defense:

> I admit that my tone is hard and grim. The struggle of my life has always been hard and grim. My tone is frank and open. I am used to calling a spade a spade. I am no lawyer appearing before this court in the mere way of his profession.
>
> I am defending myself, an accused communist.
>
> I am defending my political honor, my honor as a revolutionary.
>
> I am defending my communist ideology, my ideals.
>
> I am defending the content and significance of my whole life.
>
> For these reasons every word which I say in this court is a *part of me*, each phrase is the expression of my deep indignation against the unjust accusation, against the putting of this anti-Communist crime, the burning of the Reichstag, to the account of the Communists.[4]

Knowing that much of the world would be reading along, Dimitrov used the trial as an opportunity to speak out against the rise of fascism across Europe, including that in his own country. German newspapers tried to discredit him, calling him a "savage and barbarous" Bulgarian, but Dimitrov twisted the open racism of the Germans to his own purposes. Dimitrov painted a heroic portrait of his countrymen who had been colonized by the Ottoman Turks for five centuries:

> It is true that Bulgarian fascism is savage and barbarous. But the Bulgarian workers and peasants, the Bulgarian people's intelligentsia are by no means savage or barbarous. It is true that the standard of life is not so

high in the Balkans as elsewhere in Europe, but it is false to say that the people of Bulgaria are politically or mentally on a lower scale than the people of other countries. A people which lived for five hundred years under a foreign yoke without losing its language and its national character, our working class and peasantry who have fought and are fighting against Bulgarian fascism and for Communism—such a people is not savage and barbarous. Only fascism in Bulgaria is savage and barbarous. But I ask you, *in what country does not fascism bear these qualities?*[5]

Much to the displeasure of Hitler, the German court acquitted Dimitrov of all charges, and his principled opposition to National Socialism in Germany made Dimitrov an instant political celebrity. A popular saying at the time was "There is only one brave man in Germany, and he is a Bulgarian."[6] His success at the Leipzig Trial in 1933 also gave him a powerful voice with which to promote the communist ideal. Stalin made Dimitrov the head of the Comintern in 1934, just two years before the outbreak of hostilities in Spain.

While Dimitrov's quest fascinated Frank Thompson, it was the Spanish Civil War that would crystallize his antifascist sentiments. Two sons of a family close to the Thompsons had left Oxford to become international brigadiers in Spain. Frank, still too young to fight, followed events in Spain between 1936 and 1939 more closely than the other boys of his age. He saw firsthand how popular democracy was being crushed by the greed and political machinations of the wealthy.

Spanish politics were polarized. On one side were the rich landowning classes and businessmen who supported the Nationalists. On the other side were the urban workers, rural peasants, and middle-class intellectuals who supported the Republicans. The Republicans consisted of a wide coalition of left political parties that formed a Popular Front coalition for the 1936 elections. In a new era of universal suffrage (Spanish women finally got the right to vote in 1931) workers and peasants could take power through free and fair elections. The Popular Front defeated the Nationalists in a closely watched poll. But the Popular Front government was in office for less than six months before the Nationalists supported a well-orchestrated military coup d'état on July 17, 1936.

The Spanish Civil War was a brutal and bloody conflict that would claim hundreds of thousands of lives.[7] General Francisco Franco assumed control of the Nationalist forces and called for international help. Both Hitler

A statue of Georgi Dimitrov in Sofia

in Germany and Mussolini in Italy sent troops, tanks, and arms to assist the Nationalists. Mexico and the Soviet Union sent material aid to the Republicans, and over sixty thousand international volunteers came to Spain to support the Republican cause, including two of Thompson's childhood friends.

It was Georgi Dimitrov and the Comintern that had first spearheaded the idea of the Popular Front (a broad coalition of anarchists, communists, socialists, and social democrats). Frank Thompson would have known that it was Dimitrov who helped to organize the international brigades. But even with the support of the Soviet Union, the Republican cause was doomed. The Nationalist forces were far superior, and the Republican cause was undermined by violent infighting between leftists of different stripes. Anarchists and communists fought each other almost as much as they fought the Nationalists, even as Stalin purged his own ranks back in the USSR.

After his victory, Franco assumed control of Spain. The Nazis consolidated their power in Germany and Mussolini was emboldened in Italy. Leaders in Britain and France seemed unperturbed by these developments. Across Europe, many politically inclined, intellectual youth grew frustrated with mainstream politics. When Neville Chamberlain signed the Munich Pact with Hitler on September 30, 1938, there seemed little political will in Britain to take a firm stand against Germany. With Dimitrov at the helm of the Comintern, many Europeans, and particularly members of the upper-middle-class British intelligentsia, came to believe that communism was the only real alternative to fascism. Democratic elections had failed. Frank Thompson became restless with the British desire to preserve the status quo. Even his classical education at Winchester seemed unsuited to the political demands of the modern world. In 1943, Frank wrote:

> The culture one imbibed at Winchester was too nostalgic. Amid those old buildings and under those graceful lime-trees it was easy to give one's heart to the Middle Ages and believe that the world had lost its manhood along with Abelard. One fell in love with the beauty of the past, and there was no dialectician there to explain that the chief glory of the past was its triumph over the age that came before it; that Abelard was great because he was a revolutionary; that had he been alive today, he would have been writing for the Labour Monthly or carpeted by the Labour Party Executive for left-wing tendencies.[8]

As his political conscience blossomed, Frank Thompson graduated from Winchester. His exceptional aptitude for languages and his passion for poetry had won him another scholarship, this time to attend Oxford. Thompson started university in the fall of 1938 after a summer working on an archeological dig in Greece.[9] Like most university students, he spent a lot of time getting drunk at parties and brooding over the meaning of life. He had a tight group of friends and became active in various political clubs. Then one day, he encountered a fellow student who would change the course of his life. He first saw her at a lecture, sitting at a table across from him. He wrote: "There was something about her warm green dress, her long yellow locks like a cavalier's, and her gentle profile, that gave a pleasing impression of harmony. My feeling of loneliness redoubled. 'Why didn't I know anyone like that?' I saw her again at a Labour Club Social, dancing,—perhaps 'waddling' is a better word, with some poisonous-looking bureaucrat. It wasn't until the middle of the next term that I got a chance to speak with her."[10]

That girl in the green dress was Irish and her name was Iris Murdoch. It was in an attempt to woo her that Frank first seriously flirted with far-left politics. He was drunk one night at Oxford, reclining to one side of Iris on a bed. On her other side was a rival for her affections. Oafish and intimidated by her, but feeling compelled to action, Thompson decided to engage Iris in a discussion about politics. He launched into a diatribe against the silly positions of the Liberal Club and his frustration and disappointment with the Labour Party. "What about the Communist Party?" Iris asked. It was an unexpected suggestion. Frank Thompson later wrote:

> I was dumbstruck. I'd never thought of it before. Right then I couldn't see anything against it, but felt it would be wise to wait till I'd sobered up before deciding. So I said, "Come to tea in a couple of days and convert me." Then I staggered home and lay on a sofa . . . announcing to the world that I had met a stunner of a girl and was joining the Communist Party for love of her. But next morning it still seemed good. I read *State and Revolution*, talked to several people, and made up my mind.[11]

But his active membership in the Oxford branch of the Communist Party of Great Britain (CPGB) would be very short-lived. Germany invaded Poland on September 1, 1939, and Thompson enlisted the following day. Both Iris and his parents were passionately opposed to his enlistment. He was only nineteen, and undergraduate students at Oxford could not be called up before their twentieth birthdays.[12] The senior Thompsons tried to reverse Frank's enlistment, but he was committed to joining the fight. His parents' interference only served to increase his determination.

Then there was the official line of Thompson's newly adopted party. Although initially in favor of the war, the CPGB reversed its position. Germany and the Soviet Union had signed a nonaggression pact in August 1939. The official Comintern line was that the war was little more than a conflict between German fascists and British and French imperialists. Despite this, Thompson was not dissuaded. To explain his motives, he wrote Iris Murdoch a poem, affectionately titling it "Madonna Bolshevicka":

Sure, lady, I know the party line is better.
I know what Marx would have said. I know you're right.
When this is over we'll fight for the things that matter.
Somehow, today, I simply want to fight.
That's heresy? Okay. But I'm past caring.
There's blood about my eyes, and mist and hate.
I know the things we're fighting now and loathe them.
Now's not the time you say? But I can't wait.[13]

Frank started out in the Royal Artillery. He set sail for the Middle East in March 1941 as part of a unit called Phantom and was stationed in Cairo. After Hitler's invasion of the Soviet Union in June 1941, Thompson was transferred to Syria. He fell ill as soon as he arrived in Damascus in September, and he spent two months in the hospital. During this time, the Russians were taking terrible losses. Thompson's admiration for the Soviet Union and the suffering of the Russian people ballooned. His war diaries are filled with reflections on the achievements of the USSR. On November 8, 1941, he wrote in a letter:

Who will say that, whatever we think of communism, there are a lot of things which we admire in the Soviet Union. That its government, whatever we say about its methods, is supremely concerned with the welfare of its people. That it is a land where goodwill and not selfishness is set up as the factor that should govern social relations. Where working people are accorded honour and security more proportionate to their importance. Where the talents of artists and scientists are being pooled to the public benefit with wonderful results. Where any peasant or worker can get far better entertainment than Hollywood films. A land, I am sure, that is bringing up a young generation with far fresher, less jazz-addled minds than in Britain or the USA.[14]

Throughout his time in the Middle East, Frank Thompson was a faithful correspondent with his parents, his brother, and his friend Iris Murdoch.

Frank Thompson in 1939.
This photo was given to
Dencho Znepolski by
Frank Thompson's
mother in 1947.

Almost all of this correspondence was preserved. Frank's letters and diaries provide an incredible window into his thoughts and fears in the time leading up to his fateful decision to enter Bulgaria. His writings show his deep admiration for the peoples of eastern Europe. He was fascinated by their languages and intrigued by their rich and varied culture and history, imagining them to be the martyrs of Europe. In a letter dated November 19, 1941, Thompson wrote:

> Aren't the Slavs a splendid lot? The Poles have suffered more than any nation in Europe. The Czechs, especially their students, have done far better than we had any right to expect. . . . Serb rebels are currently reported to be in virtual control of a quarter of Serbia. Perhaps it's not just coincidence that Serb resistance has been much stronger since Russia came in. There's a strong communist movement in Yugoslavia. Even the old peasant Bul-

gars will turn in the end—just you see. Nor is it the first time that the Slavs have thrown their bodies between Europe and destruction. They bore the brunt of the Turks and Tartars too. "To suffer like a Slav" will soon become a by-word in all the world's languages.[15]

After Syria, Thompson was sent to the Western Desert in North Africa, and then back to Syria and eventually to Iraq. Between August and November 1942, Frank Thompson's squadron was stationed in Persia. The squadron's job was to help protect a railway that the Allies were using to transport military and logistical aid to the Russians. It was here that he convinced a local Armenian to give him Russian lessons and began to teach himself Polish. It was also in Persia that he spent time listening to Soviet radio broadcasts. Thompson was deeply impressed by the Soviet coverage of events all across Europe as opposed to the BBC's narrow focus on British efforts in the war. The BBC's bald-faced anti-Bolshevism incensed Frank. He wrote in another letter home: "Oh damnation. Isn't it time to admit in all humility that a regime which has inspired so much sober courage, solidarity and self-sacrifice in 160 million people cannot be so terrible, after all? . . . Of course, I don't expect us to applaud or foster Bolshevism. But we might have the courage to realise that Europe's health can only be restored by the working-class movement, and do what we can to win its alliance and respect."[16]

Frank Thompson was also fascinated by the Russian radio broadcasts targeting the Bulgarians. Although the Bulgarians were officially allied with Hitler, they had not declared war on the Soviet Union. There was a natural fraternity between the two countries—the majority of the populations in both nations were Slavic-speaking, Orthodox Christians. Moreover, the Bulgarians would have never been able to achieve national independence without Russian military support. The Russians were viewed as "liberators" to most Bulgarians, and some radio broadcasts tried to play on the heartstrings of the Bulgarian workers and peasants. In a diary entry dated January 21, 1943, Thompson wrote: "The last half-hour I've been listening to a communist station, probably Russian, talking to Bulgaria. Bulgarian, of course, is nearer to Russian than most Slavonic languages. I can understand about as much as I can of Ukrainian, and the languages of communists is much the same in all the Slavonic languages. The broadcast was very stirring, challenging the Bulgars to rout the venal and traitorous Fascist clique that had sold the freedom-loving Bulgar people to the German-Fascist highwaymen. I think we shall hear from those lazy old peasant Bulgars before long."[17]

Despite his ever-growing admiration of the Slavs and their great sacrifices during the war, Thompson was, as his brother E. P. would later come to suspect, becoming wise to the brutality of Stalin in the USSR. In December 1942, he wrote: "It was an eye opener to me to learn how many people Stalin had personally poisoned. . . . Old Bolsheviks, it seems, never die. They only get bumped off by Stalin."[18] It is possible that Frank Thompson, although deeply enamored with the ideals of communism, would become truly disgusted had he lived long enough to see what the Russians ended up doing with them in practice. But during the war, the Soviet Union was an ally in the fight against fascism. There were few premonitions of the Cold War that would emerge after the hot war was over.

During the war, Frank Thompson wrote many letters to Iris Murdoch, whom he might have married had he survived.[19] Iris Murdoch was also a dedicated correspondent, sharing her own life and fears on paper.[20] Their letters to each other were filled with playful tenderness. They were also saturated with references to classical literature and youthful idealism about the world that might follow the war. Compared to Thompson, Murdoch believed that her dedication to the ideals of workers' revolution and class equality was more fanciful. In March 1943, she wrote to him: "Oh Frank, I wonder what the future holds for us all—shall we ever make out of the dreamy idealistic stuff of our lives any hard & real thing? You will perhaps. Your inconsequent romanticism has just the requisite streak of realism to it. I think I am just a dreamer. Shout in my ear, please."[21]

Thompson's unit participated in the Sicilian landings in June 1943. Although he survived unscathed, he witnessed the deaths of many in his unit. As the war continued, he knew that many of his old Winchester classmates had lost their lives. After spending two weeks in a now-liberated Sicily, Thompson was sent to Libya. His letters and diary entries show that he was restless and exasperated with the Allies for not opening a Second Front. The Soviets were taking heavy losses in the East, but Churchill was refusing to move.

In April 1943, Thompson heard about the Special Operations Executive (SOE), a unit that sent British officers to work together with local resistance movements. The strongest of these partisan movements was in Yugoslavia where Josip Broz Tito and his communist comrades were successfully wreaking guerrilla havoc on the Axis forces. In Greece, both communist and nationalist partisans were trying to liberate the country from Nazi and Bulgarian occupation. Frank Thompson volunteered to be transferred to the

SOE, where he argued that he could put his knowledge of Modern Greek to good use.

But Thompson was suspicious of the British operation in Greece. In theory, the British hoped that right-wing and left-wing partisans in Greece would work together to defeat the Nazis. As the tide of the war began to turn, however, it became increasingly clear that Churchill was opposed to the communists in Greece. When the time came, Britain would throw its weight behind the nationalists in the Greek Civil War, crushing the communist partisans who had fought bravely against the Nazi occupation. The enemy of my enemy is my friend only until my enemy is defeated.[22]

The SOE was also looking for someone to work with the partisans in Bulgaria. There was little quality information about their numbers and effectiveness, although the partisans were credited with several successful acts of sabotage. Partisan bands had removed train tracks in Bulgaria, disrupting Nazi supply lines to Greece. If the SOE could establish contact with the partisans, equipping them with arms, uniforms, food, medicines, and other essential supplies, the British hoped the partisan detachments would grow in size and inspire a local peasant uprising against Boris III, the Bulgarian king. In Bulgaria, the partisans were almost all communists.

Thompson was sent to SOE headquarters in Cairo for parachute training. Here, he taught himself Bulgarian, a language that he deemed "simply Russian as a Turk would talk it."[23] During his time in Cairo, he had the opportunity to meet some Yugoslav partisans who were brought in to advise the SOE. His meeting with these men inspired Thompson. On December 26, 1943, just a month before he dropped into Bulgaria, Frank Thompson wrote in a letter to Iris Murdoch:

> With the passing of the year I seem to have come to a watershed in my life. In the past few days I have had some profoundly moving experiences. I have had the honour to meet and to talk to some of the best people in the world . . . people whom, when the truth is known, Europe will recognize as among the finest and toughest she has ever bourne. Meeting them has made me utterly disgusted with some aspects of my present life, reminding me forcibly that all my waking hours must be dedicated to one purpose only. . . . Nothing else matters. We must crush the Nazis and build our whole life anew.[24]

Thompson was to be dropped into Serbia where he would make contact with Major Mostyn Davies, an SOE officer already on the ground and working with the partisans. Davies was leading his own mission, but with limited success. With Thompson's remarkable language skills, his youth, and his strong leftist sympathies, the SOE officers in Cairo had high hopes that his Bulgarian mission, code named "Claridges," would increase guerilla activity. In the lead up to his departure, Thompson was full of hope and dedication to his dream of a new world emerging after the horrors and brutality of the war. It was during this time that he sent a letter to his younger brother, E. P., then serving in Italy. Thompson wrote:

> My eyes fill very quickly with tears when I think what a splendid Europe we shall build (I say Europe because that's the only continent I know really quite well) when all of the vitality and talent of its indomitable peoples can be set free for co-operation and creation. Think only of the Balkans and the beauty, gaiety and courage which their peoples have preserved through the last 600 years—years which have brought them little else but poverty, oppression and fratricide. When men like these have mastered their own fates there won't be time for discussing "what is beauty?" One will be overwhelmed by the abundance of it.[25]

In late January 1944, Frank Thompson was on board an airplane flying to a drop point over Tsrna Trava in Bulgarian-occupied Serbia. His final mission of the war was about to begin.

4 | THE BROTHERS LAGADINOV

As the more than twenty Wellington bombers carrying Thompson and British supplies flew toward Bulgarian-occupied Serbia, three brothers—the Lagadinovs—huddled together in the mountains of Pirin Macedonia. They were Bulgarian partisans in the first partisan brigade formed in Bulgaria, a brigade that would later be referred to as the "Parapunov Brigade."[1] Their initial leader, Ivan Kozarev, was famed to be the first partisan in the country, and they desperately needed the food, guns, clothes, and ammunition that would be dropped from the sky that night. But these were not the partisans Frank was supposed to meet. It would only be much later that some of the British supplies would find their way to the Brothers Lagadinov.

The eldest of these three brothers was Kostadin Lagadinov. He was born on April 11, 1913, to Fidanka Lagadinova while his father fought on the front lines during the Second Balkan War.[2] Kostadin was the first son of Atanas Lagadinov, a humble peddler and carriage driver who had founded the Razlog branch of the Bulgarian Communist Party in the years following the Bolshevik Revolution in Russia. As a carriage driver, Atanas Lagadinov traveled to and from Bulgaria's cities. He saw the wealth of the landlords and of Bulgaria's small, but growing, bourgeois class. He also saw the desperate poverty of the peasants. Freedom from the Ottomans had done little to increase their living standards. They had tried to improve their lot through elections, but as would happen in Spain, democratic elections precipitated a military coup.[3] Men like Atanas saw revolution as the only answer.

After suffering defeat at the end of World War I, the Bulgarian people elected a leader from the Agrarian Union, a party popular with the peasants but threatening to the middle class and the military establishment. Bulgaria's communists, together with the Agrarians, had opposed the country's involvement in the imperialistic war and criticized the country's pro-German monarchy. After fewer than four years, however, a military coup overthrew the Agrarian government in June 1923. Under pressure from the Comintern in Moscow, the Bulgarian Communist Party, with the support of both the Agrarians and the anarchists, attempted to retake the country. The "September Uprising" failed abysmally. It led to massive political reprisals against workers and peasants associated with leftist parties, even those who had not participated in the uprising. Bulgarian state forces persecuted thousands of communists, socialists, and Agrarians.[4] Aleksandar Stamboliyski, the Agrarian prime minister, was arrested, tortured, and executed. After 1923, both the Agrarian and Communist Parties were outlawed.[5]

Unlike Frank Thompson, who had a comfortable middle-class upbringing, Kostadin Lagadinov grew up in the midst of the crushing poverty and political chaos of interwar Bulgaria. Kostadin was only ten years old in 1923 when his father participated in the doomed September Uprising. By some miracle, Atanas Lagadinov survived the government reprisals against the communists. He and his wife had three more children and raised them all to believe in the inevitability of social revolution. Kostadin found inspiration in his father's idea that workers and peasants could join forces. They could rule their own country and build a more equitable society.

Atanas Lagadinov encouraged his son to study and, like Frank Thompson, the young Kostadin was a bright and ambitious boy who did well in school. Despite his humble origins, Kostadin won a scholarship to study law at Sofia University, the country's top institution of higher learning. The son of a communist carriage driver was going to become a lawyer. His political sympathies, however, were further radicalized in Sofia. On his first university vacation, Kostadin returned to his hometown of Razlog. There he met his old friend and schoolmate Nikola Parapunov, who was printing and distributing illegal communist literature. Despite the grave risks, Kostadin became Parapunov's accomplice.[6]

Kostadin also started attending underground political meetings with

A statue of Ivan Kozarev
in the Bulgarian town of
Dobrinishte

other young idealistic men and women. He hid in dark cellars and discussed
surplus value extraction by candlelight. They asked illegal questions: Who
gave the German king the right to rule over their nation? Why should Bulgarian peasants and workers pay taxes to or fight for a leader appointed by
the Western powers? What kind of country could Bulgaria become if the
peasants collectively owned their own land? How was it that the privileged
few maintained power and authority over the oppressed masses?

Knowing that he would be expelled from the university if he were caught,
Kostadin still chose to distribute communist literature to the workers and
students in Sofia. On April 1, 1932, Kostadin was once again in Razlog visiting his parents' home. Early that morning, the Bulgarian police appeared at
the front gate; they had come to arrest Kostadin for his illegal political activism. Kostadin escaped out of the back of the house while his father stalled
the officers by telling them that his son was not at home.

The village of Razlog sat at the base of the Pirin Mountains, and it was into these mountains that the nineteen-year-old Kostadin fled. He spent the better part of a year hiding in different towns around Bulgaria: first in Dupnitsa, then in the coastal town of Burgas on the Black Sea, and then back in Sofia. At the same age that Frank Thompson would enlist to fight against the fascists, Kostadin Lagadinov became a fugitive from them.

At some point during that year, Kostadin saw his name in the state newspaper. For distributing illegal literature, he had been given a twelve-and-a-half-year sentence in absentia. In addition, the government had imposed a 500,000-lev fine, an impossible sum for the son of a carriage driver. Kostadin's friend, Nikola Parapunov, was arrested and would serve an eight-year sentence. The king's ministers, called the "monarcho-fascists" by people like Kostadin, were desperate to stop the spread of communist ideas.

Hunted at every turn by the king's police, Kostadin and nineteen other fugitive communist activists met in the port city of Burgas. Local communists gave them an old sailboat with a weak outboard motor. Their goal was the Black Sea port city of Odessa in the USSR, about 313 nautical miles to the north. It would be a dangerous journey, but it was their only choice.

It was dark when they set out. They had limited provisions, but if all went well, they were supposed to reach Odessa in about two days. Less than halfway through their journey, the engine died. Soon these nineteen men were running out of drinking water. Desperate and afraid, the fugitives took turns with the two wooden oars. They rowed on for hours until all of the drinking water was gone. Their only hope was to head back to land, but they knew they would be arrested if they returned to Bulgaria. Just when they thought they were doomed to die of thirst, a Soviet ship found them; the Russians gave them provisions and towed them the rest of the way into Odessa.

The twenty Bulgarians traveled directly to Moscow to meet with Vasil Kolarov, Georgi Dimitrov's comrade in the Communist International, and the Bulgarians were all granted political asylum. Kostadin Lagadinov was given work in a tire factory and then as a driver. Within a year, he started military training at a tank and parachute school. After graduation he became a sergeant in the first mechanized tank regiment of the Red Army, which guarded the Kremlin. In 1934, he learned that his mother had died in Bulgaria, but he could not risk arrest to go home and attend her funeral.

Kostadin Lagadinov lived for several happy years as a soldier in Moscow. But this was the Soviet Union of the 1930s. On the fifth of August 1937, the People's Commissariat for Internal Affairs (NKVD) arrested Lagadinov and threw him into prison. They charged him with being a Bulgarian spy and with participating in an attempt to organize the assassination of Joseph Stalin. Kostadin Lagadinov was guilty of being in the wrong place at the wrong time. As far as Stalin was concerned, Bulgaria was a fascist country and Lagadinov was Bulgarian. This made him untrustworthy.

Stalin was purging the ranks. The Butirka prison overflowed with high party officials and old Communist Party members. In the cell beside Lagadinov, the great aircraft designer Andrei Tupolev was being held on similar charges of espionage. Without ever setting foot in a court, Kostadin Lagadinov was sentenced to eight years of hard labor in a Siberian camp, only four and a half years fewer than the prison sentence he had fled Bulgaria to avoid. And Siberia would be much worse.

From the Butirka prison, Kostadin traveled by train across the USSR. It took a week to reach Syktyvkar in the Komi Republic. From there, the prisoners marched more than sixty kilometers to their final destination. They worked in an open asphalt pit and were only allowed to stop working when the temperature fell below negative 45 degrees Celsius (−49 Fahrenheit). Some days the temperature reached negative 60 degrees Celsius (−76 Fahrenheit). Spittle froze before it hit the ground.

It is often imagined that all inmates of the gulag were political dissidents or, like Kostadin Lagadinov, unjustly accused victims of the purges. But there were some criminals in the Soviet Union, too. The labor camp had its share of convicted murderers who were still Soviet patriots. These criminals hated the so-called spies who worked among them, and the Bulgarians were bullied mercilessly. In 2011, Kostadin Lagadinov remembered that one of his compatriots finally stood up to the Russian prisoners. "I am a Bulgarian revolutionary!" he said. "If you ever call me a spy again, I will kill you!"[7]

"For nearly two years, we ate porridge—flour and water! Without any fat," Kostadin Lagadinov recalled. The prisoners were completely malnourished and lived the labor camp nightmare so vividly described by Aleksandr Solzhenitsyn in *The Gulag Archipelago*.

"Then in mid-June 1941, they organized all of the 'spies' and told us that we were free. I was handed a note. It was to serve as an identity document so that I could travel to Moscow."[8]

This handwritten note, on the letterhead of the camp, was a personal letter of apology from none other than Lavrentiy Beria, the Soviet minister of internal affairs. After spending three long years in prison and in the Siberian labor camp, Lagadinov was freed. Even before Stalin's death, the Soviet government acknowledged that Kostadin Lagadinov had been arrested in error.

It was not a coincidence, however, that the Soviet government freed the Bulgarian "spies" at the beginning of the summer of 1941. For a short time, Bulgaria had remained neutral in the war, but King Boris III signed the Tripartite Pact after the invasion of Romania. Hitler promised King Boris III the return of territories that Bulgaria had lost after the Second Balkan War and World War I. The preliminary Treaty of San Stefano, signed in 1878, had ended the Russo-Turkish War (1877–1878). This treaty created an independent Bulgaria with a territory that stretched to three seas: the Black Sea, the Aegean, and the Adriatic. The enlarged size of the new Bulgarian Kingdom, seen as a natural Russian ally, displeased the British and French, and so the subsequent Treaty of Berlin replaced the Treaty of San Stefano and drastically reduced the size of the Bulgarian Kingdom.[9] King Boris III longed to get it all back. Once in formal alliance with the Nazis, the country was flooded with pro-German propaganda. Bulgarians accepted the Germans and tacitly supported and supplied the Wehrmacht as it marched its way into Greece and Yugoslavia.

But German soldiers did not occupy Bulgaria. Control of the country remained in the hands of the Bulgarian government. As a result, the Bulgarian people were believed to be in favor of King Boris III's decision to support the Nazis.[10] All of this changed, however, with the German invasion of Russia in 1941. With Russia's entry into the war on the Allied side, new efforts would be made to activate those Bulgarians with leftist sympathies. Georgi Dimitrov, Vasil Kolarov, and the Comintern could put men like Lagadinov to strategic use. They prepared a submarine to return the Bulgarian revolutionaries back to their country. There they could lead an underground resistance against the Nazi-allied monarchy.

In 2011, the ninety-eight-year-old Kostadin Lagadinov recalled:

The beginning of the War on the 21st of June found me on the train. Once in Moscow, I went directly to Vasil Kolarov in the Comintern. When he saw me like this, skin and bones and in prison clothes, Uncle Vasil cried. He immediately called to have some clothes made for me. At the store, four Russian beauties pampered me. For two hours they dressed me. At the end, they gave me three hundred rubles! I had never seen such a pile of money! From the store, I went straight to a restaurant. They brought me the menu. I started to order: two of this and two of that and also two of this and two of that. The boy covered the table with plates and food and bread and he asked me, "Where is the second person?" "I am the second person," I said, pointing to myself. I told him that I had been a prisoner.[11]

If anyone in the world had cause to question his commitment to the ideals of communism, and especially the leadership of Comrade Stalin, it was Kostadin Lagadinov. After being hunted in his own country for his political ideals, he sought refuge in the Soviet Union, the country that was supposedly realizing these ideals in practice. Even after years of imprisonment on false charges contrived by a paranoid dictator, Kostadin Lagadinov remained committed to the political dream of the worker's paradise. After only a week in Moscow, he left for Sevastopol to prepare for his mission to Bulgaria. On August 5, 1941, they set out. "Equipped with backpacks, weapons, food and a wireless radio, we boarded the submarine with Lieutenant-Captain Aleksandar Devyatko. The leader of the group was Tsvyatko Radoynov. About a kilometer from the Bulgarian coast, we had to wait for three nights. It happened that it was a full moon, and the night was as bright as day. Finally, the clouds hid the moon and on the night of August 11th, five inflatable boats were put to sea and we began to paddle to shore."[12]

Kostadin boarded a boat with two other men. It was only when they made it to the beach that they realized that the other four boats had not survived. The Bulgarian police had been waiting for them. Of the entire mission, only three of the Bulgarian "spies" remained. Exhausted and disheartened, they first attempted to organize a mission in the Bulgarian city of Sliven. It failed. After this, each man decided to head back toward his native city. Walking on foot across his country, a fugitive once again, Kostadin Lagadinov returned to the outskirts of Razlog in mid-October. It was in the mountains above the city that he would meet, after eight years of absence, his old, communist-literature-distributing friend, Nikola Parapunov, and Kostadin's younger brother, Assen Lagadinov.

5 | A FAILED PETITION

Assen Lagadinov was six years younger than his brother Kostadin and equally active in politics. He spent the decade of the 1930s working with the Razlog branch of the Worker's Youth Union (WYU), a left-wing student organization declared illegal in 1934. Following in the footsteps of his big brother, Assen defied the "monarcho-fascist" government. He kept the now-illegal Razlog student organization alive by moving it underground. A popular youth leader, Assen eventually became the general secretary of the Razlog organization before he left for Sofia to work as a printer.[1]

In November 1940, the Bulgarian government of Prime Minister Bogdan Filov proposed the Law for the Protection of the Nation. The Bulgarian National Assembly voted to enact this law one month later.[2] Even before Bulgaria was officially allied with Germany, Bulgaria's political elite voted to deprive Bulgaria's Jewish population of its civil rights.[3] The law also established a Commissariat for Jewish Affairs, which was charged with overseeing the enforcement of all laws pertaining to the Jewish population. These included restrictions on where Jews could live, forced name changes, exclusion from public service, confiscation of their property, and other restrictions on their economic and professional activities.[4]

At the end of 1940, the WYU sent Assen to Razlog to help organize the Sobolev campaign, a democratic effort by the Bulgarian Communist Party to sign a friendship and mutual assistance pact with

Assen Lagadinov with his fellow printers in 1939 (second from left)

the Soviet Union before the Bulgarian monarchy threw in its lot with Nazi Germany. The Soviet general secretary of foreign affairs, Arkady Sobolev, made the original proposal to the Bulgarian government in November 1940. It guaranteed Soviet support for Bulgarian territorial claims in Yugoslavia and Greece in exchange for the establishment of Soviet military bases on the Black Sea. King Boris III's government refused the offer.[5]

In response, the Bulgarian Communist Party mobilized a massive action to popularize the Soviet proposal. They circulated petitions and collected signatures in the hope of using democratic pressure to force the Bulgarian government to reverse its decision. Underground printing presses churned out leaflets by the thousands. Secret meetings were organized in schools, factories, and even military barracks. In addition to the petition, the communists coordinated a letter writing campaign so that individuals could inform the Council of Ministers and the parliament of their support for the Sobolev proposal. It is estimated that between 350,000 to half a million Bulgarians signed the petition, an impressive result for a poor country with little communications infrastructure and a population of only 5.2 million.[6]

Despite the number of signatures collected, the Bulgarian government, fearing a Bolshevik-style revolution, rejected the proposal. The Germans had already promised the Bulgarians the return of their former territories in

Adolf Hitler greets King Boris III in Berlin

Greece and Yugoslavia, and King Boris III was himself of German royal descent. Three months after the Sobolev action, Prime Minister Bogdan Filov signed the Tripartite Pact. On March 1, 1941, Bulgaria officially entered the war on the side of the Axis powers.

Assen directed the Sobolev campaign in Razlog and in the surrounding regions. The petitions and letters had been in vain, and the entire Sobolev campaign was declared illegal. Anyone who had helped to organize it was at risk of arrest. In mid-January, the police appeared at the Lagadinov home to find Assen, but he managed to escape back to Sofia. They caught up with him there. The police arrested Assen and he served a six-month prison sentence for his part in the collection of signatures.

Meanwhile, after serving his full eight-year sentence for the distribution of illegal literature, Nikola Parapunov had returned to Razlog in late June 1941, just as Germany launched Operation Barbarossa to invade the Soviet Union. Assen was released from prison in July 1941. He came back to Razlog as an illegal, someone actively operating against the king's government. Now committed to fighting the "monarcho-fascists," Assen Lagadinov and Nikola Parapunov moved underground. Later in that summer, Parapunov helped to form one of the first partisan detachments in Bulgaria with Ivan Koza-rev. Their base of operations was to be the Pirin Mountains, just outside of Razlog, those same mountains into which Kostadin Lagadinov had fled eight years earlier. Assen rallied local youth to support the nascent antifascist resistance movement. About nine months later, the youngest Lagadinov brother, Boris, would also join the partisans, leaving only their father and little sister living in the town of Razlog.

The growing number of guerrilla detachments attracted the notice of Moscow, which decided to send them assistance in the form of returning Bulgarian communist émigrés like Kostadin Lagadinov. Of the fifty-five Bulgarians parachuted or submarined into Bulgaria in the late summer of 1941, however, most were captured or killed. It was against the greatest of odds that Kostadin lived to see his brother Assen and old friend once more. In the winter of 1941–1942, the Soviets defeated the Nazis in the Battle of Moscow, and the first fissures appeared in the myth of German military invincibility. Hitler's invasion of Russia also began to turn Bulgarian public opinion against Boris III.

Russia was a fellow Slavic and Orthodox Christian country and an old ally of the Bulgarians. King Boris III and his prime minister, Bogdan Filov, had told the Bulgarian people that they were fighting for the territorial reunification of the Bulgarian populations in Macedonia and Greece. They believed that the Germans would allow Bulgaria to keep the lands it controlled in the Balkans after the war was over. But could the Germans be trusted to keep any agreement after the abrogation of the Molotov-Ribbentrop Pact? Hitler signed a formal treaty of nonaggression with the USSR, but invaded anyway.

In the spring of 1942, a controversial map was published in Germany, listing the newly annexed territories in Macedonia and Thrace as territories under *temporary* Bulgarian administration.[7] As with Molotov-Ribbentrop, it seemed that Hitler had no intention of keeping his promises. It was in this context that Georgi Dimitrov, still based in Moscow, decided to create a Bulgarian version of the Popular Front. By mid-1942, various opposition parties in Bulgaria came together to form the Fatherland Front (FF).[8] The FF demanded that Bulgaria break with the Axis powers and establish new ties with the Allied forces, switching sides in the middle of the war. As more parties joined the Fatherland Front, the number of men and women inspired to fight with the partisan detachments grew.

For Assen and Kostadin Lagadinov, life as a partisan was hard and dangerous, especially in the fiercely cold winter months. Freezing and hungry, the men and women hiding in the mountains suffered from frostbite and disease. They relied almost exclusively on the support of the local peasants for food, clothing, weapons, ammunition, and medicines. A partisan helper living in the village was called a *yatak*, and it was the *yatatsi* who faced the fiercest reprisals if the Bulgarian police discovered their clandestine activities.[9]

In Razlog, the Lagadinov brothers counted on their brave younger sister. At the age of eleven, Elena Lagadinova smuggled messages and supplies to her brothers in the mountains. Through their sister, the Lagadinovs could keep abreast of the local news and information regarding the ever-changing political situation. From Elena they learned of German military defeats and of the infamous German map that rallied ever more support for their cause.

Small partisan bands like the one led by Nikola Parapunov raided German supplies and committed random acts of sabotage and arson to disrupt Bulgarian military operations. They also organized targeted political assassinations of Bulgarian politicians and Wehrmacht officers. For the most part, however, they inflicted little damage to the Axis war machine.[10] Disorganized and concerned primarily with obtaining food and arms, their first goal was survival.

The partisan movements in Greece and Yugoslavia were better organized and had the support of local peasant populations, angered by the occupation of their lands by Axis forces. The Bulgarian peasantry could not be counted on to support the partisans when the government promoted the idea that the partisans were really brigands and thieves using the war as an excuse to justify the theft of food and livestock from the local population. Despite their sullied reputation, more men and women headed up into the mountains to join the guerrilla movement. One found young men defecting from the king's army and citizens disgusted by the Bulgarian government's decision to allow the deportation of 11,459 Jews in occupied Greece and Macedonia.[11] Indeed, after this decision was taken in March 1942, many Bulgarian Jews also swelled the partisan ranks.[12] According to the historian Frederick Chary, there were about four hundred Jewish partisans out of ten thousand active resistance fighters, a membership rate that was "four times greater than the population as a whole." The Bulgarian government used this fact to justify its anti-Semitic policies.[13]

General Hristo Lukov was president of the Union of Legionnaires, a "full-fledged fascist organization."[14] A virulent anti-Semite, Lukov called for the ethnic cleansing of the Bulgarian nation and was assassinated in February 1943.[15] Although the killers escaped, the Bulgarian government blamed the

Assen Lagadinov
in 1942

murder on a nineteen-year-old girl—a Jewish, communist partisan—and used the assassination as an excuse to step up the persecution of the resistance movement.[16] In his diary, Prime Minister Bogdan Filov recounts a conversation with the current minister of interior, Petar Gabrovski, wherein they decided to "begin a newspaper campaign against the Communists and the Jews, while tightening repressive measures against them."[17]

In April 1943, just as Frank Thompson was joining the Special Operations Executive, the leaders of the Bulgarian Communist Party attempted to organize the Bulgarian partisan detachments into a People's Liberation Rebel Army. As the rebel numbers grew, the Bulgarian government responded by further increasing its efforts to stamp out the guerrilla threat. The government created a special gendarmerie force with almost unlimited power to hunt down and persecute partisans and their yatak helpers.[18] The partisans called this force "the Black Army."

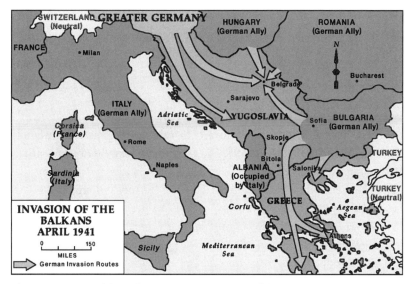

The Axis invasion of the Balkans, 1941 (map courtesy of the U.S. Holocaust Memorial Museum)

Tensions rose again on the twenty-third of May when the Commissariat for Jewish Affairs issued orders for the immediate deportation of the roughly twenty-five thousand Bulgarian Jews living in Sofia.[19] Sofia's Jews were given only three days to depart from the capital, taking with them only what they could carry.[20] Men were expected to report to the Sofia train station with their families and a complete inventory of their personal effects, leaving their homes and businesses behind. Officially, the government wanted to re-settle the Jews in smaller towns in the Bulgarian provinces, but at the time many believed (understandably so) that Sofia's Jews were being sent to their deaths. The deportation to the provinces was represented as a first step in their ultimate deportation to Treblinka. An article published in July 1943 in the *Worker's Cause*, an underground newspaper of the Bulgarian commu-nists, attempted to rally other citizens to action:

> It is the patriotic duty of every Bulgarian to unite in a powerful campaign in defence of the Jews, which will embrace all democratic and patriotic forces in this country and prevent the materialization of the intentions of the king, the government, and the remaining agents of Hitler in this coun-try. . . . We warn you that the problem of the deportation of the Jews from the country is not precluded. The government was obliged to put it off for

the time being, but, under favorable circumstances, it will try to fulfill its criminal intentions. The latter can be prevented only with a consistent, bold, and persistent struggle. . . . With joint efforts and decisive actions, the fascist beast will be crushed.[21]

If Bulgarians heeded this call, they put themselves in grave personal danger. Anyone caught aiding the resistance could be arrested and summarily executed. The gendarmes and the local police also took to burning the family homes of known partisan fighters. The gendarmes committed many atrocities—gang rapes, decapitations, and bodily mutilations.[22] They often displayed the severed heads of dead partisans on the tops of long pikes in village squares as a warning to those whose sympathies lay with the resistance. People were frightened into submission by the sheer brutality of the Bulgarian government's reprisals.[23]

If the "monarcho-fascists" were liberal with the stick, they were also generous with the carrot. Later in the war, the government offered up to a 50,000-lev reward for the head of any dead partisan, and between 1943 and 1944 the government spent more than 28 million levs on such rewards.[24] As a result, many peasants became informants for the gendarmes, betraying the partisans when they came into the villages to ask for food and supplies. Vigilante bands of villagers hunted partisans in the mountains for profit. Isolated and without support, some partisan detachments started raiding villages for food and ammunition, further alienating them from the peasants. In order to survive, the Lagadinov brothers and their partisan comrades would need another source of support.[25]

This is what Frank Thompson and the Special Operations Executive hoped to provide.

6 | LAWRENCE OF BULGARIA?

"If we should meet again, why then we'll smile." If not, why then those that follow us will be able to smile far more happily and honestly in the world that we all helped to make.

—FRANK THOMPSON TO IRIS MURDOCH, DECEMBER 1943

A little before midnight on January 25, 1944, just weeks after a devastating Allied carpet bombing of Sofia,[1] Frank Thompson and a signalman parachuted into a drop zone near the village of Tsrna Trava in Bulgarian-occupied Serbia. Also falling out of the night sky were dozens of boxes of boots, clothing, rifles, handguns, grenades, and ammunition. The British SOE command in Cairo had sent hundreds of forty-eight-hour ration packs, food desperately needed by the partisans.

Frank Thompson hit the ground with his revolver drawn. Shadowy figures rushed up to him in the darkness. "Are you Bulgarian partisans?" he said, trying out his newly acquired Bulgarian.

They were.

Major Mostyn Davies and three other British SOE operatives were already on the ground with the partisans when Frank dropped out of the sky. The successful supply drop, in particular, would have been a great relief for Mostyn Davies. According to the Bulgarian partisans who had been working with Davies before Frank joined them, Davies had not been very successful at coordinating supply drops.[2] He was supposed to send instructions to SOE headquarters in Cairo about where to make the next drop of supplies. Once he received and decoded the return message, he would arrange with the Bulgarian partisans to create a drop zone at the appointed time. This meant lighting bales of hay on fire, which made it easier for the Bulgarian army and police to discover their location. The partisans often waited in vain for planes that never came, risking their lives for no reward. What was worse, the Bulgarian gendarmes would sometimes raid villages near the drop zones looking for the weapons that they assumed had been dropped.[3] Raicho Takov Mitov, a partisan in the Tran detachment who had worked closely with Davies, did not have a high opinion of him: "Honestly speaking, Major Davis [sic] seemed not to have a favorable attitude to us and our cause. Properly speaking he was unpunctual. Throughout January 1944 we expected the transport but it did not arrive. Davis [sic] explained the delay was owing to bad meteorological conditions which had prevented the planes from taking off. At the same time, however, the British bombers took off twice from Cairo to bomb Sofia, despite the bad weather."[4]

Frank Thompson was ten years Davies's junior. He surprised the partisans with his slow, but grammatically correct Bulgarian. Although he never admitted his own membership in the Communist Party (perhaps thinking that he would not be believed), he told the partisans that he greatly admired the achievements of communism and the ongoing importance of the struggle against fascism. Some of the Bulgarians thought Frank Thompson was a secret agent because of his language skills, and they kept their distance. But he impressed many others. His manners and demeanor led Raicho Takov Mitov to assume that Frank was "a man of high culture."[5]

"Captain Thompson I remember very well," recalled the female partisan Vera Nacheva: "He was tall, slim, with clear eyes and a small and expressive face. He spoke slowly, seriously, with a concentration somehow unbecoming to his age. Sometimes I saw him burn some note or lie on the ground, his eyes fixed in the sky as if absorbed in deep thought. He smoked a pipe. On the whole Thompson spoke little. I don't remember that he ever said anything about himself. I never asked him."[6]

Dencho Znepolski, a partisan leader who would eventually lead Frank and the Second Sofia Brigade to their final battle at Batuliya, also had a clear recollection of Frank and his time among the Bulgarian partisans. He wrote:

[Thompson] was very much attached to the people, and showed great interest in the peasant life. He showed a happy and kind character, both when he spoke Bulgarian and when he danced Bulgarian national dances. It was difficult to tell he was a foreigner. He got used to everything, he was hungry with the rest of us, he had to fight the second enemy of the partisans—the lice—just as everybody else did. This is what binds people together in the struggle against Fascism. This made the Bulgarian partisans and the Bulgarian people feel Thompson close to their hearts.[7]

Frank's orders were clear: to assist the partisans in wreaking as much havoc in Bulgaria as possible. To do this, he needed the British to increase supply drops from Cairo. The two wireless sets were key to their mission. These were huge fifty-volt radios in large metal casings with heavy batteries, cumbersome in any circumstances, but on wintery, mountainous terrain almost impossible to move. Lumbering draft mules bore the weight of the wireless sets, and these slowed the partisans down when they had to flee from advancing Bulgarian forces.

Challenges filled the first two months of Frank Thompson's time in Bulgaria. The partisans were constantly on the move, hunted through the mountains from camp to camp. More bad weather, and their inability to stay in one place long enough to send and receive encrypted messages, meant no supply drops for about five weeks. As the partisan numbers increased, the need for boots, warm clothing, weapons, and especially food became dire.

In mid-March, the Bulgarian forces sent in more than ten thousand troops to root out the partisans in the south Serbian plateau. The partisan detachments took heavy losses. They were brave, but also uncoordinated and in dire need of ammunition. The only thing they could do was run and hide. The six SOE officers were split up during the intensified fighting. Mostyn Davies, Frank Thompson, and a signals sergeant managed to hide their wireless set under some brush and took shelter in an old mill. Within moments of settling in, they heard boots at the door. Thompson jumped up and leapt out of a low window into the dark night before a grenade exploded in the mill. Davies and the signals sergeant were doomed.[8]

Frank Thompson scrambled up a mountain. He dug a shelter out of the snow at the base of a tree. He spent an entire night huddled up in a ball, pressing his knees against his chest, fighting off the cold, itching with lice, and hoping that the gendarmes would not find him. The following day he caught sight of a shepherd.

"Tell the partisans that I am still alive," he said to the shepherd.

Thompson waited a full day in the dugout wondering whether nightfall would bring friends or foes. He did not know how far away the partisans were. If no one came for him by the next day, he would have to make a decision. Should he try to find his way back to the Serbian border on his own or should he just wait? If the gendarmes caught him, they might shoot him on the spot. Thompson was lucky. The partisans found him, and together they retrieved the wireless set and all went back to the Serbian border where a safe zone had been established by the Yugoslav partisans.[9]

At this point, the whole world seemed to be conspiring against Frank Thompson and the Bulgarian partisans. From Serbia, Thompson sent a request for a new wireless operator. When he came, Sergeant Kenneth Scott and his decoding book were dropped at different locations. Then SOE headquarters moved from Egypt to southern Italy. Messages sent in code had to be decoded by ciphers, and the new headquarters was understaffed. This process delayed messages to and from Bulgaria by days. As a result, supply drops were infrequent in March and April, and not successful enough to justify the risks the partisans took to arrange them. The drops failed to meet the demands of the incoming volunteers who hoped to fight.[10]

Either there was a terrible and ongoing communications failure or SOE headquarters had lost interest in Thompson's mission. The infrequency of supply drops could have been due to bad weather, but may have been a deliberate attempt to forestall a popular communist uprising in Bulgaria.[11] Although the British had sent Thompson in to organize the Bulgarian partisans, Churchill was no fan of communism. Churchill would throw Britain's support behind the Bulgarian monarchy if it broke its alliance with the Nazis.[12]

The possibility of maintaining the Bulgarian monarchy became more realistic after the mysterious death of King Boris III in August 1943. Rumors circulated that Hitler poisoned King Boris III for his refusal to deport the Bulgarian Jews (who, although limited in their civil rights, did enjoy the protection of the Bulgarian government).[13] His son, Simeon II, was a young boy, too young to rule in his own right. Bogdan Filov, Simeon's uncle Prince Kiril, and a lieutenant general named Nikola Mikhov ruled as regents to Simeon II.[14] As the Germans began to lose ground in the East, the Bulgarian government put out feelers to the British and Americans through the American consulate in Istanbul. One of the conditions of their switching allegiances would have certainly been that the British stop supplying the Bulgarian guerrillas.

Frank Thompson first met Svetozar Vukmanović, also known as General Tempo (Tito's right-hand man), in partisan-controlled Serbia. Tempo commanded the Macedonian partisans and hoped to organize the Bulgarian partisans using British supplies to create a more coordinated fighting force. Many of the men joining up were runaway Bulgarian soldiers. They had basic military training and strengthened the ranks of peasants and shepherds forming the core of the guerrilla detachments. With so many new recruits, the Bulgarian partisans amassing on the Serbia-Bulgarian border were divided into two brigades: the First and Second Sofia Brigades. Frank Thompson was attached to the latter.[15]

As the resistance movement grew in strength and the Red Army advanced toward Bulgaria, the leadership of the Comintern and that of the Bulgarian Communist Party in Moscow tried to increase their control over partisan operations. Georgi Dimitrov issued orders to the resistance through an underground radio station, Radio Hristo Botev. He commanded the Bulgarian partisans back into Bulgaria to foment insurrection in the cities of Sofia and Plovdiv. When the Red Army crossed into Bulgaria, as now looked inevitable, Dimitrov hoped that the Bulgarian Communist Party could sweep into power on the back of a popular uprising.[16]

Dimitrov ordered the Second Sofia Brigade to move into Bulgaria and head toward Plovdiv. On its way, it was to meet up with another band of partisans operating outside of Sofia, the Chavdar Brigade. With regular British supply drops, the two forces would build up strength in the Sredna Gora Mountains, which had been declared "free" by Dimitrov in Moscow. From there, they would wait for the Red Army and then carry out the liberation of Bulgaria's major cities.

General Tempo was resolutely opposed to this plan. In his memoir, Tempo recalled making his thoughts on the matter clear to Thompson:

I tried, at least, to persuade the leader of the British military mission, Major Thompson, of the folly of the decision to set off for the interior of Bulgaria towards the Sredna Gora Mountains. I told him that I frankly did not believe that the arrival of a brigade in Bulgaria would provoke a general armed uprising. I suggested that his mission come along with us and promised that we would be returning to this area within a month at the latest, thus enabling him to continue his mission. He turned down my suggestion, not only because, as a British army officer, he had to obey orders (his task was to link up with the Bulgarian HQ and the OF [leadership of the Fatherland Front] which was somewhere in the mountains near Plovdiv) but also because he believed that the situation in Bulgaria was such that the appearance of Bulgarian brigades would set in motion a mass armed uprising.[17]

Tempo doubted that the Bulgarians had the discipline or the supplies necessary to carry out such a long march behind enemy lines. He understood that the politicians in Moscow were mobilizing the Second Sofia Brigade without a clear sense of military strategy. Without support from the local populations or regular British supply drops, there was no way the mission could make it to Plovdiv. The peasants feared the brutality of the Bulgarian police, who, on the orders of Docho Hristov, Bulgaria's new minister of interior, stepped up the repressive measures against the families and villages of partisans in the spring of 1944. British supply drops would be even harder to coordinate on Bulgarian territory.[18]

It is hard to imagine that twenty-three-year-old Frank Thompson, probably smoking his pipe while contemplating the beauty of the Serbian spring, didn't seriously consider staying in safe Yugoslav territory. He could have teamed up with General Tempo, leading the Second Sofia Brigade on short missions in and out of Bulgaria until the Bulgarian partisans were better armed and trained. He could have waited for clear instructions from headquarters before making any decisions.

It was during this time in Serbia that Frank Thompson wrote the last three letters of his life. In his final letter to Iris Murdoch, dated April 21, 1944, he wrote of the two priorities in his life:

1. People and everything to do with people, their habits, their loves and hates, their arts, their languages. Everything of importance revolves around people.
2. Animals and flowers. These bring me a constant undercurrent of joy. Just now I am reveling in plum blossoms and young lambs and the first leaves of the briar roses. One doesn't need anything more than these. I couldn't wish for better company.[19]

To his family back in England he wrote:

There really isn't any news about myself. I've been working hard, I hope to some purpose, and keeping brave company—some of the best in the world. Next to this comradeship, my greatest pleasure has been rediscovering things like violets, cowslips and plum-blossom after three lost springs. I'd quite forgotten how marvelously lovely leaf buds are just when they're breaking—especially beech-leaf buds. All this makes me more homesick than ever before, because England, when you've said all you like about Greece or Italy or the Lebanon, is the only place where they know how to organize spring.[20]

On April 29, Thompson tried one last time to radio SOE headquarters for instructions, but he received no reply. He had to make the decision on his own. His orders were to stay with the Bulgarian partisans, and the Second Sofia Brigade had orders from Moscow to march into Bulgaria with or without the British mission. On the nights of May 10 and 11, there finally arrived a massive British supply drop, and perhaps this reassured Thompson that his orders were still standing. He may have also been genuinely concerned about the fate of the Chavdar Brigade, which was supposedly in dire need of support.

In his recollection of the mission, Dencho Znepolski, the commander of the Second Sofia Brigade recalled: "In this move towards Stara Planina, tired from the heavy marching, Major Thompson showed himself to be a fearless fighter against Fascism. He longed to enter the heart of Bulgaria, where he watched indignantly the cruelties exercised by Docho Hristov's gendarmerie, the police, and the so-called 'hunters' groups.' He wished he could fly there and be able to give help to the partisans from the Srednogorie, who were fighting the well-armed Fascists with mere sticks."[21]

Perhaps Thompson was a little naïve and felt himself invincible. He had, after all, survived the Middle East, the Sicilian landings, and the attack that killed Mostyn Davies in Bulgaria, telling his parents that he held "the record for the twenty yards sprint for three major battle areas."[22] He may have also believed that fighting was the only honorable option. In a letter from Italy to their father, E. P. tried to make sense of his brother's motivations: "For Frank this war is a crusade for the fullest life for all human beings, and he always had—what many of my comrades have not—the conviction that the war is a right war and the outcome will be good. Frank could not do otherwise. If he had not chosen this job, he would have betrayed his own integrity. He could not have written, talked, worked, with any sort of personal honesty. He would not have been Frank."[23]

Stowers Johnson had a very different take on Thompson's motivations. According to Johnson's journalistic account, Thompson viewed the Second

Sofia Brigade as his "private army." He hoped to ride into Bulgaria like his hero T. E. Lawrence had done in Arabia during World War I. Thompson's commitment to communism and his thirst for personal glory made him long to become "Thompson of Bulgaria."[24]

Perhaps the most interesting explanation for Thompson's decision to cross into Bulgaria, on what Tempo had warned him was no better than a suicide mission, was the news that Iris Murdoch was romantically involved with a mutual friend back in England. Frank Thompson's most recent biographer, Peter Conradi, closely examined the correspondence between Murdoch and Thompson in the months leading up to his decision to cross into Bulgaria. There are certainly hints that Thompson was upset by the idea of Iris being physically involved with other men.[25]

The rationale behind Frank Thompson's decision may never be clear, but survivors of the Second Sofia Brigade recalled that it was he who argued in favor of moving into Bulgaria at the crucial strategy meeting held in the village of Kalna before their departure. On May 12, 1944, the Second Sofia Brigade received reconnaissance that the Bulgarian army was moving to attack Kalna. Frank Thompson and the Bulgarian partisans crossed into Bulgaria two days later, marching toward the embattled Chavdar Brigade. Almost as soon as they stepped over the border, the Bulgarian forces hunted the partisans like game. Frank and the Second Sofia Brigade marched for days without food or rest. They ate snails and grass and unripe berries. These upset their stomach and caused violent bouts of diarrhea. With bellies cramping and heads spinning, they forged on.[26]

Vera Nacheva was one of the partisans who had crossed into Bulgaria with Frank Thompson and Dencho Znepolski. In the late 1970s, she had vivid recollections of Frank's chivalry on that final march of the Second Sofia Brigade:

> There were two horses in the brigade. We used them for carrying the sick and wounded. Often when there were no sick or wounded people we offered Thompson to ride, but he always declined. "I'm still young," he answered, "let the ladies or the wounded ride." When Vlado Trichkov noticed that young Thompson was in low spirits, he tried to cheer him up saying, "Frank, if you help us to destroy fascism sooner, we'll give you the prettiest Bulgarian girl for a wife." Thompson removed his pipe from his mouth, smiled and answered something jokingly. During the last days of that terrible march, I never heard him complain. He endured all hardships with great fortitude.[27]

A pensive
Frank Thompson

During an ambush, the mule carrying the wireless set fell into a river, ruining the batteries. Without the wireless, they had no way to communicate with SOE headquarters. There would be no supply drops. Desperate, they plunged on. Some rumors reached them that the Chavdar Brigade, with which they had hoped to join forces, had been wiped out weeks before. Without a destination, with no way to contact headquarters, and with no local support from the peasants who betrayed them at every instance, the Second Sofia Brigade was stranded.

On the thirty-first of May, Thompson and the other partisans rested in a little space in the forest outside of the village of Batuliya, trying to recoup much needed strength. They had been marching for two weeks, hunted by the gendarmes at every turn. The rations had long run out; they had not eaten in a week. Peasants they had conscripted as guides betrayed them.

When the local police got word about the partisans, they mobilized hundreds of troops to surround the Second Sofia Brigade. Caught by surprise and vastly outnumbered, the brigade members scattered in the melee that ensued. Two British SOE officers perished in the attack. Thompson and Kenneth Scott initially managed to flee and hide in the forest. Their plan was to split up and to try to make it back to the partisan-controlled territory they had left in Serbia. It was their only chance to stay alive.

7 | AMBUSHED IN BATULIYA

Among the few sources that I unearthed about Frank Thompson and his mission in Bulgaria, the 1979 book *Grateful Bulgaria* was perhaps the most intimate.[1] This was the book that E. P. Thompson had seen when he visited Bulgaria before writing to Freeman Dyson about the latter's *New Yorker* article. It was clearly part of the greater effort to use the story of Thompson's sacrifice as a way to confer legitimacy on the rule of the Bulgarian Communist Party, particularly since Bulgaria's leader at the time, Todor Zhivkov, had himself been a partisan.

In this book, the former partisan leader Slavcho Transki tracked down all living Bulgarians who had served with Frank Thompson in the Second Sofia Brigade. The book includes many long quotes from former partisans who survived the final battle at Batuliya, and it is a moving account of Thompson's last weeks. The following quote is from Vera Nacheva who made the fateful march into Bulgaria with her husband, Nacho Ivanov, and Frank Thompson in May 1944. Her words capture the desperation and chaos of the ambush at Batuliya. It was the last time she saw Thompson alive.

We traveled nine long days and nights with very short breaks. We were hungry, exhausted, sleepless. Sometimes we made 50 km a day across pathless ground without a break, without a wink of sleep. Even when we had time enough to stop and have a nap, we couldn't close our eyes shivering with cold and fear. And to crown it all, we were pestered by lice—enemy No. 2, as we used to call them. We dreamed of reaching a larger forest or more inaccessible locality where we could stop and take a rest at our ease.

It was vital to move away from Sofia as soon as possible but our legs failed us. It happened that some of our comrades would drop asleep in a standing position. At the command "march" they would automatically start in the opposite direction. Once we had stopped near a highway to make sure there was no ambush. Seven of our comrades had been asleep and did not join us. It was not until we had walked a considerable distance away from the danger and had counted our numbers that we found they were missing. It was pitch-dark and it was impossible to find them, moreover that we did not know their exact location. We discovered them by their snoring. . . .

Once, in the area of Batuliya, nearly a whole battalion broke up and we sent a large group to find it. On our way we met two men with a donkey carrying corn or flour most likely obtained on the black market. We detained them for safety. We stopped in a scanty growth, very unsuitable for a longer stay, but it was more dangerous to move on. Besides, we had to wait for the rest of our comrades to come back. The moment we stopped, we all went off. The comrade who was guarding the peasants fell asleep too. The peasants seized the opportunity and ran away to inform the police about us. Trouble overtook us soon.

It was in the afternoon on May 24. All of us were asleep sitting, half-lying or leaning against a tree. The place was slanting, the ground was moist and cold, yet we were fast asleep. Only a few of us heard the strange rustle although it came from close quarters. I had just looked round to see who was moving so unwarily when I heard Yordanka, lying next to me, say, "Comrades, who has bandage and cotton wool?" It turned out that the enemy had rolled down two large stones to make sure we were there. The stones had injured two comrades.

The moment we stirred, a fearful fusillade shook the surrounding hills. It was clear that we had been betrayed and now a large army unit was attacking us from close quarters. We were being heavily machine-gunned. Thousands of bullets were whizzing overhead. We had no time to collect ourselves and counteract the enemy attack. Some of the more experienced comrades led by Commander Dicho Petrov made an attempt to break the ring but with no success. Dicho was the first to fall. We had to move away immediately from the enemy positions and since we had failed to make a breakthrough we directed ourselves to the nearby glen. In that moment this seemed the wisest thing to do.

A sculpture in honor of
the men and women who
became partisans

We soon reached a safer place protected by the slope and the trees. The shoot-
ing became more intense. Bullets began to come from other directions as well.
No commands could be heard. The shootings seem to have ceased after we de-
scended into the glen. I looked around to see who was with me. I wondered
where my husband was. Luckily, he was alive and had been looking for me too.
When we met almost simultaneously we said to each other, "Are you alive?"
We had hardly exchanged a couple of words when the mountain shook with an
even more frightful fusillade. The shooting came from the opposite ridge. This
could only mean that the two heights and the adjoining ridges had been occu-
pied by the enemy. At that moment I could see Vlado Trichkov, Yordanka Ni-
kolova, Thompson, Nacho, Valentin Andreev, Gocho Gopin and Bonka. Vlado
was right next to me. I saw him straighten his trousers. I passed by him and
walked away from the group.

The shooting intensified. I continued to run over the stony gorge trying to get to the small grove as soon as possible. There was no shooting there. I was making slow progress, however, because my legs did not obey me. Bullets were showering on all sides. I stumbled, fell, picked myself up again in an endless succession. When I finally got to the grove, I made a stop, threw the ground sheet over my shoulders and fell down. I thought, "Here will be my grave."[2]

8 | GUERRILLAS IN THE MIST

How many Bulgarian partisans were there? This is one of the questions that haunted Thompson's mission. Were there enough to carry off a full-blown revolution against King Boris III and his government, or just random and isolated groups incapable of any significant actions? This is a question I often pondered as I learned more about the history of the Balkans during World War II. The headquarters of the SOE determined that the Bulgarian partisan numbers were large enough to deserve British support. Certainly the king's government reckoned that there were enough guerrillas to warrant special state efforts to squash them. Sitting in Moscow, Georgi Dimitrov seemed to believe that the partisan forces were strong enough to take the country.

But the truth is that the actual number of Bulgarians fighting against their government remains shrouded in mystery. The number of men and women hiding in the mountains is hard to determine since they were operating illegally. This number grows exponentially if one includes the helpers (yataks) who were supporting the guerrillas, often at great personal risk. During the communist era, official historians often exaggerated the number to over one hundred thousand. Subsequent scholars working after 1989 have claimed that the true figure was closer to ten thousand, but once again this all depends on who is counted as a "partisan."[1] In September 1944, there was supposedly one partisan division consisting of brigades, detachments, and combat groups (*cheti*), with the combat groups being the smallest units.[2] Frank Thompson marched with the Second Sofia Brigade, which consisted of about two hundred partisans, and the First Sofia Brigade had about three hundred members. The Lagadinovs were officially part of the Nikola Parapunov Brigade, but spent most of their time operating as an independent combat group, particularly during the cold winter months when the primary objective of all partisans was merely to stay alive until spring. The British military historian Alan Ogden asserts that 9,140 partisans and 20,070 yatatsi died "as a result of torture and executions" between 1941 and 1944.[3] It is unclear how many died of exposure or starvation. At that time, no one kept track.

As to their effectiveness, once again it depends on whom you ask. Some argue that they were relatively useless compared to the Serbian and Greek partisans. Marshall Lee Miller wrote in 1975 that "the communist armed resistance movement in Bulgaria was generally poorly organized, poorly armed and poorly led."[4] In her study *British Policy in South-East Europe in the Second World War*, Elisabeth Barker also claimed that the British effort to support the Bulgarian partisans failed due to the many difficulties of the Bulgarian internal situation and inconsistencies within the Bulgarian Communist Party.[5]

Others believe that the partisans did fairly well considering their limited support and far more difficult conditions. Special Operations Executive historian Norman Davies insisted that although partisan activity was limited, the fierce reprisals against the partisans helped to turn the Bulgarian population against their government.[6] In his memoir, published in 1947 in honor of his elder brother, E. P. Thompson argued that the effectiveness of the Bulgarian partisans must be considered in relation to the many difficulties they faced. He wrote: "Partisan detachments once formed were continually in action; they had no opportunity for taking a breath or regrouping in peace; they had no contact with the outside world. They fought an isolated war, alone in a countryside riddled with informers, surrounded on every side by enemy troops, many hundreds of miles from their nearest allies, who either had not the resources or the interest to give them aid. Only a handful of those who took up arms in 1942 survived to see the liberation of Bulgaria and the revolution of September 9th."[7]

Indeed, most of the partisan units formed in 1941 and 1942 were wiped out, but the situation began to change in 1943 after the Russian victory in Stalingrad. By 1944, partisan numbers increased exponentially as more ordinary men and women, as well as defecting soldiers from the Bulgarian army, headed up into the mountains. They could see which way the tide was turning and wanted to be on the winning side of the war. When the Red Army crossed into Bulgaria in September 1944, communist insurgents took the towns, just as Georgi Dimitrov and the leaders of the Comintern had planned. The surviving partisans descended from the mountains, and it was these partisans who helped to form the people's militias that maintained order in the immediate aftermath of September 9 when Bulgaria switched sides in the war. For all the partisans and partisan helpers who survived, this was the glorious day that they had all been fighting for. They streamed into the villages and towns as war heroes, and the mythmaking began.

To this day, the historiography and memory of the Bulgarian partisans remains contested.[8] As we have seen, different sources give different estimates of their numbers and varying opinions on their effectiveness. Unlike the partisans in Greece or Yugoslavia, who had the support of the local peasant population because they were fighting against a hostile occupying force, the Bulgarians were allied with Hitler. No Germans occupied their country. The soldiers of the gendarmerie were all fellow Bulgarians in the service of their own king, and the day-to-day situation was stable and calm for most non-Jewish Bulgarians. Boris III's foreign policy succeeded in preventing any major battles being carried out on Bulgarian soil. It was very easy for Bulgarians to be complacent, especially after the tumult of the two Balkan Wars and World War I. There was little reason to stick your neck out and risk your life. Therefore, those who joined the partisans were not considered patriots or heroes but were often viewed as troublemakers and traitors. Since many later partisans were also deserters, they were called cowards as well.

Heroes or villains? It depends on whom you asked.[9] In either case, it was their almost blind devotion to communism that makes them either good or evil. Almost all of these men and women who took to the mountains, or risked their lives to smuggle food, medicines, or messages to the partisans, dreamed of a different world. Not all of them were communists—some of them were anarchists, Agrarians, or social democrats—but they all shared the common ideal of a future where workers and peasants would have a greater say in government and a greater portion of the wealth they labored to produce. Frank Thompson, the Lagadinovs, and countless other young idealists across Europe embraced this dream, a dream that gave them courage and hope.

No one has written more elegantly about this idealistic zeal than Ernest

Hemingway in his novel *For Whom the Bell Tolls*. Hemingway's protagonist, Robert Jordan, is a young American who has gone to Spain to fight as a communist partisan in the International Brigade. For Robert Jordan, fighting among the guerrillas in Spain was like

> taking part in a crusade. That was the only word for it although it was a word that had been so worn and abused that it no longer gave its true meaning. You felt, in spite of all bureaucracy and inefficiency and party strife, something that was like the feeling you expected to have and did not have when you made your first communion. It was a feeling of consecration to a duty toward all the oppressed of the world which would be as difficult and embarrassing to speak about as religious experience and yet it was authentic as the feeling you had when you heard Bach, or stood in Chartres Cathedral or the Cathedral at Leon and saw the light coming through the great windows; or when you saw Mantegna and Greco and Brueghel in the Prado. It gave you a part in something that you could believe in wholly and completely and in which you felt an absolute brotherhood with the others who were engaged in it. It was something that you had never known before but that you had experienced now and you gave such importance to it and the reasons for it that your own death seemed of complete unimportance; only a thing to be avoided because it would interfere with the performance of your duty. But the best thing was that there was something you could do about this feeling and this necessity too. You could fight.[10]

Those who took to the mountains in Bulgaria knew that the odds were against them, but they fought anyway. Despite their grand ideals, the day-to-day life of a partisan was mundane and often uneventful. Unlike E. P. Thompson's assertion that the partisans rarely had time to catch their breath, there were months spent hiding and just trying to stay alive. In the mid-1980s, Boris Lagadinov, the youngest of the Lagadinov brothers, wrote some reflections on his time as a partisan. When I first read these pages, I got a rare glimpse into the quotidian challenges of the partisans living in the mountains. Boris Lagadinov's memories are remarkable because they follow the activities of one combat group that was formed early in the war and managed to survive for years. The Lagadinov brothers did not wait until after the battle of Stalingrad to take up arms against the "monarcho-fascists," nor were they fighting for their own civil rights. They were communist activists even before Hitler's invasion of the Soviet Union because they believed that

Boris (left) and Kostadin Lagadinov

communism would end the imperialistic wars and politically enfranchise the toiling masses.

The document consisted of thirty typewritten sheets. By the twenty-fifth page, however, the ink in the typewriter ribbon started to run out and some of the words on the final pages were illegible. The text ends abruptly. The document was titled "Memories." It seemed to be a response to the memoir written by Georgi Madolev: *Parapunovtsi*. Madolev had become the political commissar for the Nikola Parapunov Brigade in 1943–1944 and had gone on to become a prominent politician during the communist era. Boris Lagadinov was apparently angered by some versions of the events that Madolev included in his memoir.

When I first started working with these pages, I did my best to render the grammatically informal Bulgarian into colloquial English while endeavoring to preserve the original tone of its author.[11] This presented several challenges. The document itself was full of typos and there were some place names that were difficult to verify. The text was clearly a first draft and was full of long digressions and nonlinear recollections of the same event, as if Boris Lagadinov would write about something and then remember that he had something more to say about it a few pages later. There were also some strange and confusing misspellings, and an excruciating amount of detail about local people and the topography of the Pirin Mountains where the Parapunov Brigade operated. In the end, all faithful translations of the document from Bulgarian into English proved too difficult to follow. Given the complications of translation, the need to edit for coherence, and my desire to only use sections of the text, the chapter that follows is an interpretive rendering of the material contained in Boris Lagadinov's short reflections. What I learned from those pages, those memories of a time long passed, was that the partisans were neither heroes nor villains. They were ordinary men and women trying to make a difference in a world turned upside down.

9 | EVERYDAY LIFE AS A PARTISAN

I was working as a woodcutter in Mrazenitsa when fascist Germany started the war against the USSR on June 22, 1941. I worked with a gang of men, and during those first days, we were very confused. We had no idea what the future had in store for us. As the war raged on with terrible force, we would look at each other in astonishment.

Six months earlier, my brother Assen had been sent from Sofia to help organize the Sobolev campaign in Razlog and the surrounding area. In mid-January, the police came looking for him, to arrest him for his participation. To avoid this immediate arrest, he decided to go back to Sofia.

The weather was very cold. The road to Simitli was buried under snowdrifts, but he was determined to go. I accompanied him to the third kilometer. He continued on foot to Simitli. Chilled to the bone, he arrived in Gradevo. Had it not been for Bai Pudev,[1] who welcomed him and helped him get warm and rested, Assen probably would not have made it to Sofia. But his departure from Razlog did not save him from serving the jail sentence for his participation in the Sobolev campaign. He was caught at the end of January and interred in a prison in the village of Sevlievo.

Assen was there until July, and from there he came back to Razlog, this time as an illegal. He immediately joined other illegals in Razlog and the region. After Assen came to Razlog and joined the underground movement, I became their yatak. It was then that

I met Ivan Kozarev, the first partisan in Bulgaria, in a cabin by the vineyard of Prifan Stoychev. Since the police were not searching for them then as much as they would in later years, the partisans visited Razlog frequently. When the weather was bad, they would come and stay in the stable during the day, hiding under the hay. Their frequent visits and one- or two-day stays at our house continued from July to October.

We had read in the newspapers that the Soviets were sending in parachutists and submariners, but we never suspected that our brother Kostadin (who had immigrated in 1934 to the USSR in order to avoid jail in connection with the action in Razlog in 1933 together with N. Parapunov) could be among them. Our brother Assen and Nikola Ratchev came to our place on October 12. After dinner and some brief conversation, they went to the stable planning to spend the next day with us. I went upstairs to my room on the second floor to sleep. Our sister Elena was sleeping in the kitchen on the ground floor.

Shortly after I got back to my room, Assen comes in, visibly worried, and asks whether I have heard the sound of footsteps and boots in the yard. "No, I have not heard anything," I said. "And I was not yet asleep." "There is someone in the house," Assen said. "Get up and let's take a look." Assen took a light in one hand, his pistol in the other, and we went downstairs to the kitchen. We were dumbfounded. There was a man in black trousers, with black boots and a black jacket sitting on the bed by our sister. Assen asked him who he was. The man met Assen's question with silence. Then, after a moment, Assen asked, "Kosta, is that you?" Brotherly embraces ensued. . . .

The time after that went by quickly. After dinner and some more conversation, Kosta went out to sleep in the stable with Assen and the others. Our father was not home that night. He was still a peddler and would go by carriage every week to the market in Blagoevgrad (then Gorna Dzhumaya), leaving on Tuesdays and coming back on Thursdays. After Kostadin's immigration in October 1934, our mother had passed away. Kosta knew this because we had exchanged letters until 1937. After that, there was no news about him. We did not know where he was or whether or not he was still alive. After he stopped receiving letters, our father had gone to Sofia once or twice a year on his carriage. There he went several times to the Soviet embassy to inquire about his son. [The embassy officials'] response was always that they had never heard of such a person.

It turned out that during the purges, Kostadin also found himself in jail. He was released only after the beginning of the war of fascist Germany against the USSR. He had been sent from Siberia to Bulgaria with the first group of submariners. After being hunted by the police in Sliven, Kosta was told to go back to his hometown and organize the fight there. After many difficulties and a twelve-day trek (at night, of course) he arrived home.

Since he was at home and he had to spend the whole winter of 41–42 here with us, taking in other illegals was impossible. It was not even possible to keep Assen at home for much longer. That is why Assen had to go back to Sofia again. He hid there over the winter. He came back to Razlog in the spring of 1942.

In order to keep Kostadin hidden during the winter, we made a special hideout for him in the stable under the hay. Its entrance was by the barn. He was there during the day. At night he came to the house to stretch and to chat with us. This went on from October 1941 till the end of April 1942, when he left the hideout. After that, he barely spent a night at home. Because he did not want anyone to know that he was back, we were not allowed to tell anyone anything about him. We would all come back home early in the evening, close the gate with an iron bar and would only open it in exceptional cases. Kostadin warned us every evening to be careful, not to slip up and mention a word to anyone that he was in Razlog.

At least once a day I would bring Kostadin tea—without sugar, of course— so he could keep warm in the hideout. I was told to always lock the gate before bringing the tea so no one could enter without having to knock first. Unfortunately, one time I went to give him the tea without locking the gate. Just as I was in the middle of the yard, the gate opened and the police burst in. I do not know what I must have looked like in that moment, but my knees went numb. In a split second, I took a left turn behind the house and threw away the tin teapot with the tea and hot water by the pile of wood logs that we kept for the wood stove. Then I faced the police officers. Luckily, everything went well. This was not their first visit to our house.

Kostadin would tell us stories every night, especially when he read about the arrests of people who had given him food or other types of assistance. He read pamphlets and newspapers. He also read books in the hideout. There was a small crack in the wall leading to the neighboring barn and with the help of the mirror, he could get some light to read. That is how the winter passed. It was the hardest winter. The Soviet army was still in retreat. Everyone was scared. Very few people were willing to provide shelter for the illegals; even fewer people were willing to give them bread. The year 1942 was not an easy one for those first partisans. Although summer was also hard for the rebels, it was heaven compared to the winter. During the summer of 1942, they made a lot of new contacts, particularly with shepherds who agreed to help them.

During the fall of 1942, people born in 1922 were going to be drafted for regular military service. When I did not receive my draft orders for the regular army in the fall with the rest of my peers, I realized that I was going to be drafted in the spring into the Black Army.[2] I received my draft orders at the end of February 1943. I had to report for duty in the village of Gigen in the Nikopol region on March 5. I had already decided that if I was drafted into the Black Army, I would run away into the mountains. There could be no place for me in the gendarmerie. Unfortunately, I received my draft notice in the winter when I had no way to communicate with my brothers.

Even though I had made the decision for myself, I also thought it would be wise to speak with some of my friends still in Razlog. Everyone's advice was that it was not a good time to go to the mountains. Earlier, I had accidentally found out from a conversation with Penka Bilyov that he might know something about my brothers. Once I received my draft notice, my first thought was to look for Bilyov and to ask him to tell my brothers (if he sees them) that I will be in hiding after the fifth of March and that I would be expecting them to look for me. I wanted him to tell them that I would not join the ranks of the gendarmerie. I found Bilyov home. I told him everything and said that I would look for him again in a few days. When I met with him the second time, he said that he had not seen my brothers in a long time. They had forbidden him—and rightly so—to let on that he had any connection with them.

But on the evening of March 4, when I returned home after a final walk on the square and a stop by the café, I found my brothers at home. My joy was great and beyond words. I was finally with them. That had been my dream all those years. I quickly packed my bags, and I followed them through the garden in the knee-high snow. We went through the meadow above the town and we headed out toward the front. They did not say a word to me along the way. I did not know where we were going and I did not ask anything. We reached a hut, and there I was greeted by Bai Nenko. He was sitting in front of the fireplace together with his two sons Ivan (Vanyo) and Georgi. We stayed with him almost until dawn. Then we went to the hideout (the Submarine) in the morning. Kostadin called the hideout "the Submarine," because life in it followed the same regimen as life in the submarine on which he had arrived in 1941.

There I was greeted by Comrade Parapunov, Gancho, and Kalinka. Krum Radonov had left for Bansko and came back after a couple of days together with Nako Avram (Alexander Pitsin). There was not enough air in the hideout once the entrance was closed, so everyone had to lie still during the day, constantly dozing off as if they were down with the chicken pox. My life went on monotonously until the snow melted: sleeping during the day, and cooking, conversing, and collecting wood logs for the stove during the night.

The Submarine was furnished very well. Given its purpose and the conditions at the time, it could be compared to a luxurious hotel. There was a cooking stove where bread was baked and food was prepared, a sink with several meters of drain pipes going directly to the gorge nearby, bunks with mattresses brought from the Yavorov cabin, pots and pans for cooking the food, a pan for kneading bread; basically all of the things necessary for spending a well-organized winter. Days went by slowly, but the nights went by quickly. It was the final few days of winter.

Several days after I joined them, they decided to organize a plan to set the lumber factory by Belitsa Station on fire. One night we packed our belongings and headed to Belitsa Station. There was still snow on the ground. The distance there was long, and we had walked most of it without a road. It was about twenty-five kilometers. We walked the whole night. Exhausted, we reached a sparse pine forest close to the station in the morning, and we stayed there. We shivered from the cold the whole day. We only had one piece of tarpaulin to cover ourselves. Shepherds were passing nearby. We had to carry out the plan in the evening. However, at the last minute, a decision was made and we went back without implementing our plan. This happened because we could not get in touch with the partisans of the Belitsa band. If our plan had been successful without them knowing about it beforehand, they would not be able to take precautions against the inevitable police raid of their village which would ensue, resulting in unnecessary victims.

So the next night we were back in the Submarine. We stayed there through the end of March. In the beginning of April, after the snow had melted, we started going outside and spending the days in the pine groves surrounding the Submarine. . . . That is how the summer of 1943 started. It was easier to breathe already. The tanks on the Eastern Front started moving westward. This lifted the spirits of our group. Our confidence was increasing day by day. Collectively, we felt like soldiers, and depending on our ability and circumstances, we took part in the Great War on the Eastern Front. We felt like we were a part of the Red Army. In 1943, we were not just relying on loyal yataks to give us food anymore. In the summer of 1943, we were no longer hiding from people. We went everywhere and had the chance to meet many different people without prearranged meetings. Unsuspected by the government, we established new contacts with people. We looked for new adherents. That is how we gradually expanded the network of aides. We met up with many men who worked in the forest along the Tishe, Mrazenitsa, and White Rivers, and with the shepherds and herdsmen. Finding food was becoming much easier. There were no betrayals in our town.

On the Combat by the Deep Water

On August 5, 1943, I was with Commander Assen Lagadinov, Georgi Dzhodzhov, Marin Staykov, and Bai Hristo from the Gorna Dzhumaya detachment. Harvest season had started in the region of Boykov Ridge. We decided to spend the day by the Deep Water [a section of a river]. The day was very warm. The sun was scorching. We had stopped by the fir trees along the river. It was horribly muggy. There was no wind.

Around five o'clock in the afternoon, we thought the danger had passed. The day was almost done and night would fall in a few hours. We started undressing, ready to wash ourselves and cool down. Bai Hristo was telling us some interesting stories and, all of a sudden, someone shouted a few steps away from us. It turned out to be a police chief. Shooting ensued. We had laid our guns aside where we had been hiding. At the beginning of the battle, Assen threw a grenade while the rest of us—some with guns and some without—ran back along the river to the Pirin Mountains. I only grabbed my rifle. Wearing only my trousers, I snuck away along the river. The police officer was heavily wounded. Not realizing where exactly we were, and hoping to give us an opportunity to get away, Assen went to the road by Raplevo and stopped the cars going to town and got the people to drive us. Then he single-handedly organized an ambush for the police reinforcements coming from Razlog. He waited for the truck full of soldiers to appear. He shot at the heads of the soldiers and then escaped through Stolavatets towards Katarino. At that time, a group of partisans from the Belitsa band was nearby. That same evening, late at night, Assen met us for a prearranged control meeting in the region of Kameno. We waited until dawn to see if our other comrades would show up, but no one came. We spent the following day over in Katranitsata in the Pirin Mountains. We almost had no food save for a small amount of sugar. During the day, a fawn grazed near us for close to an hour.

Boris (center back) and Kostadin Lagadinov (right)

We watched it and it watched us. It came almost two meters away from us, but shooting it was out of the question. We headed to Katarino at night. We had a meeting with Kostadin there. He did not show up that night, and we spent the whole next day in the fir forest along the northern slopes of Stolavatets.

A full blockade of Razlog was ordered on the day after the combat at the Deep Water. All of the shepherds and herdsmen were ordered to keep their flocks in the town. They were not allowed to sleep on the fields. The police allowed the people who went out to work on the fields only to bring enough food for a lunch for themselves.

Kostadin did not show up the following night either, so we decided to leave for the White River in the Pirin Mountains, where we hoped the police had not yet prohibited the herdsmen from grazing their flocks and where we could find food. That was exactly what happened. The following day at noon, we were high up by the White River and the Vlazka River in the Konarnika region. We could hear the cattle bells from afar. So the hunger will be over soon, we thought; whoever the herdsman is, he will not leave us hungry. We knew almost all of them.

A bit later as we were making our way through the cattle, we saw the herdsman. We called for him, told him we were starving to death, and asked him to fix us something to eat. He went to his hut and asked his wife to get some food ready. Then he came back to us. He told us that the police had left them alone for now; the police were not going to call him and his wife back to town. In a little while, his wife came with a big bowl of gruel made from corn flour. I had never had, and have not had since, a more delicious gruel. After a few days of hunger, gruel seems like a most wondrous dish to everyone.

In addition to giving us lunch, they let us stay with them for dinner. They also gave us some food to take with us. The next day we went down to the outskirts of the Pirin Mountains to meet our brother Kostadin. We stayed on the Plashka Meadow. The following day, we heard bells and thought it was a flock of sheep. It turned out that one of our yataks had taken his sheep out. He gave us three animals so that we could stock up on meat. We slaughtered the animals, and we hid the meat in the river so that we could preserve it. We buried the meat under big stones, and it stayed there for more than a month. . . .

In another few days, we found Bai Kole [Nikola Parapunov] and Kalmik. They had just gotten back from Gorna Dzhumaya. Because Razlog was still under a blockade, and we needed to have a meeting with the party organization in Saint Vrach, Bai Kole told us to get ready to travel. On the next day, August 15 or 16, 1943, we left before noon. We traveled to Babina Voda, and, in the early afternoon, we slowly made our way along the ridge of the White River by the yellow rocks. When we reached the ledge under the Koncheto, the sun was about to set. We had a bite to eat by the Vlahinski lakes. After that, under the moonlight (it was a full moon, bright as a day), Bai Kole led us off trail through Sinanitsa to Spano Pole where we were supposed to meet comrades from Saint Vrach. It is difficult to describe this nocturnal trek: off trail, such a long distance, under the moonlight, and with several hikes up and down the ridges of the precarious folds of the Pirin Mountains. We arrived close to Spano Pole early in the morning, passed by several shepherds, and settled on a ridge with large pine trees to spend the day.

Just as we settled down in our chosen resting place, and before the sun had even risen, shooting broke out around us. We thought that any minute we would be attacked. After a certain time, the shooting died down. You could only hear barking dogs and wolves. We spent that day with a lot of anxiety. We were unsure if someone had betrayed us to the gendarmes. We worried about whether we should carry on with our plan to meet with our comrades from Saint Vrach. That night we met up with some shepherds who told us what happened. There had been a hunting party trying to capture a bear.

Provisioning Campaign at Spano Pole

After we met with our comrades from Saint Vrach at Spano Pole, we decided to carry out a provisioning campaign. There was a large dairy farm owned by Karakachans.[3] They had a substantial amount of cheese. We spent the next day close to the farm to assess the area. It was determined that the farm was guarded by only one man with a firearm. At approximately five o'clock in the afternoon, Kalmik—who had on a military uniform—and Kostadin went to the farm under the ruse that they had to inspect how it was guarded. They disarmed the security guard, and without any resistance, the farm was immediately in the hands of the partisans. There were about two thousand blocks of Balkan cheese there, as well as butter and white cheese. Unfortunately, the majority of the horses of the Vlasi people were in town. There were only five horses at the dairy farm. We had not planned out how we were going to get all of the cheese up into the mountains.

There was not much to be done. We took as much cheese and butter as the five horses could carry, and we took it high up into the Pirin Mountains toward the lakes above the village Pleshki. We hid it in the rocks, and when we got a chance later, we would transport it to our region near Razlog. We had spoken with some of the local shepherds, and together we decided that the rest of the cheese had to be set on fire. The Vlasi shepherds had also taken some of the cheese and hid it for themselves in the bushes. We set the remaining cheese on fire.[4] The local women were crossing themselves and some were crying, seeing how all that cheese made through their hard work was going up in flames.

As an explanation to the police, we left a note with the Vlasi people saying that the cheese was taken and the rest burned down by the troops of Ivan Kozarev even though he was not with us. His name was well known. At the end of the year, many of the Vlasi began to sell the cheese they had hidden on the black market. The police caught some of them and sentenced them to a few years in jail. Thanks to this cheese, we had enough food for the winter of 1943–1944.

The Betrayal in the Plashka Meadow

After the cheese campaign in Spano Pole, we went back to Razlog and set up a camp in the region of Plashka Meadow. At the end of August, we caught Georgi Vuchov in the fields, a poor orphan, but also an informant of the police. Bai Kole kept Georgi tied up in ropes for several hours. After long deliberations, Bai Kole decided to let him go in the evening after Georgi promised he would not turn us in to the police. A few days later, Kostadin and I traveled from the Plashka Meadow to Predel to meet up with Assen. Along the way in Kulinoto, we ran into the woodsman Ivan Kulin. He told us that Georgi Vuchov had told the police that he had seen us in the region of the Plashka Meadow.

We met up with Assen in Predel by the Tatarska fountain. There Kostadin explicitly asked Assen to tell Bai Kole about the betrayal when he returned to the Plashka Meadow. They were to relocate immediately. Bai Kole was supposed to arrive there that night. But he and his men did not arrive until the next morning. They were all very tired, so Bai Kole decided not to move them quite yet. On his way back from a meeting in town that night, Bai Kole saw some trucks with troops on the road to Predel. Despite that, he did not move from the meadow.

The police, now aware of the place, sent their soldiers from the artillery department. They decided to surround and search the region by the Plashka

Meadow. The soldiers were headed directly to the location of our camp. We had four people there: Bai Kole, Marin Staykov, Kalmik, and Assen. They were all dead tired. But because the forest is very dense, no one could come near without being noticed. When the soldiers were getting closer, our men heard the noise. They woke up and soon afterward saw a soldier headed in their direction.

Assen and Kalmik started shooting together, almost simultaneously, and the soldier screamed so terribly, like a wounded beast, that the police and troops turned around and ran away, stopping at the Trebishta, the area at the edge of the forest. Having survived unscathed, the partisans moved higher into the Pirin Mountains.

The police and the soldiers regrouped and went back to the place where the partisan camp had been and found only an empty tin. On their way back, angry that they did not catch any of the partisans, the police officers vented their rage on the people who worked in the fields. On that day, they beat up Dragomir Belchov, a herdsman, who later passed away from his injuries. They also brutally beat Hristo Topalov, and also the older Ivan Chekanyov was severely beaten. They brutalized everyone they encountered in that region. . . .

After [a] campaign in Kremen and another provisioning campaign in Matan Dere, the issue of finding a place to spend the winter was discussed at a troop meeting above the village of Dobrinishte. There was a lot of support for the idea of keeping the brigade all together in the same place over the winter since the Red Army was advancing quickly. After the fall of Kiev, it was believed that victory was imminent. Some argued that if the brigade was all together in one place, we could conduct drills, and so forth. But it was a good thing that the final decision was to split into smaller groups. That way if one group was discovered and destroyed, there would be a greater possibility to save at least part of the brigade.

After we split up at the end of September, we started intensive preparations to stock up for the winter. At that point, we had still not decided the best place to set up our camp. There was no water in the Razlog region of the Pirin Mountains. The White River was not a good place. All of the suitable places in the Rila Mountains were too far from our region. After carefully walking through and exploring the region, it was decided to set up the camp of our group over Yavorov, under the steps in Suhodol. There was running water a few meters away from there.

Preparation for the Winter of 1943–1944

We started preparations in the beginning of October. The place was now settled, and we had to transport our provisions and all of the necessary supplies. We had moved part of the stuff we had in the Submarine over the summer and hid it in a hole in the Byala Voda region, about a kilometer up from the Submarine. The cooking stove was there as well as a large wooden chest—part of my grandmother's dowry—to store products, a pan for kneading bread and other household items. On the evening of October 12, 1943, we took two horses from our shepherd aides. We loaded the stove, chest, and other baggage and traveled through the Raplevo and Krusheto (pastures by Razlog). We arrived in Parnakov on the outskirts of the Pirin Mountains in the morning.

The weather was bad in the morning and it started snowing. About ten centimeters of snow accumulated on October 13. We kept the horses with us in order to avoid leaving tracks. Had this first snow not melted so quickly, we would not have been able to stock up on supplies. Lucky for us, the weather improved. We managed to transport all of the supplies prepared for the winter in a couple of days. It was a good thing that all of our shepherd yataks had horses or donkeys. With their help, we were able to move everything relatively quickly. For several nights, we took five to six donkeys and horses from the shepherds who had their flocks by Izvorite and would go to the village of Banya to pick up the flour prepared for us by the yatak Todor Zhelyazkov. From there we took the goods on the donkeys to the region of Bazhuro by the White River to the Lankova Hut.

We hid the products there and later on carried them on our backs over the ridge to the camp. One time, the chieftain (Nikola Ratchev) had put a large piece of rock salt in his rucksack; when we got to the camp, the cloth of his rucksack had worn through from the friction between his back and the salt. Earlier, we had also moved a couple of loads on horses and donkeys directly on the road through Suhodol. We had left obvious tracks. In order to be sure that no one went by and noticed our tracks, we kept a post at the base of Suhodol under the lime mines where two roads, the Tinkovski and the Old Road, converge. We stayed there for over twenty days until it rained and the rain washed away the tracks. After that, we transported supplies along the White River.

Later on, we got three cows from some herdsman, took them to camp alive, and slaughtered them there. We left their meat by the trees. It froze so quickly that it was hard to cut a piece of the meat even with an axe during the winter. We moved the cheese from its original hiding place. The snow was knee-deep by that point. We would leave camp early in the morning, travel on the horses horizontally along the ridge but without a clear path to the Vlashki Lakes. We would take two blocks of cheese in our rucksacks and head back to camp. It would usually get dark before we reached the ridge of Suhindol. From there to the camp we had to travel in darkness. We reached the camp usually around midnight. We had stocked up on almost all of the necessary goods for the winter. We also had a tin of pickled vegetables, gas for lighting, and enough matches. We had chopped enough wooden logs before the snowfall. . . .

The Winter of 1943–1944 under the Steps in Suhindol

We were in this camp—which we decided to name "Ina" after a friend that Marin Staykov often talked about—from December 1, 1943, to April 18 or 20, 1944. In December and January the weather was generally great. All of January was sunny and cloudless. Of course, the sunlight could not reach us, but a bit of light would appear for about twenty to thirty minutes a day by the steps. Such weather was unpleasant for us because we could not make a fire during the day. The wood logs were from fir trees—black fir—and the smoke from them was as if produced by a locomotive engine, billowing over Suhodol and all the way down to the Yavorov cabin. On nice days during the month of January, a flock of wild goats would show up every morning at sunrise on the ridge between Suhindol and Bayovi Dupki, staying on the ridge for a short time and then determinedly going downhill to Suhindol, above the Yavorov cabin.

At the end of January and the beginning of February, the snow on the field was almost gone. You could see many horse pastures. We started talking about going down by the outskirts. However, it started snowing on February 6–7. Close to two meters of snow fell. Strong storms were raging on. At one point, the snow turned yellow, a yellow shade from yellow blossoms, fringes of willow trees. At least that is what it seemed like to us. It seemed like the strong winds had brought them over from Africa. The wind was so strong that when someone popped his head out through the entrance, it felt like the wind would tear his head away from his body. After this snowfall, we could not leave the cabin to get water and had to drink melted snow. Every day, we would dig out a couple of square meters in front of the door. Everything would be buried by snow again the next day.

We felt an earthquake on April 1. We thought the boulders from the steps would fall on us. We could feel the rumbling of the ground. We jokingly decided to eat the better food we had because we did not know what might happen. The snow turned black; black ashes covered it. It was not until later that we found out that there had been an eruption of Vesuvius at that time. During those couple of days, it was impossible to open the door of the hut. We had to stay inside even for more pressing toilet needs; we collected it [our feces] in a paper and would throw it out through a small opening.

When the weather was bad during the day, we cooked and read. When the skies were clear during the day, we stayed in bed and turned the night into a day. We had breakfast in the evening, had lunch at night, and had our dinner in the morning. The days were passing by slowly. The winter proved to be long. . . . Instead of getting out in the beginning of February as we had wished—because of those several meters of snow that made it hard for us to go farther than two meters away from the hut—we left camp in April after the cuckoo started cooing. We heard the cuckoo on the first day when we went down to Parnako, on the outskirts of the Pirin Mountains by the Izvori. Since we had not been hiking for several months (almost five months), going down Suhindol, even without any uphill hikes, proved to be a difficult challenge. We stopped to camp before we reached the base. We stayed there until the first days of May. It snowed on May 1. More than ten centimeters accumulated. We could not move without leaving tracks. There were herds surrounding us, and the dogs caught our scent and were barking at us. We curled up under the tarps for a couple of days. If we stretched our legs, they would be out in the snow. We could not start a fire, but despite all of this, it was easy to breathe. The tanks from the Eastern Front were moving closer to the west. It was then that we found out about the murder of Bai Kole in Blagoevgrad and about the tragic death of Kovachev.

By the beginning of May, only Kostadin and I were in the Razlog region. Everyone else had left for Belitsa and the general convention of all partisans. On May 11, we were near the home of Pavel [illegible], a member of the White Army. We went to him in the evening. He was the first one to tell us about the fall of Razlog after the arrival of gendarmerie troops [illegible] Captain Nikolchev. He said that as [illegible] harsh torture [illegible]. On the next day, Kostadin went into town to warn part of the [illegible] . . . hid with his brother Atanas and twenty-three days later, Kostadin brought him to Raplevo. Bai Penka Kranchev also fled the police together with his two sons Samuil and Georgi. Georgi Pulin, albeit ill, also escaped the claws of the gendarmerie. Sometime later, we also found the runaway Atanas Pulin by the

Markovi Meadows. We found him covered by a wax-laden tarp of the Yugoslavian army, hidden in the beech grove and keeping a watch. My brother decided to give him the nickname "the Marshall" then.

Kostadin asked me one evening to go and at all costs to bring Atanas Popadin (the Lively One). Without much resistance, he left his flock and came to the group. Georgi Kranchev also came out to us in Raplevo, but he was frightened by the harsh conditions of partisan life and went back to town. He was arrested by the gendarmerie a few days later. My brother went to rally Kotse Levenov as well, but his wife did not let him go. He was killed together with thirteen people by Belyov Peak on May 29, 1944.

Upon the arrival of the gendarmerie, there were many arrests, and partisan houses were set on fire. Kostadin and I were on the Markovi Meadows at about four o'clock in the afternoon when we saw dense smoke in the town. Using the grove (Misheva) as a reference point to orient ourselves, we thought only our house was burning. Our house was big, fourteen rooms in total, made of black fir beams. The smoke, however, grew denser and denser and spread over a larger area. On the following day, we found that in addition to our house, the gendarmes had set alight the houses of three innocent people. It was windy and the fire grew so large that they could not contain it. They did not set more houses on fire in town after that. They started tearing them down.

On May 31, 1944, the three Lagadinov brothers were hiding in the Pirin Mountains, about two hundred kilometers away from Frank Thompson and the Second Sofia Brigade. The three brothers had come down from the mountains to find that Docho Hristov, the Bulgarian minister of interior, had placed a bounty of up to 50,000 levs for each dead partisan. As the tanks of the Red Army moved westward, Bulgaria's political and economic elites became increasingly nervous about a homegrown Bolshevik-style revolution. Bulgaria's government committed ever more resources to stomp out the partisan threat. By May 1944, both the Nikola Parapunov Brigade and the Second Sofia Brigade fought against a regime that wanted every Bulgarian, Yugoslav, and British communist dead before the Russians arrived.[1]

Having survived the initial melee in Batuliya, Frank Thompson and his wireless operator, Kenneth Scott, hoped to stay hidden until nightfall. Most of the Second Sofia Brigade had been wiped out in the initial attack. The two Englishmen hunkered down in the underbrush, the sounds of the Bulgarian gendarmes shouting all around them. The soldiers suspected that there were still partisans hiding among the trees, and they did not give up their search. Thompson and Scott would have heard the boots of the soldiers as they grew nearer. When the two Brits were certain of being discovered, they tried to run. The gendarmes opened fire. Kenneth

Scott was shot and fell injured to the forest floor. They captured Thompson at gunpoint. Both men wore the uniforms of British military officers. While the gendarmes could summarily execute Bulgarian partisans, British officers enjoyed prisoner of war status. The gendarmes marched the captured members of the Second Sofia Brigade and the two Brits to the village of Litakovo.[2]

The local police chief, Captain Yanko Stoyanov, was infamous for his savage treatment of resistance fighters. Bulgarian soldiers raped and beat to death the captured women. Yordanka Nikolova's screams were heard all through the first night, and no one ever saw her again. Stoyanov tortured some of the partisans for information about the resistance movement. Then he had them decapitated—their heads were mounted on spikes in the center of the village. Thompson was interrogated and tortured by the local general, Kocho Stoyanov (no relation to the captain). Transcripts of these sessions reveal that Thompson gave them no useful information. He insisted on his rights as a prisoner of war and was locked up in the Litakovo municipal building. Because of his injuries, the Bulgarians sent Kenneth Scott away for medical treatment.[3]

Thompson was held for weeks in Litakovo as the war raged on in Bulgaria. The Red Army drew nearer and the beaches at Normandy had by now been stormed. The endgame in Bulgaria was on. Thompson might have been able to wait out the war in prison.

Several eyewitnesses either observed or interacted with Frank Thompson during his captivity. Stories floated around about the Englishman held in the municipal building, and the picture that emerges is of a young officer confident in his safety. Dimitar Avgarski, an aide-de-camp to Captain Yanko Stoyanov, recalled:

> From my brief and occasional encounters with Captain Thompson I remember that he was slim and wore a smart British uniform; as far as I remember he did not wear any insignia. He smoked a pipe. He behaved with dignity. We were impressed by his culture. He was young but he spoke Bulgarian surprisingly well. . . . He insisted on being treated as a captured officer but his claims were only partially met. One thing, for instance, was the regular supply of food. Once he even made protest because his lunch had been delayed.[4]

A local Bulgarian woman, Raina Sharova, remembered speaking with Frank Thompson while he was held in the municipal building. She had traveled to Litakovo to obtain an official document from the notorious Captain

Stoyanov, the only authority in the region capable of issuing a document of the sort she needed. When she arrived, she found a relative in Litakovo who happened to be guarding the municipal building where Thompson was imprisoned. Sharova's relative surreptitiously allowed her in to see the Englishman. She remembered:

> I was curious to see him because I had already heard about him. I opened the door. Thompson was lying on straw scattered all over the room. He looked at me but did not rise and only leaned on his arm. He looked clean and smart. His face was serious and there was not a sign of despair on it. I did not know that he spoke Bulgarian so I spoke to him in French. "The victory will be soon ours ... Don't despair!" He answered me in Bulgarian. "I don't despair but time flies very fast." I was worried because the gendarmerie could find me with him. It is hard to remember details after so many years have passed, but one thing I remember vividly—Thompson was clean, smart and was not dispirited.[5]

Frank Thompson wrote no poems or letters in Litakovo, so one can only imagine his state of mind. After his initial torture, and the terror of hearing one of his female comrades raped and beaten to death, as well as the revulsion he must have felt at seeing his former companions' heads mounted on pikes in the square, Frank Thompson may have just accepted his imprisonment. He had followed his orders and had done his part. Now, after weeks of starving on the run, he was being fed regularly enough to complain when his lunch was late. Victory was close.

Whether or not Thompson had a real trial is unclear, but it is certain that the account that Freeman Dyson read in the *News Chronicle* was fabricated out of whole cloth. The legend of Thompson calmly smoking his pipe in front of a kangaroo court and raising his fist in the salute of the Fatherland Front before being executed by a firing squad was a later invention of the Bulgarian communist propaganda machine. With few reliable sources about what happened on the tenth of June 1944, it was the definitive account for many years.[6]

The only written accounts are from the individual members of the gendarmerie who were hauled before the People's Court after the ninth of September 1944 to account for the death of Thompson. These records were stored in the archives of the Bulgarian Ministry of Interior and remained unavailable to most scholars. In her biography, the widow of Dencho Znepolski,

Maria Znepolska, published selected transcripts of the hearings against the men charged with shooting Thompson. For rather obvious reasons, the testimonies given in these circumstances are fairly unreliable; almost all of the men called before the court tried to blame someone else for the actual shooting. Still, they provide a better picture of the circumstances surrounding Thompson's demise than the hagiographic account reported in the *News Chronicle*.[7]

Dimitar Kyufov recounted how he arrived with about forty of his colleagues from the gendarmerie at the municipal building in Litakovo with Capitan Yanko Stoyanov. He understood that they were going to shoot the imprisoned partisans, including Thompson. Kyufov was in the guard as the Englishman, together with twelve other partisans, were marched away toward a mass grave. The partisans would be shot in groups of three. Thompson was in the first group, and according to Kyufov, Capitan Stoyanov addressed the Englishman directly. Captain Stoyanov apparently asked Thompson:

> "Do you know where you are going?"
> "No," replied Thompson.
> "You are going to be shot, because you are a partisan," said Stoyanov.
> "I am a prisoner of war, and you must ensure me my rights," were the words of the Englishman.
> "You are not any kind of prisoner of war, but a filthy partisan and therefore you are going to be shot," shouted Stoyanov.
> "You will answer to my government," were the last words of Thompson that I heard. The shooting started.[8]

Kyufov claimed he was too far away to see who shot Thompson, but later heard that it was Captain Yanko Stoyanov who personally did the deed. Kyufov was probably more interested in saving his own skin than he was in identifying Thompson's true killer. It would make sense that Kyufov would try to blame his commanding officer for the death of a British prisoner of war, since it was Stoyanov who gave the immediate command. General Kocho Stoyanov, from whom the order had most likely originated, had already shot himself before he could be called to account before the People's Court.[9]

A former Bulgarian soldier, Kiril Yanev, published a biography about Frank Thompson in 2001.[10] Although he relied on Stowers Johnson's book for many details, Yanev also seems to have accessed the testimonies stored in the archives of the Bulgarian Ministry of Interior. His account of Thompson's final scene is similar to the court testimonies, but may have been embellished for dramatic effect.

> Capitan Stoyanov came forward and said, "Major Thompson, you are going to be shot."
> "Why?" asked Thompson. . . .
> "Why should I have to give you an explanation? That's it! Will you get down?" [said Stoyanov].
> Frank Thompson stood tall.
> "You will kill me, but know that my government has sent me here in Bulgaria, and it will look for me, and you, Captain, will have to answer for my death."[11]

Thompson was then pushed to the ground and shot by the firing squad.

A very different story appears in the most recent biography of Thompson: *A Very English Hero: The Making of Frank Thompson*. Peter Conradi (also the official biographer of Dame Iris Murdoch) became familiar with Thompson through his extensive correspondence with Murdoch during the war. In 1999, Conradi traveled to Bulgaria with Phillipa Foot, a dear friend of Iris Murdoch with whom she had shared a flat in the mid-1940s. On this trip, Conradi and Foot met with Slavcho Transki in Sofia and had then traveled to Litakovo. There they met with some Bulgarian villagers who showed them Frank Thompson's pipe, and who arranged for a meeting with an elderly villager named Naku Staminov, a man claiming to be an inadvertent eyewitness to Thompson's execution. Although neither Conradi nor Foot spoke Bulgarian, and it is quite possible that the following account was yet another fabrication for the benefit of the visiting British, this version of events is plausible.[12]

According to Conradi, Staminov was a twelve-year-old boy in the summer of 1944. On about June 10, he recalled seeing a group of twelve partisans being led away from Litakovo by the gendarmes. They were calm, and he later learned that they had been lied to. They were told that they were marching to a nearby village. He recognized Thompson because he was taller than the others and because Staminov later saw his photograph in the newspaper.

Staminov saw that Frank Thompson was tied to two other men, their ankles all bound together with rope. Once out of the village, one of the gendarmes tripped Thompson who fell into a ditch. The other partisans were

Frank Thompson in
his British officer's
uniform

pushed in after Thompson. Staminov remembered hearing the Englishman
shout at the gendarmes, twisting his head back with an angry countenance.
The gendarmes opened fire, shooting all twelve partisans. Frank Thompson
was the last of the men to stop convulsing. He died face down in a ditch. His
body was later tossed into an unmarked, mass grave.[13]

11 | THE HEAD HUNTED

Around the same time that Frank Thompson was marching with the Second Sofia Brigade to its final battle at Batuliya, a detachment of the gendarmes broke into the Lagadinov residence in Razlog. The police had long known that Assen Lagadinov was among the partisans, but the rumor had spread that all three Lagadinov brothers operated in the mountains surrounding Razlog—even Kostadin, still believed to be in the Soviet Union. Docho Hristov's bounty was now in effect. He authorized retaliation against the families of men and women suspected of being partisans.[1]

The gendarmes found young Elena Lagadinova, who had just celebrated her fourteenth birthday, at home by herself. The men grabbed her, throwing her out the front gate. While she watched from the street, the gendarmes tossed three incendiary bombs into her natal home. As the house burst into flames, Elena ran for the mountains. Her father was away. She needed to find her brothers, but she had no idea where they were. She had been actively helping them for the last three years, and Elena worried that the gendarmes suspected her of being a yatak. She shuddered to think what would happen if they arrested her.

Since her mother died when she was four years old, Elena was the only female in the house. She grew up with many household responsibilities: one of these had always been caring for and feeding her father's horse, so she was an excellent rider. When her father was not away at market, she would ride the white horse out to the horse pastures in the foothills of the Pirin Mountains. When her neighbors asked her why she rode the horse so far out to graze, she would say, "The grass is sweetest there."

She used these rides out to the mountains to bring food, medicine, and messages to her brothers and the other members of the Nikola Parapunov brigade.[2] She would have been killed if she was caught, but Elena was brave. The gendarmes did not suspect such a young girl. His little sister's courage impressed Kostadin Lagadinov. One day, after Elena had brought newspapers and other needed supplies, she was sitting together with the other partisans around a fire and Kostadin referred to her as "an Amazon." The other partisans did not know what an Amazon was so Kostadin explained about the fierce women warriors of the Greek myths. The others decided that "Amazonkata" (the Amazon) would be her code name.

As the Lagadinov house burned behind her, Elena ran barefoot to the foothills of the Pirin Mountains where her brothers spent the winter in some unknown hiding place. They would have broken camp by now. Did they know about all of the horrible things that had been happening in Razlog? So many men had been arrested, others badly beaten or killed by the gendarmes. The people feared for their safety and would be less willing to help the partisans now. As the Red Army advanced, the gendarmes grew more violent. Elena believed that the revolution could not be stopped, but also knew that the gendarmes wanted to make sure that the partisans would not live to enjoy it.

She glanced back in the direction of her house, the home where she had spent the last fourteen years of her life. It was in that kitchen that she had been awakened by the footfalls of a strange man in the darkness of night. Her heart pounding in her ears, she could barely hear him when he whispered, "Elena, it's your brother, Kostadin." It was also there that she spent long hours listening to Boris fret about not receiving his draft order for the regular army. "I will not join the black armies," he said. "I will not fight against my own brothers."

Elena could see the smoke. It was a windy day, and the flames would certainly spread. How many other families, she wondered, would lose their homes because they lived too close to the Lagadinovs? She thought about the pots and pans and blankets and clothing that she might have hidden away if she had known that the gendarmes were coming. Everything she owned would be lost with the house. She thought of her father who would come back in a day or two. He would be worried about her.

It was quite serendipitous that Elena's brothers were on the outskirts of Razlog on the very day that the gendarmes came to set their house on fire. If Elena had managed to escape, her brothers knew that she would go to the horse pasture where she left them supplies and messages. Kostadin, Assen, and Boris sighed with great relief when they found her waiting there that evening. On that day in May 1944, Elena joined the Nikola Parapunov Brigade. The Amazon was no longer a yatak; she was a full-fledged partisan.

Young women in Bulgarian villages in the 1940s wore long skirts made of rough wool. Elena's skirt proved to be impractical for the life of a resistance fighter. It so happened that the local tailor was also a member of the Parapunov Brigade, so he cut her skirt up the middle and created a pair of wide trousers better for running and climbing. Kostadin gave her a pistol stolen from a prison guard in one of their village raids. He attached it to a chain around her neck because pistols were too valuable to be lost. Assen taught her how to use it.

In the weeks following the ambush of the Second Sofia Brigade at Batuliya, a few scattered survivors found their way to the Pirin Mountains, and they joined up with the Nikola Parapunov Brigade. One of these was a man nicknamed "Rancho" who had marched with Dencho Znepolski and the English Mission from Bulgarian-occupied Serbia into Bulgaria proper. Rancho had been with Thompson on the evening when the British made their last supply drop and had acquired a British jacket and a hat. Rancho was a large man, so the jacket was a bit snug on his broad shoulders. The weather was also getting warmer.

Rancho spent his first few days in the brigade with the Lagadinov family. Their father had returned from market to find his house burnt to the ground. He, too, was now a member of the Parapunov Brigade—the five Lagadinovs fought together. One day Rancho watched Assen giving Elena shooting lessons. He was impressed by the young girl. She could shoot, and she knew all of the poems of Hristo Botev by heart and would recite them to pass the time. Rancho gave Elena the jacket and a cap that had been dropped to the Second Sofia Brigade by the British Royal Airforce (RAF). These, together with her modified skirt-trousers, were her uniform for the next three months.

With the destruction of the First and Second Sofia Brigades now accomplished, Docho Hristov's gendarmes were more ruthless in their pursuit of the remaining partisans. Since the Parapunov Brigade had been one of the first in Bulgaria, the heads of the "Parapunovtsi" (members of the Parapunov Brigade) were particularly attractive targets. Elena, her father, and her brothers spent the months of June and July on the run. They could not go into Razlog to acquire food. The local population was too afraid to help. Even worse, old friends and neighbors were turning each other in for the 50,000-lev bounty. No one could be trusted. Even some of the shepherds and herdsmen refused aid. The few actions the Parapunovtsi managed were quick, provisioning raids. The only way they could get food that summer was to steal it.[3]

By August 1944, rumors arose in Razlog that the Serbian partisans had successfully crossed into Bulgaria. It was said that these Serbs were working with a new British mission, and they were bringing in a wireless set. If the Parapunov Brigade could take possession of this wireless radio set, the British would be able to make supply drops to them in Bulgaria. With food, weapons, and more ammunition, the brigade could plan more aggressive actions. Word came that the Serbs wanted a meeting with representatives of the Parapunov Brigade.

It was a tempting proposition. It could also be a trap. Kostadin Lagadinov communicated with the "Serbs" through a local shepherd who had long been a loyal yatak. Kostadin arranged to meet with the Serb partisans in a small pass below a horse stable in the foothills of one of the Pirin Mountains. A wide grassy field surrounded the structure, but the terrain below was thick with underbrush. Kostadin brought his brother Assen and Rancho from the Second Sofia Brigade. Rumors spread of local gendarmes now wearing the uniforms of the dead partisans of the First and Second Sofia Brigades, but Rancho knew many of the Serbs from his time with Thompson and hoped that he would be able to identify them.

It was August 5, 1944, just a month before the Red Army arrived in Bulgaria.[4] Thompson was already dead. Kostadin, Assen, and Rancho were waiting below the appointed stable at the appointed time. No one came. Eventually, the shepherd appeared.

"The Serbs are in the field above," he said. "They want you to go up and meet them there."

Assen was eager to greet them. He suggested that they head up immediately. Kostadin was suspicious. He told the shepherd, "The agreed meeting point was down here. You tell the Serbs that they should meet us here as we agreed."

The shepherd went back up to the field. Assen turned to his brother. "One of us should go," he said. "Do you know what it would mean for our cause if we had the wireless radio? We need food and with British guns and grenades we could do much more damage."

Kostadin deliberated. "I know very well how valuable it would be to have the wireless. But they said they would meet us here. They should meet us here."

Rancho said nothing. He was probably as suspicious as the elder Lagadinov brother. No one could be trusted. Since Nikola Parapunov's death during the winter, Kostadin had become the de facto leader of the Parapunov Brigade. He knew the gendarmes were hunting him. The story about the wireless set from Serbia seemed too good to be true.

After a short while, the shepherd reappeared. "They say they have the wireless set," he said. "It is very heavy to carry down here. They do not want to leave it unguarded."

"This is a reasonable request," Assen Lagadinov told his brother. "One of us must go."

Kostadin frowned. "Something is not right," he said, looking to Rancho for support.

Rancho nodded.

"The shepherd has been our yatak for a long time," Assen said. 'He would not lie to us."

"He may not know," Kostadin said. "If it is an ambush, the gendarmes will already be hidden around the field. It is not safe. We should not go."

"Then let me go," Assen said, throwing his hands up. "You are too important, but I can go alone."

In the Lagadinov family, Assen was the most mercurial. He tended to act before thinking, and his fellow partisans perceived this as great courage. Assen's fearlessness had saved the lives of many men, and he was much respected and loved. But Kostadin knew that what looked like bravery was sometimes impetuousness. Assen could be reckless.

"I will go and make sure that everything is okay. Then you will see that we have nothing to fear," Assen said. He marched off before either Kostadin or Rancho could stop him. The shepherd followed.

A long silence ensued. For a moment, Kostadin was hopeful that Assen would return with news of the wireless radio unit. Then he heard gunshots. Kostadin and Rancho ran into the underbrush believing that the gendarmes would be coming for them as well. Kostadin knew many good places to hide

A monument to the severed head of Assen Lagadinov in Razlog in 2013. His nickname was "Dimcho."

in this part of the Pirin. Hours later, when they were certain the danger had passed, Kostadin and Rancho doubled back to a place where they could get a clear view of the field. Assen's body lay face down on the ground. The earth was stained with a wide circle of blood oozing from his neck and sinking into the dry summer soil. They had taken his pistol and his boots.

They had also taken his head.

12 | WORDS OF ONE BROTHER ON THE DEATH OF ANOTHER

The official news of Frank Thompson's death in Bulgaria took many months to reach his parents in England. For a while, Thompson was merely "missing in action," and they likely remained hopeful that their son was still alive. The sad news arrived after Bulgaria had already switched sides. If Major Thompson had been treated as a prisoner of war, he would have been on his way home to England. E. P. Thompson learned of his brother's death while he was still serving in Italy.

After the war was over, E. P. and his mother curated a selection of Frank Thompson's poems, letters, and diary entries, publishing them in 1947 as *There Is a Spirit in Europe*. The Bulgarian partisan Dencho Znepolski sent them an account of Thompson's final days, which they also included in the volume. I spent a lot of time trying to track down a copy of this little hardcover book that had long gone out of print. Thankfully, one used copy eventually became available on the Amazon.com marketplace. I charged the $69.49 to my credit card and waited impatiently for the text to arrive. When it finally came, the pages were yellowed and brittle and the blue dust jacket was frayed all along the edges. The book was discarded from the University of Kansas Library, but not a single page was missing.

Frank's father, Edward John Thompson, the famous Oxford academic, was too ill to contribute much to the preparation of this volume. The news of his son's death had coincided with the worsening of his cancer, and the lion's share of the work fell to Frank Thompson's younger brother. It would be E. P. Thompson's first book, and E. J. Thompson would be dead before it was published. E. J. Thompson did manage to write a brief note included on the last pages. "Illness has laid me aside during the writing of this memoir, and, as Frank's father, I have felt that this was better so. But I do not like it to pass without some comment from myself, and I find this best expressed in words of the fellow-soldier who in sympathy and thought was nearest to himself, his younger brother."[1]

E. J. Thompson then quoted liberally from a letter that his younger son had written to his parents while still serving in Italy on November 24, 1944.

[Frank] was lucky, as I see it, in this one thing above all others—that he had the joy of knowing that, whatever happened, his action was contributing to a great good and lasting enrichment of the life of mankind. Many men have died in this war, and I have known a few. Of the many hardly a handful can have held so much promise as Frank. And I fear that only a few have the certainty which he had—that he was contributing to a great and creative cause, as one among other comrades who, following after, will not fail to build richly on the foundation of his life. Too many men in this war are without that knowledge—they have a sense of duty, an obstinacy, a hatred of the evil they are fighting, but they are confused or cynical about anything positive being forwarded by their efforts and, perhaps, their deaths. . . .

However much we may know the world to have lost in Frank's talents and character, there is no question of "waste." For he concentrated into his one last action all the promise and achievement of his life. The extent to which he will influence and inspire men we can never know. He lives in us, and in friends we know, and in men we shall never meet; he is a strong force for the friendship of nations. "The whole earth is the sepulchre of famous men, and their story is graven not only on stone over their native earth, but lives on far away, without visible symbol, woven into the stuff of other men's lives."[2]

The final line of E. P. Thompson's letter comes from the funeral oration of the Greek king Pericles as written by Thucydides in his *History of the Peloponnesian War*. It was the kind of classical reference that Frank Thompson himself might have made. The fact that Edward John Thompson chose to quote his younger son's letter made me wonder if the sentiments expressed in that letter had somehow made the loss more bearable. Did they really be-lieve that Frank's story would be woven into the fabric of other men's lives? Did they truly think that his spirit would continue fighting on for a better world? A strong force for the friendship of nations?

Sitting where I was in 2012, I saw very little evidence to show that the early deaths of men like Frank Thompson and Assen Lagadinov had contributed anything to the "lasting enrichment of the life of mankind."

PART II | THE REMAINS OF THE REGIME

По чуства сме братя ний с тебе
и мисли еднакви ний таим,
и вярвам, че в светът за нищо
ний няма с теб да се разкаем.

Добро ли сме, зло ли правили,
потомството назе ще съди;
а сега—дай ръка за ръка
и напред със стъпки по-твърди!

We are brothers in feeling, you and I
Cherishing the same ideals,
And I believe there is nothing in this world
We shall come to regret, you and I.

Whether we have done good or done evil—
Our descendants will judge,
But for now—hand in hand—
Let's move forward, with steps more sure!

—"SHARING," HRISTO BOTEV (1848–1876)

13 | THE RETIRED PARTISAN

"I was only four years old when my mother died," she tells me across her lace-covered dining room table.[1] "I was raised by men."

I try to imagine the four-year-old girl in the face of the eighty-year-old woman who sits across from me.

"You must eat," she says.

She is exactly twice my age. I notice the brown spots on the backs of her small hands as she waves at me to eat the watermelon and white cheese. She has piled the pink cubes of melon and the white strips of feta-like cheese onto two separate porcelain plates. A knife and fork sit upon a green paper napkin in front of me. She has stacks of books, papers, and photos piled in front of her. On the top of one of the piles rests a copy of an old Bulgarian children's book. It is called *The Amazon*.

Elena Lagadinova always wants me to eat something before I ask her any questions. Elena is an easy and eager interview subject; she has a wonderful memory for details. She also knows how to tell a good story. But she always wants me to be eating. If I stop eating, she stops talking.

I carefully extract the individual watermelon seeds from the watermelon chunks with my fork and knife. Once the dark pink flesh is stripped of the little black ovals I slice off a healthy sliver. I then cut off a piece of cheese with my knife. With my fork, I stab the cheese and then the melon and bring them both together to my lips. The sweetness of the summer fruit mixes perfectly with the saltiness of the smooth white cheese.

"Very delicious," I murmur in Bulgarian. "*Mnogo vkusno.*"

"August is the best time for watermelon," Elena tells me. "And the cheese is fresh from the village."

I close my eyes to savor the combination of flavors. This is something I learned to eat in the Balkans. It reminds me of being a Ph.D. student doing research on the Black Sea in the late 1990s. This is what I used to eat for breakfast. "It tastes like summer," I tell her. "It tastes like the seaside."

She smiles at me. Her face becomes a map of her many years. Elena Lagadinova and I are separated by four decades. She was born on May 9, 1930, fifteen years to the day before the Bulgarians celebrated the Allied victory over the Axis forces. Elena, the Amazon, was one of those who risked their lives fighting to defeat the Nazis in World War II, and she became a hero to all Bulgarian boys and girls in the postwar period. "Be brave like the Amazon," admonished the *Septemberists* children's magazine in 1948. Even children in the Soviet Union were regaled with tales of Elena's courage and dedication to the antifascist cause.

"I grew up in a household with my father and two older brothers. My father was a carriage driver. He founded the Razlog branch of the Bulgarian Communist Party," she tells me after I have taken a third bite. She speaks slowly and clearly in Bulgarian. I put down my fork and knife and pick up my pen, taking notes in a thin composition book.

"Even before I could read, my father and my brothers taught me to recite all twenty of the poems of Hristo Botev," she says. "It was hard to be a child without a mother, but at least I had poetry."

I scribble "Hristo Botev poems" in the margin of my notebook. Botev is perhaps the most famous poet and revolutionary in Bulgaria. He wrote verses to inspire the Bulgarians to fight against their Ottoman overlords and gave his life in this fight when he was twenty-eight. Many young partisan fighters like Kostadin and Assen Lagadinov found inspiration in Botev's heroic death.

"Of course, Dine was already gone," she says.

"Dine?" I say.

"My oldest brother, Kostadin. He was eighteen years older than I was," she says. "He ran away to the Soviet Union before I even had a memory of him. My father told me that he was engaged in a great battle against injustice, that he wanted all children to have food and clothes and toys and books

Elena Lagadinova in 1945, wearing the hat and jacket dropped to Frank Thompson and the Second Sofia Brigade

to read. I thought these were very good ideas, especially the part about the toys and books."

Elena smiles. "My father told me that for these ideas the fascists had banished him. I did not meet him until I was almost a teenager."

"Do you remember the first time that you met him?"

"Eat," she says, waving at the watermelon. "Can I get you some cola?"

"No, thank you." I put the pen down and pick up my fork. I cut another slice of watermelon.

"My second-eldest brother, Assen, he was political, too. Since Dine was gone and my father was always traveling, Assen was like a father to me. He was kicked out of school and sent to jail for his ideas. My father was also in and out of prison. But you see people were very poor in those days. We did not have bread to eat. For most of my childhood, we ate cornmeal mixed with water. It was a hard time for the people."

I nod.

"But it did not have to be that way," she says. "Assen was already in the mountains when Kostadin returned from the Soviet Union. Because my father drove a carriage, we had a horse. I always took the horse to the mountains to graze at sunset. I told the other children that I had been too busy with work in the home during the day. I was the woman of the house because my mother was dead. I had many chores on top of my studies. So I was very busy. It made sense to them that I would only have time to take the horse out to graze at sunset."

I knew from books and articles that Elena had taken a great risk in helping her brothers, and even greater risks when she joined them in the mountains. She was a girl from legend, a national hero at the age of fourteen. I try to remember when I was fourteen.

She turned fourteen in May 1944. I turned fourteen in April 1984. When I was fourteen I was listening to Madonna's *Like a Virgin* album and wearing fishnet shirts and fingerless lace gloves, a wannabe material girl living in a material world. Mint green was the color that year. I remember shopping for school clothes with my mom, scouring the discount racks at Marshalls for anything in mint green. Of course, mint green looked awful against my olive skin. It was fashionable. I cared about fashion.

When Elena was fourteen years old, her preferred music was symphonic. She liked marches that "moved the spirit to patriotic action." Sousa was a favorite. The few clothes she owned, she had sewn herself. They were all lost

Elena Lagadinova (center right) with other partisans in 1944

Elena Lagadinova (center) with her British hat and jacket, and the pistol she wore on a chain around her neck

when the gendarmes set fire to her house. When she joined her brothers in the mountains, her skirt was slit and sewn into trousers. She inherited a jacket and a cap that had fallen out of the sky. Nothing matched. Elena probably never wondered if her British jacket suited her complexion.

"I was in the mountains from May until September. Those were difficult times," she says. "I was just a girl. But I was with my father and brothers. We knew what we were fighting for: to crush fascism, to build a better world."

Now she is eighty. I am forty. I eat watermelon and feta cheese in her dining room in a Bulgaria where the communism that she and her brothers fought for has been dead for twenty years.

Elena looks down at an open green folder of documents. She picks up each document and examines it. The documents are individually numbered. This folder is full of articles and newspaper clippings about "the Amazon," things she has collected over the course of her life, photographs and copies of the books and pamphlets written about her. They are organized chronologically from 1944 to 1988. It is a thick folder.

"I have everything," she says. "I collected everything."

After glancing at the first five or six documents, Elena closes this folder.

Partisan Brigade in Razlog in 1944. (Elena Lagadinova is squatting in the front row on the right.)

She exhales slowly. She opens a second, even thicker folder that seems to be bursting from too much content. "These are the documents about my brothers," she says. She pulls out a large photo of a young man. It is old and creased several times; long white lines bisect the man's face. He is in semi-profile, looking off into the distance. He is handsome and resembles the photos of Elena in her younger days.

"They killed my brother Assen," she says, handing me the photo. "I don't like to remember what they did to him."

She shakes her head. "They didn't tell me. Dine told me that Assen had gone off on an important mission, a secret action. I believed him."

Elena closes her eyes, pressing her right hand to her chest. "It was only on the day of our great victory that they told me the truth. Boris and Dine told me that Assen was dead."

The day of their great victory was September 9, 1944. As the Russians made their way toward Bulgaria, the coalition of parties in the Fatherland Front prepared a coup d'état to overthrow the monarchy. Political upheaval spread across Bulgaria on the sixth of September, with massive strikes declared in the major cities. Around the country, partisan detachments came down from the mountains, preparing to support their revolution. On Sep-

Kostadin Lagadinov's wedding. (Elena Lagadinova is to the left.)

tember 9, with the Red Army poised in the northeast corner of the country, the Bulgarian communists overthrew the government. The partisans secured the towns and villages. It was not the Red Army that imposed communism in Bulgaria; the capital had been seized by the Fatherland Front well before the Russians arrived in Sofia. The partisans formed the backbone of the People's Liberation Army. They were supposed to stabilize the country as the new government switched sides and joined the Allied forces.[2]

I look down at the face of Assen and then put the photo beside my plate. I take a bite of watermelon, nodding for Elena to continue. Her eyes are watery. She blinks, and one tear traces its way down the right side of her nose. She dabs it away with a green napkin.

"He died fighting for justice," she says. "He died fighting for a dream. It was a different time then, I know. It was a utopian time." She looks up at the ceiling. I wonder if she is looking up toward Assen. Or perhaps she is just looking up to drain the moisture back down into her tear ducts. I switch back from fork to pen.

The Amazon falls into silence for several moments. "We sacrificed so much," she says, still looking up. "We were fighting for something bigger than ourselves."

"Is that why you went to the Soviet Union?" I say.

Her eyes descend. "I went to the Soviet Union for my education. I finished

Dencho Znepolski (left) and Slavcho Transki

my secondary schooling in Sofia, and then I went to Moscow with Marin to study agricultural biology at the Timiryazev Academy."

"Were you already married then?"

"Yes." She smiles. It is a lovely smile, warm and inviting. "I married my first love, Marin."

"Was he a partisan, too?"

"Yes, we were partisans together in the same brigade. Most of us were poor, but Marin came from a wealthy family. His father was a lawyer. He didn't have to fight, but he believed in our great idea. He fought beside us as if he was one of us. Because he hated the fascists as much as we did."

I think of Frank Thompson and Iris Murdoch at Oxford. They, too, had come from privileged families. They, too, had joined the Communist Party because they hated fascism.

"I continued for my doctoral studies in Moscow," she says, opening a third folder. She hands me a document titled "autobiography." It is a six-page curriculum vitae in narrative form. "I also spent a year doing research in Sweden before I came back to Bulgaria. I was interested in wheat and was trying to create new hybrids. I was fortunate to be given a position as a geneticist at the Bulgarian Academy of Science where I was experimenting with different strains of wheat. In those days, seeds were my life."

Kostadin Lagadinov
on his wedding day

She smiles again. She looks over at my plate of watermelon — time for another bite. I trade my pen for the fork. I am quite happy that watermelon is not too heavy in the stomach, and the slivers of cheese get thinner as the interview wears on. I need to pace myself. I call this indentured eating. It is worth it.

"So how did you get into politics?" I say, taking a bite.

"That is a long story," she says, watching me. "You know that Georgi Dimitrov came back from Russia in 1944. He was going to lead us to that new world."

"But he died."

Elena nods. "Yes. He died in 1949. Kolarov died very soon after him. It was a bad time," she says. "Stalin had his own plans for Bulgaria."

I knew most of this story.

Dimitrov died under mysterious circumstances, and some believed that

General Kostadin Lagadinov

Stalin murdered him. After the Tito-Stalin split in 1948, Stalin suspected any leader interested in pursuing an independent form of socialism. Stalin wanted Eastern Europe for himself. Dimitrov and Kolarov were both Bulgarians who had worked in the Comintern, both seasoned politicians who may have disagreed with Stalin's brutal methods. Both were dead by 1950.[3]

The country's next prime minister, Valko Chervenkov, embraced Stalin's methods. Bulgaria saw a period of intense political repression and purges during Chervenkov's rule. Prominent members of the Bulgarian Communist Party were accused of "nationalist deviationism." Men like Dencho Znepolski, who had fought beside Frank Thompson in the Battle of Batuliya, were imprisoned for their previous connections to the Serb partisans. Anyone accused of "Titoism," or of dreaming of an independent Balkan federation, became the enemy of both Stalin and Chervenkov.

"I was far away in Moscow," Elena says. "But Dine and Boris were here. There were troubles."

My pen runs dry for a moment. I draw three spiral squiggles until the ink starts to flow. I need to remember to buy a new pen.

"Everything was changing so fast," she says. "Bulgaria was a very poor country before the war. There was so much to do. We all had to do our part. It was especially important for those of us who were Active Fighters against Fascism and Capitalism. We were the role models."

Chervenkov did not last long. In 1954, the Bulgarian Communist Party elected a new leader, one who would manage to hold on to power for the next thirty-five years. Todor Zhivkov had been a partisan in the Chavdar Brigade,[4] the brigade that Frank Thompson had hoped to reach during that final march into Bulgaria. After he became the first secretary of the Communist Party, Zhivkov extended special privileges to all those Bulgarians who had participated in the antifascist resistance. They were referred to by a special acronym: AFFC (Active Fighters against Fascism and Capitalism). Many AFFCS rose to positions of power within the Communist Party.[5]

For instance, Kostadin Lagadinov married immediately after the war. As a great hero of the partisan resistance, he was given the opportunity to finish his legal studies. Kostadin became a general and a judge in the military court in Bulgaria. He had a promising military career in front of him. But political elites always risked falling out of favor. In 1965, rumors and accusations emerged that Kostadin and other military officers were plotting against Zhivkov.[6] Although his status as a war hero protected him from prison or the labor camp, his military career was over. The Zhivkov government forced Lagadinov into retirement. He was the youngest general in Bulgaria at the time.

Elena and her husband had been sent to Moscow for their educations, and they returned to prominent careers. Like Kostadin Lagadinov, Elena's husband worked his way up the ranks in the military, and she returned to a prominent position as a research scientist. She had two children and earned her *habilitation* (a higher scientific qualification after the doctorate). For the first two decades of Bulgarian communism, Elena managed to stay out of politics.

All of that would change in 1967.

14 | A WOMAN'S WORK IS NEVER DONE

The housewife in the home does the work of a cook, of a seamstress, of a medical nurse, and of a servant, all in one. This is a socially useful labour. . . . Why is it then that we usually attach much less importance to this work than to the work of women in the factory who produce commodities and of an employee who does her important work in the office . . . ? The great role played by the mother, the creator of new life, should be honoured. It should be honoured not only by speeches, not only by messages of greeting. . . . Give your attention to our mothers. They take care of everything, themselves, but let us help every mother have the minimum which she needs.

—GEORGI DIMITROV, SPEECH BEFORE THE PLENARY SESSION
OF THE BULGARIAN WOMEN'S UNION, APRIL 6, 1948

"It all started because I wrote a letter to Brezhnev," she says. "But you must eat. You have barely eaten."[1]

She folds her hands over the table. I take a quick bite of the watermelon. "You wrote a letter to Leonid Brezhnev?"

"I had ideas for how to improve the system," she says. "It was my duty as a citizen to share my ideas on how to make socialism work more efficiently."

Elena proceeds to tell me the story about a letter that might have landed her in a labor camp or, at the very least, precipitated her early retirement. She had a disagreement with one of the party cadres assigned to oversee the research at the Bulgarian Academy of Science. These party cadres were politically loyal subjects of the government, but knew nothing about the technical aspects of research. One of these cadres began interfering with Elena's research program on political grounds. The supervision of educated experts by party activists with little technical expertise, Elena believed, created massive inefficiencies in the socialist economy. She wrote a letter detailing the outline of a new scientific policy to the leader of the Soviet Union.

The Bulgarian government, of course, intercepted the letter. It was brought to the attention of Zhivkov. It was the 1960s and, luckily for Elena, Zhivkov was also beginning to question the efficacy of promoting loyal cadres over educated experts.[2] Zhivkov apparently understood that a modern economy required men and women with the technical knowledge to fuel innovation and growth. Fidelity to Marxism-Leninism was not going to help genetically engineer the seeds needed to increase crop yields on the now collectivized farms. Scientific socialism needed scientists.

"One day, they sent a car for me while I was at the academy. I was in my lab coat in the middle of an experiment. I told them to wait but they told me to come immediately. I thought I was being arrested," Elena says. "Instead, I learned that they were making me the first secretary of the Fatherland Front."

"What year was that?"

"1967," she says. "And a year later they made me the new president of the Committee of the Bulgarian Women's Movement. My career as a geneticist was over."

I hear regret in her voice.

"Why did they want a biologist for the women's committee?"

"It is a long story." She glances at the watermelon.

Elena explains that Bulgaria had a big problem in the late 1960s. Before 1944, many Bulgarian peasants had been illiterate, especially women. Communism promised to free women from their economic dependence on men. To achieve this, women had to be educated. Once they had the training, they would be given jobs in the formal economy, including in traditionally male dominated spheres like science and engineering. The Bulgarian Communist Party also liberalized divorce laws and laws prohibiting abortion. Women gained full legal equality with men and joined the project of building the bright communist future.[3] By 1965, Bulgaria could boast more women in the workplace than almost any other nation in the world.[4] Women were educated and employed, but they stopped having babies.[5]

This created a problem. Todor Zhivkov's plans for expanding the industrial economy required more workers. Bulgaria suffered a significant demographic hit during World War II, and the labor shortage was one important impetus for fully actualizing communism's grand agenda for sexual equality. But if incorporating women into the workforce meant fewer children, the labor shortage problem would only get worse. All of the communist countries faced a similar problem by the 1960s.[6] The Romanians solved this problem by outlawing abortion and all forms of contraception.[7] Other countries toyed with the idea of forcing women back into the home. The demographic crisis created a sensitive political problem in need of a solution.

For Todor Zhivkov, Elena represented the ideal choice—a war hero from a family of celebrated partisans; she was a scientist with an advanced degree from the Soviet Union and many years of practical research experience. She was the mother of two children. And perhaps most importantly, Elena was not afraid to think outside the box.

"Was it hard to leave the academy?"

"Of course. I was a scientist. I loved my research. But my country needed me. It was a great honor to be given this position. I could not refuse," she says.

She pauses. I wonder about her choice of words: "I could not refuse." Is she speaking idiomatically? Or does she mean it literally?

"I got to work right away," she says. "The first thing I did was get pregnant." I raised an eyebrow.

"If I was going to convince women to have more children," she says, "I had to be a role model. Communist leaders must lead by their good example."

The tone in her voice changes for just long enough for me to catch an underlying moment of exasperation.

"A political system is only as good as its leaders," she says. "If I was going to solve this problem, I was going to solve it scientifically. When I started I knew nothing about women's problems. We had to collect data. I worked together with the editorial board of the *Woman Today*, the Central Statistical Agency, and some of the research institutes to create an anonymous survey. In the end, we received over sixteen thousand responses from working women. It was the first survey of its kind in Bulgaria."[8]

I write furiously in my notebook. Elena pauses long enough to let me finish writing. I nibble on a piece of watermelon, without cheese.

Elena Lagadinova with her family

"We found that women were completely overworked, and that they wanted to have more children but did not have the time. Twelve percent of children under the age of seven were left at home alone while their mothers were at work. Something had to be done. We came up with a plan. I had to present our research to Todor Zhivkov and some members of the politburo at a special meeting in Lovech in 1970. I took all of the data and I had some placards made. I still have them. Do you want to see them?"

"The originals?" I say.

"Yes, I have them somewhere in my closet."

"That'd be great. I'd love to photograph them."

Elena pushes herself up from her chair, leaning into both of her hands on the table. She is careful but spirited as she walks from the dining room down two low steps to the sitting room. She crosses through a corridor and is out of sight.

I look around her apartment. It is rather humble considering that Elena was so high up in the Bulgarian Communist Party for such a long time. In addition to being the president of the women's committee for twenty-two years, she was a member of the Central Committee and the Bulgarian parliament.[9]

The apartment is in a desirable location in Sofia, right in the heart of the

Elena Lagadinova (with an image of Georgi Dimitrov on the wall behind her)

Oborishte neighborhood, near Sofia University and the National Library. This block of flats was once reserved for the highest communist functionaries. I expected it to be quite luxurious the first time I went to visit her, but the only luxurious thing about the apartment is its address. The apartment is small, especially by American standards. As with my ex-in-laws, the furnishings date from the late seventies. There is nothing ostentatious about the place: a small kitchen, a dining room, a sitting room, and a few bedrooms tucked away on the other side of a narrow corridor. Elena once lived here with her family, but her husband passed away and all of her children are grown. Now, she spends most of her time in this apartment alone.

Still, the desirable location of the apartment and her once unlimited access to a government Mercedes with a driver marked Elena as a former member of the communist *nomenklatura*. Her extensive foreign travel was also a privilege that the ordinary Bulgarian women she represented did not enjoy. In a people's democracy, the population resented the material perks and privileges awarded to the political elite. Domestic leaders like Lagadinova were envied and derided for their supposed hypocrisy. Glancing around her humble apartment, I wonder how Bulgarians now feel about the gargantuan palaces being erected by the country's post-1989 oligarchs, who clog the streets of Sofia with Hummers that cost more than many Bulgarians will be able to earn in an entire lifetime. There was inequality under communism, but it was a pale shadow of the vast inequalities that would follow its collapse.

I stand up to stretch my legs and walk down into the sitting room to examine her bookshelves. She owns a good collection of books, all in Russian or Bulgarian, and quite a few new volumes scattered among the old communist-era books. I can tell these by their colorful spines. In front of the books sit a variety of tchotchkes, souvenirs and gifts, most likely from her diplomatic visits abroad. Each one of these must have a story. I make a mental note to ask her about them on another visit. A photo of her late husband hangs on the wall along with three paintings by her youngest daughter, an artist who now lives in Poland.

"Here, I found them," she says. She is carrying four large placards wrapped in clear plastic. She slides each one out. The first graph shows declining birthrates in all East European and several West European countries. The others are graphic representations of the survey findings, including a detailed time budget of how Bulgarian women spend their time each day. Between their jobs, their commutes, and their various household and childcare responsibilities, women worked about fourteen hours a day.

"You see," Elena says, pointing at the time-budget placard. "We had found the root of the problem through our research. Then we had to come up with the solutions."

She leans the placards against the wall and walks back up to the dining room table.

"Would you like some water? Some cola?" she says.

"No, thank you."

"I have some fresh juice. Would you like juice?"

"No, I still have some watermelon."

"Coffee?" she says.

I shake my head. "So what kind of solutions did you come up with?"

She disappears into the kitchen and returns with a glass of juice. "It is fresh," she says, putting the glass in front of me. I take a sip.

"It was clear that we needed to give women paid maternity leaves and to build more crèches and kindergartens for the children." She sits back down in her chair. "Women needed help. We developed a comprehensive plan. I went to Lovech with my placards and gave a three-hour lecture on the situation of women in Bulgaria and what our party needed to do about it."

Elena's eyes fill with excitement as she explains that Lenin believed that housework needed to be socialized in order to free women from the domestic burdens of the home and fully incorporate them into society. Georgi Dimitrov, too, wrote about the heroic labor of women in the home.

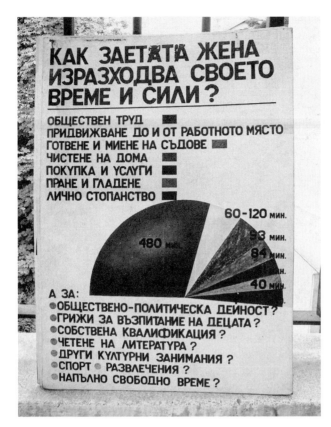

КАК ЗАЕТАТА ЖЕНА
ИЗРАЗХОДВА СВОЕТО
ВРЕМЕ И СИЛИ?

ОБЩЕСТВЕН ТРУД
ПРИДВИЖВАНЕ ДО И ОТ РАБОТНОТО МЯСТО
ГОТВЕНЕ И МИЕНЕ НА СЪДОВЕ
ЧИСТЕНЕ НА ДОМА
ПОКУПКА И УСЛУГИ
ПРАНЕ И ГЛАДЕНЕ
ЛИЧНО СТОПАНСТВО

60-120 мин.
480 мин.
93 мин.
84 мин.
40 мин.

А ЗА:
● ОБЩЕСТВЕНО-ПОЛИТИЧЕСКА ДЕЙНОСТ?
● ГРИЖИ ЗА ВЪЗПИТАНИЕ НА ДЕЦАТА?
● СОБСТВЕНА КВАЛИФИКАЦИЯ?
● ЧЕТЕНЕ НА ЛИТЕРАТУРА?
● ДРУГИ КУЛТУРНИ ЗАНИМАНИЯ?
● СПОРТ ● РАЗВЛЕЧЕНИЯ?
● НАПЪЛНО СВОБОДНО ВРЕМЕ?

A placard
handmade
in 1969
summarizing
how Bulgarian
women spend
their time

"It was time that the Communist Party did the things Lenin and Dimitrov said they were supposed to do," she says. "They had an obligation to women."

"So were they convinced?" I say.

"Well, they agreed with my scientific analysis of the problem. They did not agree with my solutions. The solutions would cost a lot of money from the state budget, money the men preferred to spend on other things. They said it was less costly to outlaw abortion."

"Like they did in Romania."

"Yes, exactly like Romania," she says, raising her voice. "But what kind of country are we to make women have children that they do not want? These children will be unloved because women have no time for them. They will become a problem to society. Or wives will avoid being intimate with their husbands to prevent pregnancy, and we will have more broken families! What kind of solution is that?"

Elena Lagadinova with Angela Davis, who visited Bulgaria in 1972

She makes her hand into a fist and presses it into the table. I imagine her forty years younger, the only woman in a room full of men. Even four decades later, her eyes burn with the certainty that she is right. I see the righteous indignation.

"I told them, Kristen, I said, 'If you are not going to listen to me, then send me back to the Academy where I belong.'"

My eyes widen. "You said that to Zhivkov?"

She nods.

"And what happened?"

"They agreed to our plan. When they rewrote the constitution in 1971, they elevated the right to maternity leave as a constitutional principle, and in 1973, there was an official politburo decision on women," she says.

I knew that this decision guaranteed women maternity leave and promised more childcare facilities and other socialized services for families.[10] "So that decision was in place *before* the International Women's Year?"

"Oh yes," Elena says, nodding. "We were well ahead of all of the other countries when we went to Mexico City in 1975 for that first World Conference on Women. The United Nations even recognized Bulgaria as a model country for women's issues, as I have told you before."

I nod. My first interviews with Elena concerned her international activism during the United Nations International Decade for Women.[11] I knew this part of her past quite well.[12] During her years as president of the women's committee, Elena became a prominent international voice for women's issues.[13] She was elected as the general rapporteur at the third World Conference on Women in Nairobi in 1985 and was appointed to serve as a member of the board of trustees of the United Nations Institute for Training Women (INSTRAW) from 1985 to 1988.[14] Activist women from the developing world as well as Western women acknowledged her to be a pragmatist who did not allow politics to interfere with the concrete challenges that women faced around the world.[15] Elena believed that socialism was the best political and economic system for women, but she eagerly learned from the experiences of other countries, even those in the capitalist camp. She studied the layout of supermarkets in the United States and France to explore ways that grocery shopping in Bulgaria could be made more efficient.[16]

Of course, her work was not always successful. Zhivkov remained in power for about thirty-five years; he feared popular figures like Elena. As her career progressed, she won the support of the ordinary women but earned herself the animosity of many influential party members. They resented the amount of money spent on women, especially when Bulgaria's once vibrant economy stagnated in the 1980s. In 1985, Elena helped to push through a new Family Code, one very favorable to wives.[17] The backlash from men was inevitable, especially from men high up in the Bulgarian Communist Party. By the 1980s, many of Bulgaria's ruling elite cared little for the original ideals of communism. They sought mostly to preserve their power and privileges. In a supposedly classless society, the extra perks reserved for the *nomenklatura* were a blatant hypocrisy.[18]

Although Elena also enjoyed some privileges, many perceived her as a threat. She openly opposed the party's "administrative intervention" in the lives of Bulgaria's Turkish minority, forcing them to change their Turkish names to Bulgarian ones.[19] The secret police bugged her apartment, but she had friends in the Ministry of Interior who called to tell her when the police would be listening in. Zhivkov tried to replace her, but she used her international contacts and her reputation as a global women's activist to maintain her position. She was too widely known, and too well respected, to be so easily pushed aside. She was, after all, "the Amazon."

"For twenty-two years, I worked for this committee," Elena says. "You know all the work that I did."

I smile at her. Elena had been a force of nature where women's issues were concerned. One of the journalists on the editorial board of *Woman Today* referred to Elena as a "miracle."[20] In a relatively short period of time, Elena transformed the daily lives of millions of ordinary Bulgarian women.

"Of course, there were still problems that needed to be solved," she says. "Our work was not finished. We had to work within the constraints of the system. There were limited resources, but we did the best we could."

"So why did you give it up? There were so many new women's organizations after the changes. They could have used your expertise."

Elena shakes her head. This is delicate territory. I eat some cheese and watermelon. "Perhaps I will have some water," I say.

"Yes," she says. "I would like some water as well."

Elena disappears into the kitchen. I can hear her pulling glasses down from the cabinets. I eat the last bites of melon. I wonder if I have overstepped my bounds. She has never spoken with me about those final years. All I know is that she retired in January 1990 at the age of sixty. It was not an "early retirement," since all Bulgarian women had the right to retire by fifty-five.

She brings two glasses of water into the dining room. "Drink," she says. "The cheese is salty."

The water is tepid. Bulgarians do not like to drink overly cold water, believing that it is bad for the throat. Elena sits across from me sipping her water. I regret asking the question. I am about to suggest that I come back tomorrow when she says, "It was a putsch from the inside. They called themselves reformers. They were all thieves."

She takes a breath. She takes another drink of water.

"In my years working with the committee, I helped many people," she says. "There were some that I helped even more than others, young women with ambition who needed a head start. In the end, they put a knife in my back. It was a bad time, Kristen. They said they were bringing democracy, but what did they bring? They brought ruin to everything we built."

"Is that why you retired?" I say. "Because of what happened in 1989?"

"I told them, 'This is not my party.' I called the general accounting office to do a full audit of the committee's accounts, and then I retired. We had a lot of money in the committee, you know. I didn't want anyone to say that I stole anything. I turned it over to the new women's organization, the one they had formed behind my back. And then the money was gone. Our offices were restituted. Our archives were scattered. I kept as much as I could for my private archives, but there were many things I wish I had kept. There were so

Elena Lagadinova just one month before the fall of the Berlin Wall

many letters from world leaders and women's activists that were written to me in thanks for my international work. They were all kept in the committee's archives. I never kept a single letter for myself. Imagine, I did not make one extra Xerox so that I could bring a letter home."

Her face falls. For the first time she seems like an ordinary eighty-year-old woman. I look around her apartment. If she had been an American, Elena would have settled into a comfortable retirement by now. She would have a decent social security check after working for over thirty years. But the last twenty years had not treated her well. Her pension is a pittance, and I assume that she, like so many other Bulgarians of her generation, lost her savings in the banking collapses and the rampant hyperinflation of the 1990s. In the winter months, she turns off her central heat. She relies instead on small electrical heaters, and then only on the coldest days.

Many Bulgarians in her position would have stolen the money from the committee. In the chaotic years that followed 1989, a lot of government money disappeared because no one was keeping track. Anyone in a position of authority could have easily diverted resources to their private accounts. Those who helped to drain the communist state's coffers now lived

A delegation of Ethiopian officials visiting the grave of Assen Lagadinov in 1984

comfortable lives in their villas outside of Sofia. They sent their children to study in the West. They saw the opportunity and seized it. They were entrepreneurs of a sort, the kind of people necessary for building the new free market economy.

I look across the table at her, this woman who was the youngest female partisan fighting during World War II.

"A lot of people think communism was about equality," she says. "But it was not about equality; it is impossible to have perfect equality. People are too different."

Elena looks down at the second folder, still open in front of her, brimming with articles and clippings about her brothers. She runs her hands across a photo of an Ethiopian delegation at a commemorative ceremony marking the fortieth anniversary of Assen's death.

"It was about justice," she says. A tremor fills her voice. "It was about building a society that would work for the many rather than enriching the few."

Elena waves her arm at the window. "And now you see what we have? So many people are without medicine. So many children are on the street; they are not going to school. Prostitutes make more money than doctors and judges. The young people leave to the West and never come back. People are

Assen Lagadinov's grave in 2013 in Razlog

poorer now than they were before the war, while the rich live in mansions with swimming pools in Boyana and Dragalevtsi."

I look down at my plate. A scattering of black seeds soak in a thin film of light pink juice. Beside my plate I have laid the old, creased photo of Assen Lagadinov.

I pick up the photo, reach across the table, and return it to Elena. She gazes down at the young face of her brother. She places it on top of the other photos and newspaper articles. Elena closes the folder.

"This is not what we fought for," she says.

15 | HISTORY IS WRITTEN BY THE VICTORS

In March 2012, I attended a planning seminar hosted by a local women's nongovernmental organization (NGO) in Sofia. The organization recently learned about an opportunity for European Union funding to support scholarly research on women's lives under communism. The NGO convened a group of leading scholars in the disciplines of history, anthropology, and sociology—mostly Bulgarian women in their fifties and sixties—to discuss the possibility of working on the communist era.

The women grappled with the question of whether they would be able to write an "objective" account of the period between 1944 and 1990, given that they had lived most of their lives during that time.[1] They were concerned about how their personal memories of the era might affect their scholarship, but they all agreed that young scholars who had not lived in that era should not write the history of women's lives under communism. While they recognized the diversity of their individual experiences, the scholars also agreed that communism was not as bad as most people wanted to believe it was.

They were particularly wary of West European scholars whose writings might perpetuate Cold War stereotypes. One woman recalled reading something written by a British scholar about how gray life was behind the Iron Curtain.

"My life was full of color. I didn't know what she was talking about," she said.

Another woman in the room explained, "I was young and went to university and had my children during that time. How could I not look back on those years and feel happy?"

"So the question is," the seminar leader, a woman named Ivanka said, "How can we best achieve objectivity?"[2]

"There is no such thing as objectivity in history," said one of the professors of history, Dr. Gancheva. "Historians have come to accept the subjective nature of most historical accounts."

"There is historical truth," said Dr. Meneva, an older historian. "Events happened or they didn't happen. There are ways of finding the truth if you look in the right places."

Dr. Antanasova, a sociologist, cleared her throat. "There is nothing objective about communism. During that time, all of the statistics on women's empowerment were manipulated by the government. How will we even start?"

Ivanka sighed. "The statistics today are manipulated, too. Democracy doesn't bring objectivity," she said. "Statistics are just as subjective as historiography. Subjective positions inform the questions that are asked."

All of the women nodded in agreement.

The eldest woman in the room, Mrs. Popova, was a former English teacher and an occasional interpreter who once worked for the communist era women's committee. She was in her late sixties. "How can we study something that we lived?" she said.

"I cannot believe that something I lived is now considered 'history.'" Ivanka said. "It makes me feel old."

"I was only a child when communism ended, but I have wonderful memories of that time," said Margarita, Ivanka's assistant, a woman in her midthirties. "I think that everyone was happier then. They had a purpose and they understood what was expected of them."

She shifted in her chair, her eyes cast down at her feet.

"I wish I had grown up before the Changes," she said.

"The Changes": this is how most Bulgarians refer to the transition from state socialism to capitalism. In German this translated into Die Wende. In Bulgarian, it is *promenite*. It is an ambivalent term. In the West, we refer to 1989 as the "democratic revolutions," "the collapse of communism," or "the fall of the Wall." In the former Eastern Bloc, people merely say "the Changes."

"I was only in eighth grade when everything changed," Margarita said. "I had no one who could advise me on how to live in a market economy. Things were so much simpler before."

Silence followed her words. The older women looked uncomfortable. I was the only non-Bulgarian, and I was trying to take notes on everything that was said. I felt new tension in the room.

It was still difficult to speak about communism in Bulgaria, even twenty-two years after its demise. The history of the People's Republic of Bulgaria was long and complex, but I knew the basic outline.[3] When the Red Army crossed into Bulgaria in 1944, three key leaders oversaw the political ascension of the Bulgarian Communist Party: Georgi Dimitrov, Vasil Kolarov, and Traicho Kostov. To a certain extent, all three may have harbored dreams of an independent Balkan Federation. After being pawns in the grand plans of the Great Powers for so long, the leaders of countries like Yugoslavia, Bulgaria, and Greece imagined that the postwar world would allow them political self-determination for the first time. But Churchill wanted Greece, and Stalin coveted both Bulgaria and Yugoslavia.[4]

Josip Broz Tito of Yugoslavia refused to be Stalin's puppet in the Balkans. In 1948, Tito and Stalin split. Tito was accused of "anti-Sovietism," of "nationalistic deviation," and was expelled from the Comintern. According to the Yugoslavs, Dimitrov himself sympathized with the idea of an independent Balkan Federation, and he tried to negotiate around Stalin and his megalomaniacal dreams of world domination.[5] Others believed that Dimitrov conspired with Stalin in the purge of "anti-Soviet" members of the Bulgarian Communist Party.[6] This was a purge that would lead to the show trial and execution of Traicho Kostov at the end of 1949.[7]

The facts were these: Kostov was removed from the politburo on March 31, 1949, while Georgi Dimitrov visited the Soviet Union. Kostov was subsequently appointed as the director of the National Library and finally accused of anti-Soviet deviationism in mid-June. The death of Georgi Dimitrov was announced on July 2, 1949. Although Dimitrov was already sixty-seven years old, his death was unexpected, giving rise to rumors that Stalin had him poisoned. In the six days that it took to transport Dimitrov's body from Moscow to Sofia, his devotees built the mausoleum in the center of Sofia that held his embalmed body for the next four decades. In the months following Dimitrov's death, Vasil Kolarov assumed power, although he, too, died within six months. In December 1949, Traicho Kostov was tried with ten other high-ranking Communist Party members. They were each found guilty of anti-Soviet deviationism. The government executed Kostov. All of the others were sent to jail or to labor camps.

In 1950, Stalin installed Valko Chervenkov to rule Bulgaria. Under Chervenkov, the purges continued unabated. Many Bulgarians, most of them committed communists, were disgraced and imprisoned. Chervenkov targeted anyone who questioned the Soviet orthodoxy.[8]

The trial of Traicho Kostov killed the dream of many partisans like Dencho Znepolski, the commander of the Second Sofia Brigade, who believed that communism could bring democracy and self-determination to Bulgaria. Stalin stopped at nothing to make sure that Bulgaria remained firmly under Soviet control, hijacking the cause for which Frank Thompson and Assen Lagadinov died.

In 1956, the Bulgarians finally rid themselves of Chervenkov. Without Stalin to support him, Chervenkov was replaced by Todor Zhivkov. The Bulgarian Communist Party quickly moved to rehabilitate Kostov and his associates. Zhivkov recognized that innocent people had been unjustly accused and persecuted, that Chervenkov had nurtured a dangerous "cult of personality." In April 1956, a Sofia court reversed all of the sentences. The court released all those unjustly imprisoned, including Znepolski. Only Kostov's sentence could not be reversed.[9]

Exoneration could not undo the damage. Just five years after the revolution that was to bring social justice to all Bulgarians, Georgi Dimitrov, Vasil Kolarov, and Traicho Kostov were all dead.[10] Gone, too, were Frank Thompson and Assen Lagadinov, and many partisans who lost their lives to the gendarmes. The promised people's utopia devolved into a brutal dystopia ruled by paranoid dictators. But far beneath the realm of high politics, the planned economy started Bulgaria on a path to rapid modernization. For ordinary people, apparently, not everything was black.

"Perhaps we should start with some personal stories," Ivanka said. "For instance, I was divorced during that time. I had two children to raise on my own, and I had a lot of support from the government. I know that it would be much harder to be a single mother today."

"Much harder" was a bit of an understatement, I thought as I listened to Ivanka. After 1989, Bulgaria became a democratic country, but it also became a miserable one. After January 1, 2007, Bulgaria officially joined the European Union and earned the distinction of being its poorest member state. By 2011, the European Commission found that 44 percent of Bulgarians had experienced "severe material deprivation."[11] In that same year, 49 percent of the total population was at risk for poverty or social exclusion. Democracy and free markets promised freedom and prosperity. Communism was not the only political dream that disappointed the Bulgarians.

"I was the first person in my family to earn a university degree," said Dr. Meneva. "I came from a poor peasant family, but I had many opportunities under the old system that I would never have today. The education for women: that was a good thing."

"Of course, there were the shortages," Ivanka said. "It was almost impossible to find Pampers or feminine products."

The older women in the room nodded.

Mrs. Popova laughed. "I remember once that I was sent to the airport to meet a visiting female dignitary from Ethiopia. It was sometime in the eighties. I was going to be the interpreter for her visit. She was very tall and elegant. I remember that she was wearing sunglasses and jeans."

Mrs. Popova paused. Jeans symbolized the West and were widely coveted during the communist era. To Mrs. Popova, the fact that this Ethiopian wore sunglasses and jeans meant that she was wealthy and glamorous, and perhaps slightly intimidating.

"I was riding in the car to the hotel with her and she turned to me and asked me if we could go to a pharmacy." Mrs. Popova said. "The Ethiopian said she needed to buy some tampons. I had heard of these and I knew what they were for. I was too embarrassed to tell her that we did not have them in Bulgaria. So I nodded and told the driver to stop at the pharmacy. And you know what I had to buy her . . ."

Ivanka and Dr. Gancheva groaned with the memory.

"That massive roll of unrefined cotton that we used to have to use," Mrs. Popova said.

"That had the little filaments still in it." Ivanka rubbed her thumb and forefinger together as if rolling a tiny thread between them.

"I got back into the car and gave it to her. She looked absolutely horrified by it, but she said nothing," Mrs. Popova said. "I was so embarrassed."

Ivanka smiled. "That is a wonderful story."

"I hated communism," said Dr. Peeva, who had until now remained silent. She was also a historian. "I was an intellectual and I hated all of the restrictions on free thought. Not being able to get the books that I wanted to read.

Not being able to get journal articles from the West. Always having to use Marxist theory."

Ivanka leaned in toward Dr. Peeva, nodding for her to continue.

"Most of my research has been against this regime," Dr. Peeva said. "You know that."

Dr. Peeva sighed. She directed her next words to Margarita, who still sat with her eyes looking down.

"Recently, I have come to see that perhaps I did not understand it so well. I saw it only from the university. But for ordinary people I suppose it was different. I think there were some good things about the system that I couldn't see because I was so angry about the books."

I knew Dr. Peeva socially, and I had wondered why she had agreed to come to this seminar. Her words signaled that she was willing to participate in any grant proposal they wrote to the European Union.

I flicked my eyes over to the face of Dr. Meneva. She was the senior Bulgarian historian and had always been more favorably predisposed to communism. She had written several articles about the status of women during the previous era, always pointing out the real achievements. From her terse expression, I guessed that she was silently seething at what she perceived to be the opportunism of some of the other historians in the room. Now that there might be EU money available to support scholarship on the era, they were suddenly interested in thinking about the history of communism.

I also knew that Dr. Meneva disapproved of what she called the "marketization of historical scholarship." She hated the fact that Bulgarian historians, who earned only a fraction of what their colleagues in the West earned, had little choice but to sell their skills to the highest (foreign) bidder in order to make a living. Dr. Meneva complained that some of her colleagues had become "mercenary historians," scholars dispatched into the archives to find evidence for whatever thesis Western donors wanted proved.

And then there was me, the American ethnographer. I was the oddball of the bunch, the one of these things that was not like the others. I had never lived in communist Bulgaria. I had, however, written three books on gender issues in the post-1989 era.[12] Ivanka invited me to attend the seminar because she knew that I was interested in the Bulgarian partisans and the work that the Bulgarian communists did for women. I did my own research in the Bulgarian archives.[13] I had also been interviewing Elena Lagadinova and other women who worked with her at the national committee. For me the past was still alive in the people who had lived through it. Any "truth" about that past had to be created in dialogue with its survivors. Too often, I thought, historical "truth" was merely a tool to justify contemporary political arrangements.

"What about you, Kristen?" Ivanka asked. "Can you tell us a story about communism, maybe from the American point of view?"

The women all turned to me; even Margarita lifted her eyes.

"Well," I said, "In school, they taught us that communism was very bad."

I smiled. Ivanka and Margarita laughed.

"I was also very afraid that we were all going to die in a nuclear war," I said. "It wasn't looking very good with Reagan in office in the 1980s."

Ivanka nodded at me to continue.

"I remember that well," said Margarita. "We used to write letters for world peace in school."

"We did, too." I said. "I was terrified of this: the whole Warsaw Pact versus NATO nightmare scenario. I grew up in San Diego, and we had four big military bases and a nuclear power plant nearby. If there was a nuclear war, we would've been the first to go."

"We always thought that you would start shooting first," Dr. Meneva said. Her tone was cool. She was always polite with me, but she did not like Americans.

At that moment, I realized that the Cold War stereotypes went in both directions. But "we" (the West) had won that Cold War and this meant that "we" largely controlled how the history of communism could be written. I thought about the lives of Frank Thompson and the Lagadinov brothers. I thought about Elena. Would anyone care about their stories? And what about the achievements of the women's committee? Would I become an apologist for totalitarianism if I tried to document the progress of women in Bulgaria between 1944 and 1989?

There were big risks in trying to tackle Cold War stereotypes. In a supposedly democratic era that celebrated political rights and the freedom of speech, I knew that it was still difficult to produce a more nuanced historical account of the communist era. There was little intellectual or ideological pluralism when it came to the historiography of the recent past in Eastern Europe, even if it was just talking about childcare and maternity leaves.

Doubt haunted me. It might be foolish to pursue my project. Had I gone too far with that favor for Professor Dyson five years earlier? I was not a historian. It would be safer to focus on what I knew best: the post-socialist period. If I wrote the book that I wanted to write, my academic colleagues might begin to question my credentials, wondering whether I had lost all "objectivity." What if I was wrong? What if I was just naïve? Perhaps my fondness for two kind octogenarians had gotten the better of me.

I glanced around the room. The women assembled felt this fear just as well as I did. There was no need for official censorship when all of the scholars learned to censor themselves. What I learned that day in the seminar is that it might be easier to assert that the moon landing was staged than it would be to argue that there was anything good about the communist past.

16 | ON CENSORSHIP AND THE SECRET POLICE

"Elena told me you like tea," A. said, pointing to an electric kettle. "But perhaps I can offer you a vodka?"

I glanced at my mobile phone. It was just after noon. She looked hopeful.

"Sure," I said. "Why not?" This was my first meeting with the woman to whom I would give the pseudonym Anelia.[1] She was my host.

"Wonderful," she said. "I'll get the ice and tonic water."

She disappeared into the kitchen, leaving me alone with a wheezing pug. The little dog waddled up to my feet, and I scratched behind one of his ears. I looked around Anelia's small apartment. I sat on a low couch in front of a square coffee table. Eight small dishes of various snacks were laid out in front of me: thin slices of *kashkaval* (Bulgarian yellow cheese), salami, batter-covered peanuts, almonds, two different types of cracker, some cookies and potato chips. Across the table was a single lounge chair. To my left was a tall bookshelf.

Behind the lounge chair, an open floor-to-ceiling unit of shelves divided the room into two sections. A variety of porcelain statues and snow globes and a hand-painted Dutch wooden clog were carefully centered on each shelf, giving the room a cozy feel. On the other side of the room, a glass-paned door led out to a balcony. The apartment was built during the communist era, but I could tell by the new aluminum window frames that it had been remodeled recently. Images flicked on a small television in the corner. The sound was muted.

Anelia reentered the room with a bottle of Bulgarian vodka, a local Bulgarian brand of tonic water, and a glass bowl full of ice.

"Do you smoke?" she said.

"Only when my daughter isn't around," I said. When I did life history interviews in Bulgaria, I often smoked if my interview subject smoked. Sitting around and chatting over cigarettes was a popular pastime in Bulgaria. Not only do Americans have a reputation for not smoking; we also have the image of being intolerant of smokers. This national stereotype I could easily avoid by smoking a few cigarettes now and then. If I didn't, some people would eventually become self-conscious about their smoking and would try to rush the conversation.

"Oh, wonderful," she said, smiling. "I like to smoke."

From one of the bookshelves, she brought down two ashtrays. Then she sat in the chair across from me and said, "Please, eat something."

I grabbed a handful of almonds. "Your dog is adorable. What is his name?"

"I call him 'Smart,'" she said. "He was a present for my grandson, who was supposed to take care of him. But you know how children are. And he is at school all day long. So now Smart lives here with me."

"He's very affectionate!"

"If he's bothering you, please let me know."

"No bother," I said. "I'm fond of dogs. And he's a cutie." I continued to scratch Smart behind his ear. He collapsed in pleasure at my feet.

"I like you already," Anelia said, smiling.

"Elena told me you worked for the committee in Berlin for eight years."

"Yes, thanks only to Elena," Anelia said. "She sent me there because she supported people with skills, not just members of the Communist Party."

I jot two letters in the margin of my notebook followed by a question mark: "CP?" From what I know about Bulgarian communism, it would have been very difficult for Anelia to live in East Berlin for eight years without being a party member.

"Elena speaks very highly of you," I said. "She told me that there was no way I could write about the committee without speaking to you."

Anelia was born in 1942, which made her twelve years Elena's junior. She had no firsthand recollections of the war. By the time she was a teenager, communism was well established in Bulgaria, the political reality she was born into. I had interviewed many of the women who worked with Elena at the women's committee, but Anelia was the youngest. She had inherited the world for which Frank Thompson and the Lagadinovs had fought.

"Elena is very kind. She is not the kind of person who forgets her friends from before, like so many others these days," Anelia said. "She was very good to me. I'll always remember that. I'll help you in whatever way I can."

Anelia poured two drinks. I was relieved to notice that there was only a little vodka poured over the ice. She filled the rest of the glass with tonic water and placed one drink in front of me. "*Nazdrave*," she said, raising her glass.

I lifted my own glass and looked her straight in the eyes. In Bulgaria, when you say "cheers" it is considered bad luck not to look a person directly in the eyes.

"*Nazdrave.*"

We each took a sip. The drink was cool. The quinine tingled on my tongue. It was only lunchtime, but I had no other appointments for the day.

She lit a cigarette. "So where should we start?"

"I suppose you could tell me a little about your background: where you grew up, where you went to school, and how you came to be involved with the committee."

"Well," she said, sipping on her vodka tonic. She pulled a long drag through her cigarette. For a sixty-eight-year-old woman, I thought Anelia was rather attractive. She wore her thin hair in a short bob, dyed a dark brown. She was dressed in dark-blue jersey pants and a T-shirt. She was lively and articulate, always pausing to give me time to write when she saw that I was scribbling frantically in my notebook.

"I am a true child of the state," she said. "From the very first grade, my family could not afford to pay the five levs school tuition fee, because we were so poor. I was fortunate to be born in this country after the ninth of September. The state paid all of my school fees all the way up to university. This was a privilege that anyone could take advantage of, boys and girls, Bulgarians and Turks," she said. "I remember being in the first grade at school and sharing a classroom with the son of an attorney, the daughter of someone who had been an officer in the king's army, and many other children of the educated and upper classes. I was very scared to be there. Who was I? I was the daughter of peasants. But the teachers made it very clear that I had the right to be there just like any of the other children. I learned that I had the right to an education like everyone else."

"Did you enjoy school?" I said.

"I loved school. I could not wait to go in the morning. I did not want to be a farmer, and the only way to avoid that was to get educated."

"Elena told me you graduated in English philology, is that right?"

"Yes," she said.

"Did you want to become a teacher?"

"No, I just wanted to learn English. I loved the language, and it was English that would bring me to the women's committee." She tapped the end of her cigarette into the ashtray. She picked up the box. I noticed the brand; they were inexpensive Bulgarian cigarettes.

"Will you smoke?" she said, holding the box out to me.

"Thank you." I drew a cigarette out of the box, and she offered me a lighter.

"I never wanted to work with women," Anelia said, "I much preferred the company of men. I spent the first decade of my career working in a forklift manufacturing facility. All of my colleagues were men."

"Forklifts? Isn't that an odd career path for an English philologist?" I puffed on the cigarette lightly. The taste of this Bulgarian tobacco was strong and leafy.

"Well, you know, in that time you didn't really have a choice about your job. You went where you were needed. My family didn't have any connections or anything so no one helped me. The government wanted to hire more women in traditionally masculine professions. So I decided that I would like to go work in a Balkankar factory for heavy machinery. I liked building things. I was very happy there for ten years with the forklifts."

"From forklifts to politics?" I took another drag. "How did that happen?"

Anelia laughed a deep, sonorous laugh. Her smile was wide as she sat comfortably in her casual clothes, smoking and drinking vodka at noon. She struck me as a woman with a predisposition for great joy.

"It is a funny story," she said, exhaling a lungful of smoke. "Bulgaria was importing some hydraulic machinery from England. They needed someone to translate all of the technical manuals into Bulgarian. Of course, there were many qualified translators, but there wasn't anyone who both knew English and all of the technical terms for hydraulic mechanisms. These are very specific terms, you see." She took a sip from her drink.

"I had a complete knowledge of hydraulics because of my work in the forklift factory. I had learned the words in English out of curiosity, to keep my English active. In the end, I was the only person they could find capable for translating those manuals."

I crushed out my cigarette. I had not smoked even half of it, but I realized that I could not write and smoke at the same time. It was a similar problem to the one I had with Elena and the indentured eating. I wished for a moment that I could use a digital recorder, but I knew that Bulgarians of a certain generation were uncomfortable being recorded. The interviews never went as well because they censored themselves. Taking notes was more informal. It put people at ease.

"After that," Anelia said, "Bulgaria started exporting forklifts and other equipment, and they needed someone who could translate technical manuals from Bulgarian into English. So that is how I also became a translator. At some point, I was asked to do some translations for the *Woman Today* magazine. That is how Elena discovered me. She wanted me to come to work for the committee, but I did not think they would accept me because I was not a party member."

"Couldn't you just join?" I said.

Anelia laughed. "It wasn't that easy. You had to be active in the Komsomol first, and then you had to be nominated. You had to read all those books: Marx and Engels and Lenin. Then there were the meetings and all the boring speeches. It was so tedious. You couldn't just join," she said. "You had to really believe. I was happy with my forklifts. I didn't care about politics."

Anelia shifted in her chair, leaning her elbow on the armrest and pressing her cheek into her fist.

"I never dreamed that I would be working as a translator and interpreter for Elena, or that I would have the chance to travel to the West. You know that it was almost impossible for ordinary Bulgarians to travel outside of the Eastern Bloc, right?"

"You had to have special permission."

"You had to have permission," Anelia said. "And hard currency. Traveling to the West for most of us was the same as traveling to the moon."

Anelia smashed out her cigarette.

"The committee was different," she continued. "When I got there, I realized that there were other women who were not members of the party. There were some divorced women, too. Elena did not care about your family or your politics; she just wanted competent people. After some time, I took on more responsibilities with the committee. I worked very hard. It was good work for me, even if it meant that I had to be surrounded by women instead of forklifts."

She paused. I finished writing a sentence in the notebook. She waited, taking a sip of her drink. I looked up and nodded for her to continue.

"At that time, the women's committee was affiliated with the Women's International Democratic Federation in the GDR. The treasurer of this organization was usually a Bulgarian. In 1981, the current treasurer was preparing to return to Bulgaria. The WIDF asked the committee to send a replacement. Elena decided to send me, but this was a big problem."

"How so?" I said.

"Because I was not a party member. The president of the Federation of Women in the GDR called Elena to personally protest my appointment. You know the Germans weren't like the Bulgarians on these matters. The Germans were strict. They didn't accept me."

"But you went anyway?"

"Yes, and I stayed there for eight years. Elena supported me because she knew that I could do the job. I went there as treasurer, but in my first year I was doing translations, conducting research, attending international seminars, and writing articles for *Women of the Whole World*."

"Really?" I said. *Women of the Whole World* was an international women's magazine with a massive global circulation during the communist era. It was issued in five languages—Russian, English, French, Spanish, and German, with occasional issues in Arabic—and was sent to progressive women's organizations in over 150 countries.

"Really," she said. "But they rarely let me have a byline. The German government controlled the magazine. They didn't like to acknowledge individual authors. And it was censored, of course. But I tell you I wrote a lot of good articles for that magazine based on real research. It was all my work."

"What kind of research were you doing?"

"I traveled to all of the socialist countries in the Eastern Bloc to learn about the situation of women there. You know, people think that all of the socialist countries were the same, but there were a lot of differences. When I was working for WIDF in Berlin, I traveled to Poland, Hungary, Czechoslovakia, Romania, the Soviet Union, and Yugoslavia to meet with women's committees and talk about best practices. Different women faced different problems in different countries because there were different government policies. In Romania abortion and birth control were illegal but there was less support for single mothers than in the GDR." Anelia paused to light another cigarette. "The Hungarians had a very good system."

Smart was now dozing at my feet. I took a sip of the vodka tonic.

"Would you like another cigarette?"

"Not right now," I said. "I need to be able to write." I held up my pen.

"I learned so much from those trips, but I couldn't write about everything that I wanted to. You know, in the GDR there was no freedom of the press at all," she said. "Everything that went into that magazine had to be approved by the GDR censors. In other countries it was not so strict. There were ways to publish criticisms, and of course there was always the *samizdat*."

Samizdat referred to banned literature, distributed through clandestine networks.

"We also didn't have nongovernmental organizations like you have in the West, organizations that were independent of the state and which could criticize national policies. We were all state employees, and we had to keep our mouths shut. I traveled to many countries to do research and the research was good research. I had a lot of facts about the conditions of women's lives in other countries, even Western countries. It was idiotic that we could not publish everything we wanted. This was stupidity."

Anelia laughed. "It reminds me of a joke," she said. "Why did the Stasi operate in groups of three?"

"Why?"

"One could read, one could write, and the third could keep an eye on the two intellectuals," she said, chuckling.

I laughed.

"Can you give me an example of something that was prohibited?" I said.

"Sure," she said, leaning her right elbow on her right knee. "We could write anything about the political situation in South Africa or in Central America, but we never wrote any articles about Northern Ireland."

"Why not?"

Anelia shrugged. "It wasn't allowed."

"But why not?"

"I don't know," she said.

"So the magazine was mostly just propaganda?"

"Sure, it was propaganda," Anelia said. "But everything was propaganda in those times. The West had its own propaganda, too. We knew Radio Liberty and Radio Free Europe. And we knew about the United States Information Service. Everyone had their own propaganda."

Anelia leaned forward with both elbows resting on her knees.

"But my articles were good," she said. "I wrote a lot about women in Vietnam and the women in the southern African countries, fighting against colonialism, neocolonialism, and apartheid. We published many stories on

Nicaragua and El Salvador. Your magazines focused on Afghanistan. We wrote about the American invasion of Grenada."

"There were newspapers in the U.S. that wrote about Grenada as well."

"Yes," she said. "You had freedom to criticize your leaders. We did not have this right. But your country was still responsible for many great evils in this time, even though there were people speaking out against them. So in both cases the government did what it wanted."

"But there were many Americans who tried to change things," I said. "I remember the divestment campaigns in the 1980s."

Anelia nodded. "Yes, I know. There were Americans who came to our events in the GDR, who supported freedom for the black South Africans." She snorted. "We thought they were all spies."

I laughed.

"It's true," she said. "They came to us in good faith. I treated them with suspicion. But what else could I do? Everyone in Germany was being watched. We all knew it. It would be dangerous for us if we were too friendly with these progressive Americans. We could get in trouble. It was especially bad for me because I was a foreigner. The Stasi were watching me all of the time."

"So why did you stay for so long?" I said. "Didn't it bother you?"

Anelia takes a large swallow of her drink. "Sure it bothered me. I worked in the GDR for eight years and I never had one East German friend. I was never invited for dinner at a colleague's house," she said. "It reminds me of another joke. Why do the Stasi make the best taxi drivers in Berlin?"

"Why?"

"Because you just give them your name, and they already know where you live."

Anelia laughed for a moment, shaking her head.

"There were so many jokes about the Stasi, you know," she said. "It was terrible, but at least we could laugh about it."

I nodded. "So why did you stay?

"I had to stay. Elena had nominated me. After one year, the general secretary of the WIDF didn't want to let me go. I worked so hard, you see. I was very valuable to them. Elena had been proven correct, so I felt I had to stay. Plus, my daughter was young and in school there. I thought it would be good for her to study in German schools. So I stayed for eight years. You got used to it. You had nothing to worry about if you weren't doing anything illegal. What did I have to hide? In the end, I was happy in the GDR. I probably would have stayed longer if it hadn't been for the Changes."

"So you came back to Bulgaria?" I said.

"Yes, in 1990," Anelia said. "I didn't have a choice. Everything was changing so fast."

"What did you do then?" I said.

"It was a hard time," Anelia said. "I was still in my forties. I got divorced. I couldn't find a job at first. The committee was gone. Elena had retired. You know, the first years after the Changes were very hard."

"Yes."

"When did you first come to Bulgaria?" she said.

"Technically, I was first here in 1990," I said. "But that was only on a transit visa. The first time I spent a few weeks in the country was in February 1998."

"So you know how bad things were in those years," Anelia said. "Do you remember?"

"I remember the *mutri*," I said, using the colloquial term for "Mafia."

"Oh, the mutri were only part of it," Anelia said. "You know, I knew many people from the research institutes. They had very high education and a lot of experience. Many of them were women. They lost their jobs in the middle of their careers. Some got kicked out of the university, because they were communists. They had to go out on the street and sell thong underwear to make some money. They were experts with scientific training. I was so embarrassed for them."

"I remember that," I said. "I came right after the hyperinflation."

Anelia threw her hands up. "Oh my god, the hyperinflation! So many people were ruined. Good, decent people who had worked hard for their whole lives."

"Did you lose money, too?" I said.

"No, I was lucky. I had traded in my East marks, and I had everything saved in deutsche marks. And I spoke English and German. I had valuable skills for this thing called the market economy. And I had never been a member of the Communist Party. Finally, that was a good thing."

She paused and crossed her legs. "You see, there were so many Western companies that needed translation services. I started working for one firm, but I quit when I realized that I could do freelance translations. I could make more money at home doing translations in a week than I could in that firm for a month. My communist education was, how do you say it?" she said, switching to English. "The gift that kept on giving?"

Anelia finished her cocktail and examined my glass. "Would you like more ice?" she said.

The pug named
"Smart"

"Yes," I said. "That would be great."

"This capitalism is a very good system for people who are hardworking. In Germany, I was not appreciated. They never let me have a byline for the articles that I wrote. I hated that."

The front door clicked. Anelia popped up and greeted her now-adult daughter, Angelina, who came in to take Smart for a walk. There were introductions and the conversation quickly turned to lighter things: dogs and gardens and summer holiday plans. Angelina joined us for a cigarette. I finished my vodka tonic and was poured a second. We spoke briefly about shopping, and then the three of us started showing each other pictures on our mobile phones. I showed them pictures of my daughter. Angelina showed me pictures of her son. Anelia showed us photos of Smart in awkward positions. I decided that pugs were both adorable and ridiculous. Vodka tonics were delicious.

I left a little tipsy at three p.m. with a promise that I would come again.

17 | THE POLITICS OF TRUTH

I would end up visiting Anelia twice more in that first summer. Because I did not have a car, I took a taxi out to meet her in her apartment. Anelia lived in a not-so-luxurious district of Sofia called Youth No. 2. There were also neighborhoods called Youth No. 1, Youth No. 3, and Youth No. 4 that looked exactly the same as Youth No. 2. These neighborhoods were a collection of concrete buildings called "residential blocks" left over from the communist era. The suburbs of Sofia had rather unimaginative names, perhaps because the communists were rationing interesting words. Not so far from Youth No. 1, No. 2, No. 3, and No. 4 was the neighborhood "Friend-ship," also produced in multiple copies. There was the neighborhood "Hope" as well as "Student-town," which is where many of the university students lived. There was a neighborhood near the airport called Enemy. This neighborhood, according to some Sofia residents, was not a very friendly place.

In these outlying Sofia neighborhoods, there are rarely street names. There are merely block numbers. The blocks in Youth are so massive that they have seven or eight different entrances. In order to find someone's flat, you needed to give the taxi driver a neighborhood name and number, then a block number and an entrance letter. This would sound something like: "Please take me to Youth No. 2, Block 207, Entrance B." "Do you know where that is?" The taxi driver would say.

Try as I might to find some landmark, all of the Youth blocks looked the same to me.

"No," I would say.

This would produce sustained grumbling from the driver. He would have to pull out a big book of Sofia street maps to try to figure out where Block 207 was. Even the Sofia taxi drivers had trouble finding the right entrances. On my third visit, I remembered that Anelia's entrance was directly across from a furniture repair shop. Since the buzzer on her downstairs door did not work, I would have to call her mobile phone. She would come downstairs and open the door for me. She was always delighted to see me, as was Smart, the wheezing pug. Our conversations were both fun and informative, with Anelia regaling me with jokes and stories about her time in the GDR and the vicissitudes of being an international women's activist during the Cold War.

I returned to Bulgaria the following March in time for International Women's Day. It is customary in Bulgaria to give flowers on Women's Day, not only to your mother, but to any important woman in your life. I was bringing Anelia a bouquet of roses. I called her from the taxi just as we made the turn into Youth No. 2 so that I would not have to stand outside for too long in the bitter cold. When she met me at the door, she looked pale and tired. Her face was thinner, but multiple layers of sweaters made her body appear larger.

"Kristen, it is so nice to see you," Anelia said. She smiled a half smile as if her facial muscles were conserving their energy.

"Nice to see you as well," I said, pressing my cheek against hers.

"How have you been? How is your daughter?" she said. We climbed the stairs up to her flat. The elevator needed repairs, she explained, but no one had the money to pay for it.

I gave her a brief update as we walked up the four stories. When we got into her apartment, it was only slightly warmer than the chilly hallway. Anelia had turned off her heat. I took off my hat, gloves, and scarf. I unfastened only the top two buttons of my coat.

We sat across from each other. "Would you mind if we spoke in English?" she said. "I would like to practice a little bit and I don't often get the chance."

"Sure," I said. "So how have you been?"

She shook her head. "Not so good," she said, lighting up a cigarette. "I've not had any work since January. You know I do translations, and for years I had more work than I could accept. But with the crisis, things are bad."

The "crisis" she referred to was the global financial crisis that started in 2007–2008. It began in the United States with subprime lending and mortgage-backed securities and then spread like a cancer around the globe. It took a few years before it hit Bulgaria, but when it hit, it hit with the full force of a hurricane. The global recession was the worst economic crisis since the Great Depression in the 1930s. It was also a major global economic shock that could clearly be traced back to the irresponsibility of Americans on Wall Street.

"Maybe things will pick up soon," I said. It was difficult to speak with Bulgarians about the crisis. "People need translations."

Anelia puffed on her cigarette. For the first time, I noticed the deep wrinkles that appeared around her lips when she pursed to inhale. When I saw her last summer, her face had seemed softer. It was one of the terrible ironies of aging for women; after a certain age every pound lost on your body adds lines to your face.

"I hope so," she said. "I took a credit on my apartment. I'll lose my flat if I cannot make my payments. I've lived here for more than twenty years. This is my home."

As Anelia spoke these words, I felt sick. I understood immediately that she had taken a loan that she should not have taken. She was now sixty-nine years old, a member of the age group that was the prime target of one of the cruelest legal scams of the post-socialist era.

I saw the Xerox fliers all over Sofia beginning in 2006. The fliers were frayed at the bottom with a phone number written sideways on the strips of paper, and bold advertisements for things called "easy credit" or "fast credit." It was the beginning of the Bulgarian version of the mortgage crisis, which had its own local flavor. In the United States, the banks swindled the poor. In Bulgaria, they targeted the elderly.

Unlike other communist countries, the vast majority of Bulgarians owned their homes under communism. The government provided fixed mortgage rates of 1 or 2 percent, which allowed even young couples to buy an apartment. Although the demand for housing always outstripped the supply, a residential construction boom in the 1970s and 1980s, especially in the new suburbs like Youth, Hope, and Friendship meant that many Bulgarians found flats. Mortgage payments were made via salary deductions throughout one's working life. The idea was that all workers could pay off their mortgages by the age of retirement. Since the communist government subsidized all utilities and basic foodstuffs, and health care was free, Bulgarian pensioners could count on a secure retirement lived in the comfort of their own homes.

An advertisement for "Creditland," which offers free consultations

With the Changes in 1989, the government liberalized food price controls
and privatized state-owned utilities, resulting in drastic price increases. Although the national health care system remained intact, the cost of medicine skyrocketed. The Bulgarian pension system was never designed to deal
with the new market realities. Post-socialist governments could not afford
to increase payments to senior citizens. Men and women who had paid into
the system for their entire careers were cheated out of the decent retirement
they thought they had earned.

The one bright spot in an otherwise bleak scenario was that many pensioners fully owned their homes. In the worst case, elderly Bulgarians could
rent out their flats and move in with a child or have their children move in
with them to help pay for food and utilities. This is how many families survived the economic chaos of the 1990s. By the mid-2000s, the local economic situation in Bulgaria seemed to be improving and Sofia, like so many
other national capitals, experienced a housing bubble. Fueled by easy credit,
the value of residential real estate increased exponentially in a few short
years.

The home equity loan was a relatively new concept for most Bulgarians
raised under communism, who were shocked to learn that they could receive

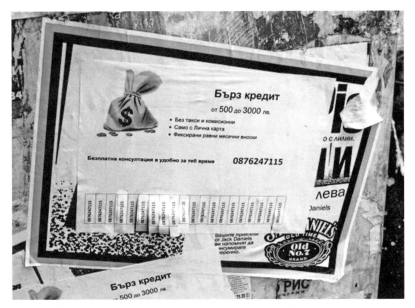

A flier for "fast credit," offered with "no fees or commissions." Interest rates are as high as 30 percent per month.

thousands of levs in cash against the estimated market value of their flats. All they had to do was use their homes as collateral to secure the loan. As in the United States, Bulgarian lenders proved unscrupulous. They approved loans to Sofia residents regardless of their income. In many cases, these predatory lenders *hoped* for a default. The banks targeted pensioners because they owned some of the most desirable real estate. When the elderly could no longer service their loans, the lender could foreclose on a previously unavailable piece of real estate in a market where housing prices were skyrocketing.

"I wanted the money to go to Russia to visit my sister, to help my grandson, and to make some small renovations," Anelia said. "I didn't think I would have any trouble paying it back. I have always had steady work."

"Have you spent it all?"

"Most of it," she said. "I still have some left, but the interest on the loan is monthly and it is quite high. The amount is growing faster than I thought possible."

She crushed out her cigarette and immediately lit another. "I wish I had never done this. I should have waited to save the money. That's what I've done all of my life. Not spend money that I didn't have. And I wouldn't have done it if I thought that I wouldn't have work."

"No one can see the future," I said.

"Maybe they could," she said. "Those young men in suits. They're taking our flats away. It's already happening to some of the people in this block."

Anelia's face twisted around her cigarette. She looked up at the ceiling and then back to me.

"You know, Kristen, I was thinking about an article that I wrote for *Women of the Whole World* when I was living in Germany. I remember that I once wrote about the psychological damage caused by unemployment. It was based on some journal article from the United States. I remember hating this article, because I believed that the source was fabricated. It was just more anti-Western propaganda. I mean, for us, the idea of unemployment meant being on holiday, and being on holiday was a good thing. It wasn't a bad thing. I didn't have any exposure to your system where you cannot live if you do not have a job. We were always forced to work. I'd read Western papers about unemployment, but I didn't understand. The West was so rich."

"You had access to papers from the West?" I said.

"Yes, of course," she said. "We had a research division and we had affiliated organizations all over the world. We read a lot about the problems of life in the West, but we didn't believe it. I didn't understand."

"There are a lot of problems in the West," I said. I'd been lucky during the crisis. Somewhere in graduate school I had come to understand that borrowing other people's money was something to be avoided: student debt, credit cards, car loans. I'd seen too many of my fellow students spend themselves into a hole. "Banks are a big problem."

"But we thought that everything in the West was perfect," she said. "I thought that everyone was rich. When I went to international meetings, I saw that the Western women always had such nice handbags and clothes and jewelry. They had cosmetics and beautiful shoes. We had nothing like that. I was very envious."

I heard this same observation from many women in Eastern Europe who traveled to the United States before 1989. They saw the clothes and forgot that American women have no paid maternity leave or guaranteed access to health care. And Western women often bought all those nice clothes and bags with high-interest credit cards.

"Not everything was propaganda," I said.

"How would we know?" she said.

"Did you think that everything you read about the West was a lie?"

"Not all of it," she said. "But most of it. I worked at this magazine for eight years. I knew that everything was censored. They didn't want us to be able to think for ourselves."

I reached into my bag and pulled out a pack of Karelia Lights. The Greek cigarettes were much smoother than the Bulgarian ones that Anelia smoked. I opened the box and pulled out a cigarette. Anelia leaned over and lit it for me. I put the box down on the table and gestured for her to take one.

She lit it and took a long drag. Her exhalation combined with a deep sigh. "Can you imagine how many articles I wrote about the evils of capitalism, quoting Lenin and Marx? All those years, I was forced to write about unemployment and exploitation and imperialism and neocolonialism and apartheid and military dictatorships in Chile. I was a good writer. I could write passionately. But I didn't believe a word of it."

Anelia shook her head.

"Now I am sitting home alone with nothing to do. Every day, I'm sending out e-mails. I'm ready to work. I speak four languages fluently and have many years experience. I look every day, but no one will hire me. I cannot understand a world in which people that have skills and who are willing to work can't find employment. How can I pay my bills? Now I remember those articles that I wrote: about how capitalism is wage slavery, about how the rich benefit from the suffering of the poor, about how unemployment is necessary to keep wages down."

Anelia tapped the end of her cigarette on the rim of the ashtray. I looked up at her. She had never fought for the Communist Party. She had never met in secret in a basement to discuss the works of Lenin, risking arrest to debate strategies for creating a different world. She had never distributed an illegal newspaper. Anelia grew up in a world where Marx's critique of capitalism was official government dogma.

"I thought it was all lies." She shook her head, pressing her cheek into her palm. "Can you imagine that all that time I was actually writing the truth?"

In 2012, I returned to Bulgaria for the summer. Five months had passed since I last saw Anelia. This time when I took the taxi to the Youth No. 2 neighborhood, I knew exactly where to go. It was late afternoon on a hot, muggy July day. The humidity was so dense it felt like you could scoop a ball of it out of the air. I had spent the entire morning writing in an air-conditioned café on Vitosha Street. I felt like I had done enough work for the day and was ready to share a couple of cocktails with Anelia. I brought with me a good bottle of Ruski Standart vodka and Schweppes tonic.

The downstairs door was wide open. I climbed the stairs and knocked. An old woman opened the door. She had lost a lot more weight. Her T-shirt hung on her like a drapery. Her eyes were sunken. Her lips were drawn. I immediately feared for her health.

"Welcome," she said, as Smart barked at me from between her legs, wagging his tail and wheezing like he always did when he got excited.

"I brought some goodies," I said, giving her the vodka and the tonic.

"Wonderful. I love Ruski Standart," she said. "You will have drinks with me, right?"

I nodded.

"Come in, come in. How have you been?" Her voice was soft, but she seemed happy to see me.

All of the windows in her flat were wide open, but the room still felt like it was filled with smoke.

"More or less," I said. "I have been very busy, but things are more or less." In Bulgarian, people almost never say that they are "fine" or "good." They say "*gore-dolu*," which literally translates to "up-down," but figuratively translates to "more or less," meaning not bad, but not great either. There are traditional superstitions about telling other people that things are good in your life. Envious people are prone to cursing you if they know that things are going too well. One can wear a blue talisman to protect from the evil eye, but fate should not be tempted.

On the other hand, Bulgarians willingly share their misfortunes with everyone they meet. In the United States or Great Britain the polite "I'm fine, thank you, and you?" is the standard and appropriate response to the question "how are you?" It does not matter what you are really feeling. In Bulgaria, you could ask someone "*Kak ste?*" (how are you?), and they could appropriately reply, "*Mnogo zle*" (very bad). This would not be considered rude.

"*Kak ste?*" I said.

"*Zle*," Anelia told me. "*Mnogo zle.*"

"Have you been ill?" I said.

"Ill in the mind," she said, pointing to her temple. "But let me get some ice. Sit down and I will be right back."

Anelia disappeared into the kitchen. I sat down on the couch across from the chair where she always sat. Smart pressed against my legs. I scratched behind his left ear. He stood immobilized, lightly wheezing with pleasure, his eyes popping out of his head in that ridiculous pug way.

I examined the table in front of me. There were two empty packets of cigarettes, and an ashtray filled with cigarette butts. Anelia had been smoking more than usual.

In 2001, there was a study on smoking in the Czech Republic. Like Bulgaria, the Czech Republic had a national health care system. The Czech government feared that the popularity of smoking among Czech citizens placed an enormous burden on the state budget. The government was considering a large public relations campaign to prevent smoking among its citizens. Fearing the loss of more markets to health concerns, the Philip Morris corporation commissioned a study by Arthur D. Little International, a London-based consulting firm.

The study examined the budgetary impacts of smoking in the Czech Republic with relation to the rising costs of national health care.[1] The report,

Public Finance Balance of Smoking in the Czech Republic, found that the prevalence of smoking among Czechs actually had *positive* budgetary impacts. First, the government collected significant tax revenues from the sale of cigarettes. Second, and most important, smoking resulted in the earlier mortality of potential pensioners. The report pointed out that since smokers tended to die earlier than nonsmokers, the percentage of smokers in the Czech Republic was a fiscal windfall for the national budget from which the pensions of these people would otherwise have to be paid.[2] The conclusion was simple: let Czechs smoke as much as they want. Philip Morris could maintain its profits and the Czech government would have fewer pensions to pay out in the long run. It was a win-win situation for the government and the corporation.

Anelia returned. She carried a bucket of ice and two short, frosted whiskey tumblers. She sat and poured two drinks. We exchanged a little small talk about Smart and Anelia's grandson. She asked about my daughter and my research. I complained about my increasing administrative duties at work.

"At least you have work," she said. She took a long drink of vodka tonic. "It's been over seven months now."

"Nothing?" I said.

She shook her head. She lit a cigarette. Anelia looked wobbly and tired.

"It isn't that I haven't been looking," she said. "No one will hire me. It's not because I am old; the young people can't find jobs either. It's this crisis. So many firms are closing. Every day there are more people looking. And the more people who are looking, the less they are willing to pay."

"I know," I said, feeling both guilty and thankful for my employment. "It's bad everywhere. Look at what is happening in Greece."

"Yes," Anelia said, "and the Greeks were so far ahead of us."

"Did you hear about the man who shot himself in front of the Greek parliament?"

Anelia nodded. "Yes, he was a pensioner like me."

I felt uncomfortable. I lit a cigarette.

"I am almost seventy," she said. "I worked for forty-five years. My pension is not enough to pay for the water and electricity. How am I supposed to live?"

"The crisis can't last forever," I said.

Anelia shook her head. "You're so American," she said. Her tone was angry. It was not a compliment.

"Why do you say that?"

"You are so optimistic. You believe that the crisis will end and the whole system will be well again. But what about the lives that'll be ruined by this crisis? The lives that will be lost, and the people who'll give in to despair. Is that just a part of *your* system?"

"It is not *my* system," I said. "I have nothing to do with this." I swallowed.

"No," she said. She snorted at me. "We never felt that communism was *our* system either. It was always the government's fault. Ordinary people could do nothing. We all knew how bad it was: the censorship and the travel restrictions and the secret police. But we did nothing. It was not our problem as long as we were not the victims. We didn't care."

"But people do care," I said. "There's the Occupy Wall Street movement. There are protests. Look at all of the protests in Greece. And in Spain, too."

"Have the protests changed anything? What did Occupy Wall Street do?" she said. "Nothing."

I sat across from her, feeling helpless. The weight of her depression was heavier than the muggy air. "It's hard to change things," I said. "It's hard to know where to start."

Anelia didn't reply. She seemed lost in her thoughts, her eyes focused somewhere in the middle distance between us. I looked down at Smart who was asleep at my feet. Even the pug was subdued by the darkness of Anelia's mood.

"Do you know the Greek myth of Cassandra?" Anelia finally said.

"You mean from *The Iliad*?"

"Yes," she said. "You know that Cassandra was given the gift of prophecy. But this was a curse, because no one would ever believe her. She knew the truth. She foresaw the Trojan horse and the fall of Troy, but she couldn't prevent these misfortunes because the world thought her mad."

Anelia looked me straight in the eyes. She sighed. "Communism was like Cassandra," she said. "It told the truth. But it couldn't change the future because no one believed it."

"Breasts do not have politics," V. told me in July 2011. Although the simple declarative sentence seemed self-evident, it had the weight of a great profundity.

I made plans to meet V. for the first time in front of the Bulgarian National Library. We would wait for each other under the statues of Saints Kiril and Methodius, the monks responsible for the invention of the Cyrillic alphabet.

"How will I know you?" I had asked her in Bulgarian.

"I have a lot of white hair," she told me. "I do not dye it."

I took a microbus from Iztok and hopped out across the street from Sofia University. Elena had given me the contact information for this woman whom I would call "Veneta." I was thrilled that she had agreed to meet with me.

Veneta was in her late seventies. She was the general secretary of a nongovernmental organization that still celebrated the contributions of the Balkan partisan movements to the defeat of Hitler in World War II. I had called her a few days earlier, and she was busy touring around Bulgaria with a group of Greek pensioners. She had taken them to visit the graves of their relatives who had fled into Bulgaria during and after the Greek Civil War in 1946–1949. This was the war in which the British and Americans supported the National Republican Greek League, which crushed the Greek communists, many of whom had been partisans fighting during World

War II. Since the nationalists sent the children of communists to "reeducation" camps, many Greek leftists smuggled their sons and daughters north to Bulgaria during the war. When the victorious nationalist government outlawed the Greek Communist Party in 1949, many more Greeks fled north in the face of domestic persecution. A third wave of Greeks flowing into Bulgaria came during the era of the military junta between 1967 and 1974. The junta arrested and imprisoned thousands of so-called communists or "enemies of the people."[1]

With Western support, the nationalist forces in Greece were ever vigilant against the domestic threat of any form of communism. Those fleeing Greece were considered political refugees by the Eastern Bloc (and some Western) countries that welcomed them. Of those who came to Bulgaria, many grew old and died in the country. Veneta's organization preserved the memories of those who lost their lives during World War II and the Greek Civil War, and kept careful registries of refugees for their relatives still in Greece. Those left behind came in busloads to lay flowers at the graves of those who were forced to flee.

When I got to the statues of Kiril and Methodius, I scanned the benches, and recognized Veneta immediately. She had a full head of thick, white hair, which fell to her shoulders, and she wore a simple but elegant cotton dress and soft leather clogs.

"Good day," I said.

"Are you Kristen?"

I nodded. She reached out and grabbed my hand.

"It is so nice to meet you," she said. Her eyes were a very pale blue. Their color was cool, but they burned with warmth and welcome. Deep lines around her mouth suggested a lot of time smiling. I made a mental note to smile more often: better to have smile wrinkles than frown lines.

"Shall we go to the Artist's Union?" I asked.

"Yes, of course," she said. She was only four years younger than Elena, but she seemed ten times less frail. She walked with energy and purpose. Before 1989, Veneta worked for over twenty years with Elena on the Committee of the Bulgarian Women's Movement. Veneta had been responsible for all domestic organizational activities. Elena told me that Veneta was a "human archive."

"Elena told me that you are writing about the committee," she said as we walked.

"Yes," I said. "Until now I've only been researching their international activities, but I'm interested in their domestic work as well."

"You know the committee was governed by its bylaws," Veneta said as we crossed Shipka Street. Learning about the communist era was like trying to find the center of an onion. The official layer of history told by the professional historians was wrapped around the remembered experiences of those who lived through it. Veneta was one of the people who had helped to build communism.

"The first bylaws were passed in 1968, but they were amended in 1973, 1979, and 1988."[2] Veneta spoke quickly and with few pauses. It was going to be difficult to get everything down in my notebook. I wiggled the fingers of my right hand in anticipation of the cramp that I knew would come.

"The committee worked in a way similar to all other societal organizations in Bulgaria at that time," Veneta said. "There were elections at every level of society to determine who would attend the national conference. At the national conference, they elected the members of the national committee and approved any changes in the bylaws. Have you seen the bylaws?"

Before I could answer, she said, "I have brought you copies of all of them." She stopped and began to dig through her bag.

"Perhaps," I said, "we can wait until we sit down?"

Veneta looked up at me. She smiled. "Yes," she said. "Of course."

Just down from the main building of Sofia University, across the street from the park called Doctor's Garden, one found the café of the Union of Bulgarian Artists. The day was warm and sunny but not too hot and not humid. We found a table outside where we could sit across from each other.

"What will you have?" I said. I did not want her to start again until I had the chance to get out my notebook and pen.

"Iced coffee," she said. "And water."

I wanted a cola. I opened my notebook to the first blank page.

"Before you continue about the internal structure of the committee," I said. "Maybe you can tell me a little about yourself? I always like to start with some personal background."

She didn't miss a beat. "Yes. Fine. Between 1972 and 1975, I was the president of the Regional Council in the city of Lovech. After that, I went to work in the political bureau of the women's committee in Sofia, in the section that dealt with organizational matters. I worked with the women's committee at the national level from 1975 to 1990, until the very end. I oversaw all of the procedures for the holding of the conferences at the national, regional, and municipal levels, as well as the preparation of all of the reports and decisions and the sending and receiving of information to and from the regional committees and the municipal committees."

"Are you a lawyer by training?" I said.

She shook her head. "I am a pedagogue," she said. She told me that she studied education at university and would have been a teacher if she had not gone to work as a women's activist.

Veneta spoke with her hands. Her fingers opened and closed and waved around to illustrate specific parts of her speech. She liked to point and to spread her palms, and she often gesticulated with a closed fist. Her white hair was stiffer than the hair of a younger woman, but she often brushed it back off of her shoulders, a very feminine gesture.

"My job was a very important one," she said. "I had to make sure that our organization had a diverse representation of women. Our national conference was organized with great care. The delegates to the conference had to be representative of Bulgarian society. This meant that there had to be a diversity of ages, professional backgrounds, educational levels, labor activity, and party affiliation," she said.

As she spoke these last words, she drew an imaginary list of parameters in the air with her right hand. The skin on her hand was almost translucent; I could make out every vein. She wore no rings, and her nails were cut short.

"This was very important because in order to make the decisions of the national conference valid there had to be a quorum," she said. "This quorum had strict rules about representativeness in terms of different regions and women from different social positions. It could not be a conference of elites. Of course, there were members of the intelligentsia present, and many of the women were winners of special orders and medals. But there were also many women who were rural cooperative members or factory laborers."

"Were most of them members of the Communist Party?" I said.

"There were many, but not all of them. We were very open to all women in Bulgaria," she said. "Unlike most other organizations in Bulgarian society, you did not have to be a member of the Communist Party in order to join. Any woman could join, no matter what her affiliation. Women were free to choose their own politics, and people were allowed to have their own opinions. As long as they wanted to work for the cause of women, politics didn't matter."

"Were there men on the committee?"

"No," she smiled again. "You had to be a woman. It was *our* organization." I laughed.

"The men had their own organizations," she said. "We had the right to have ours, too."

"So there was just one?" I said.

"Yes. We concentrated all of our efforts so that we could be more effective. There is greater power in greater numbers," she said.

I nodded. Many women's organizations had been founded in Bulgaria after 1989, all part of the emerging civil society created with foreign funding, much of it from the United States. I had written my first book about this and I knew that these new organizations had few successes.[3] Living standards and opportunities for women declined in the last two decades. The old committee had been effective in its own way. This fascinated me.

The young waitress brought us our drinks. Veneta gulped down her water and cleared her throat.

"I have a lot of experience advocating for women and their specific problems," she said. "We had to protect women in the workplace and make sure that they were being supported as mothers. We wanted to be sure that women could take the maternity leave they were guaranteed by law. Sometimes employers put pressure on women not to take the full two years, but it was their right." She spoke with passion, waving her hands around the table. She almost knocked over her glass of iced coffee.

I had the urge to pull the glass away from the edge of the table like I would do for my daughter. I resisted this urge by focusing on my notebook.

"In sectors of the economy where women did not traditionally work, the committee made sure that work sites had women's bathrooms and special rooms for them to relax in so they could get away from the men they worked with." Her face brightened in a smile. "You know Bulgarian men are very patriarchal."

"Yes, I know." I smiled back at her.

"We tried to support activities for women, so they could get out of the house in the evenings to have some free time. We were going down to small villages and to little towns where there were these cultural clubs. We held dances. We sponsored singers and poets. We arranged social meetings so that women could get out of the house. In the rural areas most women were very isolated from other women and from society because they were so busy in the home with their housework. These local activities were sponsored and organized by the national and regional and municipal committees. We gave women a chance to meet each other and discuss their common problems. We would sometimes invite academic speakers to talk about parenting or pedagogy or basic things like home hygiene and sewing."

Veneta's eyes widened. She leaned across the table toward me, her hands still gesticulating dangerously close to that glass of iced coffee.

"These were things that women cared about. These were the things that they were interested in learning," she said. "We did so much. It wasn't political. It was cultural. That's why we were so different from the other social organizations in Bulgaria. Women came to our events with pleasure. We did things that spoke to their daily lives. For instance, we taught about embroidery and making lace and other crafts that were traditional to women. We also had lectures on local folklore and customs and holidays. We sponsored festivals. We hosted women who were heroes of the Great Patriotic War or who were heroes of labor."

In my notes I circled the phrase Great Patriotic War. She was referring, of course, to World War II. The Great Patriotic War was its Soviet name. Since Veneta was the current president of an organization that celebrated partisans, I imagined that she maintained strong links with Russian organizations commemorating the history of resistance on the Eastern Front.

"All of the ideas for the women's programs came from the local women's organizations themselves. They could initiate the things they wanted, and we would sponsor them. We worked with a lot of different partners in society to realize these programs. And we made a lot of progress in increasing the cultural level of women in the rural areas. It was very inspired work."

Veneta spread her hands out on the table in front of her. The thin skin was lined and spotted with wide brown freckles. They were the hands of an old woman. Veneta's energy made her seem so much younger.

"We worked with a lot of idealism and romantic notions in those days," she said. "Every epoch has its own worldview. Ours was very different than the one today. We had a lot of hope. People didn't become prostitutes or drug addicts. They didn't have to."

"Because there were other economic opportunities?"

"No. Because there was a safety net to catch people when they had problems," she said. "You know, Kristen, the committee was empowered to have societal control or people's control. We had the right to represent women to other state agencies. We wanted women to feel that they had someone who would help them; that they had somewhere to go to complain where people would listen. We would help in all sorts of ways; even the smallest problem was something that we would concern ourselves with. It was this practical work that built the women's movement. Women all across the country could write us letters of complaint, and we brought their complaints before all of the other social organizations in Bulgaria. We also met with women and listened to their concerns. We wrote protest letters on their behalf."

"Can you give me an example?" I said.

"For instance, we could make sure that pregnant women were moved to a more suitable work post if their current jobs were too strenuous. Also, when they passed the new Family Code in 1985, we spent a lot of time helping women to figure out the new laws and how they could be applied to their personal lives. We were very democratic."

She paused at the word "democratic." She studied my face.

"This is a form of democracy," she said. "To talk to the population, to listen to their concerns, and to act on them. It was not all black at the time. Yes, it was a totalitarian government, but we took a lot of initiatives to work on behalf of women, and the work that we did was very valuable."

She took a few swallows of her coffee. The ice had long melted, so I imagined that it was not so cold. I waved to the waitress.

"Would you like something else?" I said to Veneta.

"No, thank you," she said.

I ordered another cola and a bottle of mineral water.

"You know, we had a lot of good programs," Veneta said. "There were some British visitors before 1989 who came to learn about Bulgaria's polyclinic system. They wanted to use our model for their country. We had a lot of good practices in health and medicine. And of course for women's issues. Then after 1989 there was another group of British experts who came to give advice on democracy. I learned a very important phrase: when you are dumping out the water from the bath, do not lose the baby."

"Don't throw the baby out with the bathwater," I said in English.

"Yes, exactly," she said. "There was a man in this delegation who warned me about the baby in the bath. He saw what was going to happen. There were a lot of good things that were achieved by socialism, but we threw the baby out in the water."

She gestured with her arms as if she were dumping a tub of water out on the left side of our table.

"We lost everything," she said. "Democracy brought a lot of bad things."

"What did you do after the Changes?" I said.

"I joined the Democratic Women's Union for a while, but it was never the same," she said. "Social work is only effective if it truly helps people. A social organization has to be helpful to people. If it is not, it has no purpose."

The Democratic Union of Women (DUW) was supposed to be the successor organization to the Bulgarian Women's Committee. After 1989, the "reformist" elements of the Bulgarian Communist Party renamed themselves the Bulgarian Socialist Party (BSP) and won a majority in the first free elections in 1990.[4] Many communist-era social organizations were renamed and subsumed under the party structure of the BSP. The DUW was reimagined as a "nongovernmental organization," and as such, it could finally advocate for women's needs outside of the rigid structures of the communist state. As with so many women's organizations after 1989, however, the DUW accomplished little. It mostly served as the women's political arm of the new BSP.[5] Its primary "nongovernmental" purpose was to ensure that women voted for the "reformed" socialists.

Veneta told me that the DUW no longer existed.

"Those women are all gone now, making their own political careers," she said. "They cared only for themselves; selfishness justified in the name of democracy."

"What about some of the new women's organizations?"

She shook her head. "I cannot work for any organization that doesn't actually do something. Now I am working with two social organizations that are doing something for society," she said. "You know, I am the general secretary of the Antifascist Union. This is my political work. But I also have work for women. I travel around the country as an advocate against breast cancer. My organization asks oncologists to volunteer their time to travel around the country to the rural areas. There are many women who cannot travel to the big cities to have mammograms. Most of these doctors are highly trained oncologists who are volunteering their time to help their country. The young ones volunteer on the weekends, but we have some retired oncologists who work with us throughout the week. We give free breast exams to any woman who comes to us."

The waitress came with my cola and water. I passed the bottle of water across the table and set it down in front of Veneta. She ignored the bottle, looking me straight in the eyes.

"I am a socialist," she said. "That fact is not hidden. I once went to meet with a doctor to ask him if he would volunteer his time for us. He told me, 'I am a member of the UDF.'"

The Union of Democratic Forces (UDF) opposed the Bulgarian Socialist Party (BSP) in the 1990s. They were a right-leaning, pro-Western party whose members were often called "Democrats" as opposed to the "Socialists." The political rivalry between these two parties defined the decade immediately after the fall of communism. Tensions between "Democrats" and "Socialists" were often high; families and friendships broke apart because of opposing political allegiances, especially after the UDF erected a memorial wall to the "victims of communism" and demolished the Georgi Dimitrov mausoleum in defiance of public opinion.

"I told him that it didn't matter. I told him that breast cancer affects socialist women as well as democratic women in Bulgaria. I told him: breasts don't have politics," she said. Her voice was earnest. I could not help but laugh.

"They don't!" Veneta grinned. "He agreed to work with us, and he has been one of our best volunteers."

She drained the last of her water. "On a recent trip to Yambol, there were two rival politicians competing for the position of mayor," she said. "They were both women, and they both came to have their breasts examined by our doctors. Women's issues like this should not be politicized. Women's work is the same no matter what their political affiliations: cooking, cleaning, caring for children, and caring for the elderly. Medicine must also be beyond politics. And even though I am a socialist, and they call this a socialist operation, women from all political parties come to have their breasts examined. In fact, in Yambol, the UDF mayoral candidate was the owner of a toy factory. She was so impressed with our work that she brought toys for all of the doctors for their children and grandchildren."

Veneta opened the bottle of mineral water and poured some into her empty glass. She drank about half. We had been sitting out in the sun for an hour. She had done almost all of the talking.

Bulgarians now filled the café of the Artist's Union. Out on the terrace where we were sitting, every seat was occupied. Young people surrounded us, perhaps students from Sofia University. They smoked and chatted, their mobile phones displayed on their tables. A couple to my right seemed to be flirting with each other. At another table, four girlfriends exchanged gossip. My hand throbbed.

"Well—" I said, about to thank her for her time.

"We worked for a lot of humanity's problems that were not political," she said, interrupting me. "We worked for a better life. That is the only thing that matters. This is the main purpose: to improve the quality of life of the people, of the society, and of the state."

She brushed her hair back over her shoulder.

"I have spent my life working for women," she said.

I looked up at her. She sat back in her chair.

"Do you think it was worth it?" I said.

She raised her brow.

"I mean after all of the things you did for people who probably don't even remember you now." I was thinking about Elena and Anelia, alone in their apartments.

Veneta tilted her head in thought. She remained silent for a moment.

"Of course it was worth it," she said. "I have spent my life working to help others. What is worth more?"

20 | THE PAST IS A FOREIGN COUNTRY

And now, what? Capitalism has defeated our socialism, but today we can see that this system is not fair. I am certain that sooner or later people will come to realize that only through public ownership [of the means of production] will we have social justice!

—GENERAL KOSTADIN LAGADINOV, AGE NINETY-EIGHT, IN 2011

"Kristen, you are here in Sofia? Where are you? You must come over right away," Elena said over my mobile phone.

"I am at Orlov Most," I said.

"You are close," she said. "You must come quickly. There is someone here I want you to meet."

"Okay, I'll come now. Give me about fifteen minutes." I shoved the phone back into my purse. Elena rarely sounded so insistent. I wondered whom she was with. I gathered up my notebook and sunflower seeds. I walked to the underpass at the metro stop and crossed under Tsar Osvoboditel Street. From there, I walked around Sofia University to Shipka Street to buy some flowers.

It was an unseasonably warm afternoon. I had arrived in Bulgaria the evening before, on March 8, for International Women's Day. The jet lag made me stay up too late. The seven-hour time difference between Boston and Bulgaria meant that when it was midnight in Sofia it was only five p.m. for me. On Saturday the archives were closed, so I let myself sleep until one thirty p.m., a mistake that meant my body clock would stay confused longer.

After having coffee with my ex-in-laws, I walked down Major Thompson Street to the new metro stop in Lozenets. I had gone first to visit the protest camps recently set up across from the Bulgarian parliament. It was March 2013, and the political situation in Bulgaria was chaos. Massive street protests against skyrocketing winter electricity bills had forced the government to resign on February 22. Parliamentary bureaucrats scrambled to form a caretaker government until snap elections could be held in May. The protests had continued, with citizens variously calling for the renationalization of the electricity distribution companies and changes to the constitution. In the last month, four men had set themselves on fire.

I set out that afternoon to conduct interviews with the protestors, and to find out when and where the following day's protest was going to begin. I spent three hours with the protesters in the small tent city. They were a mixed bunch: pensioners, students, and a few political loonies expounding various conspiracy theories to anyone who would listen. I could not identify any leaders per se, but the young men and women whom I deemed to be coordinating the following day's protest were friendly and competent.

"Do you see any drunks here?" a young man asked.

I looked around the camp, at groups of people talking. Everyone seemed rather sober and serious. "No," I said.

"You have to write about this," he said. "The government is spreading lies that we are all drug addicts and drunks. They're trying to discredit us."

"I'm not a journalist," I said. "I'm a scholar."

"It doesn't matter," he said. "You're a foreigner. People will listen to you. You have to write something for a newspaper. We're not drug addicts."

I gave a vague promise and walked on. Another man, an elderly gentleman in a military uniform, asked that I take his photograph with his handmade sign. It read "Banks — Bloodsuckers! You have no place in Bulgaria."

"Put it on Facebook," he said, pronouncing the word Facebook as if he knew it was important, but had no idea what it meant.

I spoke to some students sitting on the ground in front of one of the tents. There was a sign in Bulgarian. It read "This is not a protest. This is a process. Revolution for a New Bulgaria."

I asked the students why they were protesting. One young woman said, "I love my country, but I have no future here. While the Mafia governments

A handmade sign reading "Banks — Bloodsuckers! You have no place in Bulgaria!"

stay in power, Bulgaria will never develop. I don't want to leave. I want to stay and fight to make my country a better place."

"Do you have any concrete proposals?" I said. The protestors I had spoken to thus far all had very different ideas about what needed to be done.

"Free university education," she said. The other students nodded. "And practical training placements for three years after you graduate."

"You mean like it was before?" I said. Before 1989, the state paid for all university education, and all students completed three years of national service upon graduation. The state guaranteed a job in the student's area of specialty, although the student had no control over where that job would be. Sofia residents hated the system because they often got sent out into the rural areas. Students also had little control over exactly what type of enterprise they would be placed in, and their salaries only covered the most basic

A protester in March 2013. The sign reads "Bulgaria wants morals, nature, and solidarity!"

expenses. It was basically a guaranteed, three-year, state-sponsored internship.

"Yes," the woman said.

"And better post-privatization control," said one of the young men.

"And changes to the electoral code," the first woman said. "We need a majoritarian system."

A second woman in the group waited until there was a lull in the conversation before she spoke. "There should be more kindergartens," she said. "Every mother should have a safe place for her child while she works."

"You mean like they had under communism?" I said.

At the word "communism," the students tensed.

"We don't want communism back," the first young woman said. "We just want a normal country."

I wondered exactly what a "normal country" looked like, but I was still too jet-lagged to try to sort that out.

I left the camp at around five p.m. and walked across the park to the Billa supermarket in the underpass in front of Sofia University. I bought myself some sunflower seeds and a Coke Zero in a one-liter plastic bottle. I needed some time to sort through my thoughts. Sitting and shelling sunflower seeds was my preferred form of meditation. That was what I was doing when Elena called me.

I arrived about seventeen minutes later, clutching a large bouquet of roses. I pressed the button on the panel to the right of the main door. None of the buttons had names next to them, but I knew that Elena was number 5. She buzzed me in. I walked up the stairs to the third floor and found her waiting at the door with a wide grin.

"My dear. Welcome to Bulgaria!" she said.

"Happy Women's Day!" I said, giving her the flowers. She put her hands on my shoulders and we kissed each other's cheeks.

"Come in, come in," she said. "I am so glad you came. When did you arrive?"

"Last night," I said.

I followed her into her dining room, a room where I had spent many hours. Another woman sat at the table. She wore her gray hair cropped short and donned a thick brown and tan sweater.

"Kristen," Elena said. "This is my dear friend, Maria Znepolska. The one who wrote the book I told you about."

It took me a minute to remember. I had bought the book last summer at the Sofia headquarters of the Bulgarian Antifascist Union. It was the most recent, and perhaps most comprehensive, biography of Frank Thompson written in Bulgarian.[1]

"I loved your book." I extended my hand. "I am very interested in Major Thompson."

"Yes," Maria said, taking my hand and clasping it between hers. "Elena told me. Elena says that you are writing a book of your own."

"Sit," Elena said, gesturing to my usual chair. She put the flowers in a vase and placed them on the table. "Have some wine. Do you want anything to eat?"

"No, thank you," I said.

"I have fruit and some very good chocolates," she said.

"Fruit," I said. There was no way to avoid it. Indentured eating.

Elena went back into the kitchen. I sat in the chair to Maria Znepolska's immediate right. "You must have done so much research," I said.

She smiled. "It was many years work," she said. "But I was lucky. I had all of my late husband's papers. He wrote many pages about Major Thompson."

Maria Znepolska with
her book about Frank
Thompson, published
in 2012

Maria Znepolska was the widow of the partisan commander Dencho
Znepolski. Her late husband led the Second Sofia Brigade from Bulgarian-
occupied Serbia to its final battle at Batuliya. It was Znepolski who wrote the
first account of the final march for Frank Thompson's mother and brother.
It was this account that was published in English together with a collection
of Frank's letters, poems, and diary entries in 1947. Znepolski had great af-
fection for Thompson, particularly after he learned that Thompson was a
member of the Communist Party of Great Britain. Maria Znepolska's new
book was called *Da Se Znae*, which translated as *To Know*. It was a well-
documented and emotional account of Thompson's life.

"I love the photo you have on the cover," I said. It was a young Frank
Thompson smiling directly at a camera, his arms crossed against his chest.

"It was given to my husband personally by Frank's mother," Maria said.
"She came to Bulgaria with her son. They were guests of Georgi Dimitrov."

Elena came back with a plate of sliced peaches, a fork, and a napkin. She placed it down in front of me. She took a wine glass out of a sideboard.

"Do you want wine or *mastika*?" Elena said.

"What are you drinking?" I said, looking to Maria's glass. It was filled with a clear liquid.

"We have been drinking mastika since lunchtime," Maria said. She gave a sheepish smirk.

Mastika is a licorice-flavored spirit—considerably stronger than wine.

"I'll have wine," I said. I wondered exactly how much Elena and Maria had had to drink. Here were two women in their eighties. I surmised that they might be a bit tipsy. That might explain Elena's unusual insistence on the phone.

"It's homemade," Elena said. She poured my glass full of dark-red liquid and poured herself another small glass of mastika. She motioned to fill Maria's, but Maria put her hand on top of her glass. Elena put the bottle back on the table. She picked up her own glass and said, "To Georgi Dimitrov."

We all said "*nazdrave*," looking each other directly in the eyes as we clinked glasses.

"Things would have been different," Maria said.

"Things would have been better," Elena said.

"If what?" I said.

"If Dimitrov had lived," Maria said.

I looked at Elena. She nodded.

"So was he poisoned?" I said. "I know that a lot of people say he was."

"Maybe," Elena said.

"I don't know," Maria said. "But I like to believe that if he had still been alive, my husband would not have suffered so much."

"He suffered a lot," Elena said.

"He was never the same after that," Maria said, shaking her head.

I wanted to ask for more details. I decided against it. Elena and Maria had seemed very happy when I arrived. I did not want to plunge the conversation toward dark memories. This was always a problem when speaking with people who lived a certain history. I could learn a lot from them, but it came at a cost. When women like Elena and Maria told me stories about World War II or about the communist era, they had to relive those times. Sometimes this was joyful. Many times, it was full of pain. I looked from Elena to Maria and back to Elena. If I pressed them, I felt that this would become an instance of the latter.

Maria Znepolska's favorite photo of her late husband, Dencho Znepolski

Dencho Znepolski had been caught up in one of the earlier internal convulsions of the Bulgarian Communist Party. He was arrested in 1951 for being an associate of Traicho Kostov. His crime was "fraternizing" with the Yugoslav partisans and with Frank Thompson in the spring of 1944. The Bulgarian government accused him of "nationalist deviationism" and Znepolski spent three years in prison and in the forced labor camp at Belene. Maria had published a posthumous memoir in her husband's name.[2] It was a fascinating tale of how a good man got crushed by the maelstrom of history.

"Do you know where Dimitrov is buried?" I said, trying to change the subject. I wanted to go to the grave site and take some photos.

"In the Central Sofia Cemetery," Elena said. "Do you remember when we took him there?"

Maria nodded. "It seems like yesterday."

After 1989, the body of Georgi Dimitrov had been removed from the mausoleum and cremated. His remains were interred beside those of his parents

✝ **Тъжен помен**

Девет месеца

без

оз. ген. майор
Костадин Атанасов Лагадинов

11.04.1913 - 29.10.2011

Антифашист, партизанин в Разложкия партизански отряд "Никола Парапунов"
Революционерът - юрист Костадин Ат. Лагадинов посвещава живота си за укрепване на законността и правораздаването в българската народна армия и държавата.
Остана верен на своя светъл идеал, на обичта си към своя измъчен народ и родина - България.
Напусна ни с вяра в борбата на народа ни за социална справедливост.
Твоя достойно извървян път остава пример за нас!
Прекланяме се пред светлата ти памет.
Обичаме те!

От семейството, роднините и приятелите

An obituary poster for Kostadin Lagadinov who died in 2011 at the age of ninety-eight

and other relatives in the Central Sofia Cemetery. A procession of thousands walked from the center of Sofia to the cemetery, bearing their once great leader to his final resting place.

"But do you know exactly where his grave is?" I said. "The Central Cemetery is very big."

"Do you want to go there?" Elena said.

"Yes," I said. "I've been thinking of writing an article about the mausoleum, and I would like to see where he is buried now. The only person who knows exactly where to find it is [Veneta], but she is not in Sofia now."

"It has been so long," Maria said. "I don't remember. But you can call the administration office. They know where all the famous graves are."

Elena Lagadinova and Maria Znepolska in March 2013

"Is your brother there?" I said to Elena.

Elena nodded. "Yes, but he is in a different section. With the urns."

Her eldest brother, Kostadin Lagadinov, had died two years earlier. He was ninety-eight years old: the oldest living general in Bulgaria in 2011.

"So many of us are gone now," Maria said. "That is why we must write."

"Is that why you wrote about Thompson?" I said.

Maria took a sip of her mastika. "Thompson was a great man," she said. "A hero who died fighting for a cause that he believed in. It is important to remember that there were once such people. We need to remember that sometimes you need to fight."

I suddenly remembered Frank Thompson's poem to Iris Murdoch back in 1939.

Sure, lady, I know the party line is better.
I know what Marx would have said. I know you're right.
When this is over we'll fight for the things that matter.
Somehow, today, I simply want to fight.

"Look at these protestors," Elena said. "They are against the monopolies and the corruption and the foreign capitalists. These are the same things that Dencho and Thompson were against."

"It is the same fight," Maria agreed. She looked to Elena and then back at me. "But it is not enough to protest *against*. Nothing ever changes until the people have something to fight *for*."

Maria's words hung in the air. Again I thought of Frank, like an old friend somehow whispering profundity at me across time.

That's heresy? Okay. But I'm past caring.
There's blood about my eyes, and mist and hate.
I know the things we're fighting now and loathe them.
Now's not the time you say? But I can't wait.

21 | A MOMENT OF REDEMPTION

I could never be so mad as to turn knight-errant, for I am aware that the customs of those days when famous knights roamed the world no longer prevail today.

—MIGUEL DE CERVANTES, *DON QUIXOTE*

About eight days later, Elena decided to accompany me to the Central Sofia Cemetery. "I want you to take some historic photos," she said over the phone.

"But today is very cold," I said. "Perhaps we should wait until I come back in the summer."

"No, we should go today," she said. "I called the Central Cemetery Administration. I have the information."

"Are you sure?" I said. "I was out this morning. The wind is terrible." The weather in Sofia had changed drastically since I arrived. The Bulgarians call March a "woman's month" because the climate is so mercurial. A week earlier I had been able to march with the protesters for three hours without a coat. But that morning, even three layers of clothing failed to keep out the biting cold. The stray dogs huddled together in piles to try to keep warm.

"I am healthy today," Elena said. "I am dressed. We can go whenever you are ready."

"Okay," I said. "I will call a taxi and come right over."

Elena rarely ventured forth from her apartment. Her husband

was dead and her children were all grown and gone. She still had many friends and former colleagues, but they always came to visit her. Elena went out in her neighborhood for basic groceries and medicine from the pharmacy. I guessed that she did not wander too far from home because she feared being hassled. So many younger Bulgarians were rude or even hostile to what they called the "red grandmothers," and there were plenty of youths who would not hesitate to snatch the purse of an older woman too frail to run after them. If she was willing to go with me today, it might be my only opportunity. I hoped that she would not get sick.

I was not feeling very well myself. It had been a difficult ten days. A caretaker government ruled Bulgaria after the February protests had forced the resignation of the prime minister and his cabinet. The government resignation had done little to stem the political discontent, and a spate of suicides and self-immolations filled the newspapers. On March 13, while I was working in the Central State Archives, I had gone out to get a Coke Zero at the exact moment that a fifty-one-year-old man set himself on fire in front of the offices of the Bulgarian presidency. I had smelled the scent of human desperation. I felt maudlin. But if Elena was willing to go out, I needed to get going.

Within the hour Elena and I were dropped off at one of the side entrances to the Central Sofia Cemetery. We were both wrapped like mummies with sweaters, coats, tights, hats, gloves, scarves, and thick-heeled boots. The wind shrieked. The tops of my shoulders almost touched the bottoms of my ears, and my teeth were clenched. My breath was shallow through my nose. My gums hurt if I tried to inhale through my mouth.

"We must buy flowers," Elena said. She led me across the street to where a Roma woman sat inside a small enclosure with three glass walls. Elena had a cane, which she leaned her full weight upon with each careful step. She walked like someone afraid to fall down.

The flower seller had white lilies, red and white carnations, and some premade bouquets of what looked like wild flowers picked from a backyard garden. Elena picked out three red carnations. I asked for two red and three white carnations. I tried to pay for all of the flowers, but Elena insisted on paying for her own.

"Please," she said, "I want them to be from me."

We crossed back to the other side of the street and entered the cemetery. Inside, at a little kiosk, a woman sat selling candles and boxes of matches. Elena stopped here and bought five candles and some matches. I did the same.

Protesters on the streets of Sofia in March 2013

"Now we have to find plot twenty-two," Elena said. She reached into her bag and pulled out a map of the cemetery. She gave it to me.

"Find the plot," she said. "I don't have my glasses. Look for the Catholic chapel."

I unfolded the map. From where we were standing, it looked like plot twenty-two was a third of the way into the cemetery. I had never been here before. Looking at the scale of the map and then looking around, I realized that the cemetery was massive.

"I think it is down this way," I said, pointing ahead.

We walked together in silence. Elena moved slowly, leaning on her cane. I bowed my head against the wind.

"After the Catholic chapel, we turn up to the right," I said after we had been walking for about ten minutes.

The Catholic chapel was a small building at the base of a long lane of plots. "It should be around here," Elena said.

We found the wooden sign with the number twenty-two and surveyed the graves. None of them stood out as being the grave of a famous person. Somehow I had expected that the grave would be big and spectacular. Dimitrov had, after all, spent the first forty years of his death embalmed in a large, white marble mausoleum in the middle of Sofia. I walked up and down the length of plot twenty-two. Elena stood on the paved pathway, scanning the names on the graves that she could see.

"Do you see it?" she said.

"No," I said. "I don't see it anywhere. Are you sure this is the right plot?"

"That is what they said."

"Maybe we should ask at the chapel. There might be someone inside."

"Yes," she said. "That is a good idea."

I met her on the pathway, and we walked back to the chapel. Her steps were already heavier.

"It is very cold," she said.

"Yes," I said. "I think I heard them say that today will be the coldest day of the winter so far. Because of the wind."

As I said the word "wind," it came blowing all around us. We both squinted and put our heads down. I cupped my gloved hands over my nose and mouth.

"I made soup," Elena said. "We will have hot soup for lunch."

I smiled at her. "Hot soup will be perfect."

The chapel was close. It would have taken me less than a minute to walk there at my pace, but with Elena, it took almost five.

When we got to the chapel there was a woman tending the candelabras.

"Good day," Elena said.

The woman smiled at us. "Good day," she said.

"Can you tell us where we can find the grave of Georgi Dimitrov?" Elena said. "I was there many years ago. But I do not remember."

The woman looked at Elena and then me. She noticed the red and white carnations that we held. We did not look like vandals. "It's very hard to explain," she said. "I'll take you there. Just give me a minute."

The woman left the chapel and returned a moment later wearing a coat, hat, and gloves. "It's very cold," she said.

"Maybe the coldest day this winter," Elena said.

"Follow me," the woman said.

The woman from the chapel had shoulder-length gray-blonde hair. I guessed that she was in her late fifties or early sixties. Her pace was initially fast, but she slowed when she realized how difficult it was for Elena to walk. She was accustomed to dealing with the elderly.

"The grave is not well marked," the woman said. "They didn't want it to be disturbed."

I knew that Veneta brought buses full of Greek tourists to the grave site in the summers, so it could not be that well-guarded a secret. But the possibility of vandalism was probably higher than I imagined. While many Bulgarians saw Dimitrov as a national hero, others thought he embodied everything wrong with Bulgaria. He was a great man to some and a villain to others.

The woman led us down the pavement. She turned into plot twenty-two. The narrowest of footpaths divided the graves, which were crammed close together in the plot. She led us three rows deep, and I let Elena go in front of me so that I could steady her if she lost her balance.

"Here it is," the woman said.

She pointed to a roughly cut granite tombstone jutting out of a raised granite platform. The center of the raised platform was filled with earth and there were weeds growing out of it. On the top of the headstone was a picture of the leader, head turned toward the viewer, smoking a pipe. The words on the stone read "Georgi Dimitrov 1882–1949." There were no other inscriptions. The headstone was not very big. No wonder I had not been able to find it. It was a humble grave.

"Here it is," Elena said.

"I'll leave you," the woman said. She hugged herself against the wind.

"Thank you," I said.

"Thank you very much," Elena said.

"My pleasure," the woman said. She smiled at us.

Elena stooped down and began clearing some of the weeds from the front of the tombstone. She snapped the long stems of each of her three red carnations, leaving only about eight inches of the stem below the flowers, and drove each stem into the earth in front of the tombstone. I shortened the stems of my carnations, handing them to Elena one by one. She arranged the flowers so that they formed a colorful little cluster below the etching of Dimitrov.

"Let me light the candles," she said, "And then you can take your photos."

Elena removed each of her gloves. She pulled the candles out of her purse. She took a match from the box and struck it. The wind blew the flame out. She lit another match, trying to cup the flame from the wind with her hand. The candle lit. Elena pressed the candle into the earth among the flowers, but the wind blew the flame out again. She lit a third match; she relit the candle. This time the wick was already primed. The flame wobbled and bent, but did not go out. She took a second candle, lit it from the flame on the first, and shoved this candle in closer to the headstone.

"There," she said. She stood up.

I took the lens cap off my camera. I set the dial to continuous shooting and snapped a series of pictures of the grave site.

"Elena," I said, "Why don't you stand next to it. I'll take a few of you."

Elena adjusted her hat. She dropped her cane off to the side, and steadied herself by placing a hand on the top of the tombstone. She looked down at the burning candles.

I shot several photos. The sky was white through the bare branches of the trees behind her. Elena seemed lost in her own thoughts.

"He had a great dream," she said in a low voice. "A great idea."

"Do you think you can take one of me?" I said.

"You can show me how," she said.

I walked to her and gave her a quick lesson with my camera. She took a photo of me. "A historic photo," she said.

The wind blew the candles out. Elena clenched her fists. She replaced her gloves. We spoke for a few moments about the difficulty of getting a grave in the Central Sofia Cemetery. She was very pleased that her brother had been given a place in the new section.

"Shall we go there next?" I said.

Elena smiled at me. "I would like that," she said. "I have saved some candles for him."

"Is your husband here, too?"

"Yes, but in a different section. That one is on the other side. I don't know if I could make it there on a day like today."

"It is really cold." I wanted to get inside as quickly as possible. The muscles in my body were all tense.

We left the grave site. Elena walked with great labor, her cane clacking against the pavement with each step.

"We should thank that kind woman once more," Elena said, as we neared the chapel.

We found the woman inside. "Thank you very much for your help," Elena said.

"We never would have been able to find it without your help," I said.

The woman heard my accent. "You are not Bulgarian?" she said.

"She is an American," Elena said. "She is going to write about our Georgi Dimitrov."

The woman tilted her head, intrigued.

"You must be very cold," she said. "Why don't you come inside to my office? I have a heater in there. You can warm yourselves."

Elena Lagadinova at the grave of Georgi Dimitrov in 2013

I looked to Elena. She nodded. She would be happy to sit down for a while. She had been on her feet for about an hour.

We followed the woman to her office. It was at the top of a short flight of steps in a low administrative building behind the chapel.

Elena struggled up the stairs. A space heater warmed the small room, and a man sat behind a desk looking through a catalogue. He appeared to be in his late twenties.

"Please sit down," the woman said, gesturing to two chairs in front of the desk.

Elena and I sat. The woman stood behind the young man. "This is my son, Chavdar. He is the resident sculptor here," she said. "And I am Emilia. It is very nice to meet you."

"This is my friend, Kristen, from the United States," Elena said, "And I am Elena Lagadinova."

The woman's face went pale.

"Elena Lagadinova?" she said. Her eyes were wide. "*Elena Lagadinova*?"

Elena seemed frightened. She did not go out very often. "Yes," she said. "My family were the Lagadinovs from Razlog."

"Oh my God," Emilia said. Her mouth hung open. "I didn't recognize you."

Elena looked down. "The years have changed me."

"I didn't know you were still alive," Emilia said.

"I'm still standing," Elena said.

"Chavdar," Emilia said to her son. "This is Elena Lagadinova. The Amazon. She was my hero when I was a child."

Chavdar looked up at Elena. He seemed unimpressed.

Emilia looked to Elena. "It was my favorite book, about you and your white horse," she said, pressing her hand against her chest. "It's such a great pleasure to meet you in person."

"It was many years ago," Elena said.

Emilia turned to her son. "I had three years' maternity leave when you were born because of this woman."

Chavdar nodded to Elena. His eyes were distant.

Elena rested both of her hands on the top of her cane. "We were trying to do something for Bulgaria. For the people. To make a good life. It was a different time."

"It was a better time," Emilia said.

Chavdar looked back down at his catalogue, then to me. "Would you like to see some photos of my work?" he said.

"Sure," I said, glancing at Elena. She sat watching Chavdar.

I took the catalogue. I spent a few moments looking through the pages at a variety of different models of tombstones, commenting on how elegant they were. There was a photo of two exquisite white marble angels watching over a modern-looking grave. I realized that Chavdar had real talent, but very few people in Bulgaria could afford to commission this type of elaborate sculpture for their grave sites.

"We should be going," Elena said. She stood, leaning into her cane to rise to her feet.

"It's beautiful work," I said to Chavdar.

"Is there work like this in the United States?" he said.

The truth was that I didn't really know; I didn't hang around many cemeteries taking in the sculpture. "I guess so," I said, shrugging.

"I would like to go to the United States," Chavdar said. "But they won't give me a visa."

Emilia shot him a look.

"Oh," I said.

"Thank you for letting us come in and get warm," Elena said to Emilia. She offered her hand.

Emilia took Elena's hand between both of her own. She shook her head in disbelief. "Elena Lagadinova," Emilia said. "The Amazon. Really, from my heart, it was an honor to meet you."

I watched Emilia's face. She had tears in her eyes. I looked to Elena. She was smiling up at Emilia. A silence filled the room as they stood together, their eyes locked.

Chavdar slid his card across the desk toward me. "If you know of anyone who needs any sculpture done, please give them my contact information."

I took his card. I put it in my pocket. "Yes, I will," I said.

He stood up. He offered me his hand, and I shook it. He turned to Elena. "It was nice to meet you," he said to her.

She nodded to him, but did not remove her hand from Emilia's cupped palms.

"Have a pleasant day," Emilia said. "You must keep warm."

Elena removed her hand. I went to the door and held it open while she slowly made her way through.

"Good-bye," Elena said. "And thank you."

"No," Emilia said. "Thank you."

Emerging from the heated office was painful. The air outside was so raw it felt like I was inhaling knives. I hunched forward, pulling my collar up around my scarf.

Elena walked with even greater effort. "My brother is down this lane," she said. "And then we will go home and have soup."

I nodded. I would be leaving Bulgaria the following day. I had to pack, but I would have some time in the morning before the flight. I just really wanted to be indoors. The day seemed to be getting colder.

We walked together, side by side, without speaking for a few hundred meters.

Elena's breath became heavy. She stopped to rest, leaning on her cane. She looked at me.

"She knew who I was," Elena said. "She remembered."

I nodded.

Elena smiled. It was the wide grin of a proud child. She lifted her chin, then turned to walk on, still smiling.

There is a spirit abroad in Europe which is finer and braver than anything that tired continent has known for centuries, and which cannot
be withstood. You can, if you like, think of it in terms of politics, but it
is broader and more generous than any dogma. It is the confident will
of whole peoples, who have known the utmost humiliation and suffering and have triumphed over it, to build their own life once and for all.
— MAJOR FRANK THOMPSON, CHRISTMAS DAY, 1943

On a scorching hot morning in August 2013, I caught a bus from
the Poduene bus station in Sofia to the city of Botevgrad. Once in
Botevgrad, I hired a taxi driver who called himself Sincho to drive
me out a few kilometers to Litakovo. I wanted to visit the grave
of Major Frank Thompson. I brought red carnations. I was feeling
lost and frustrated with the political situation in Bulgaria and in
Greece and back at home in the United States. In all of these places
politicians seemed dangerously out of touch with their constitu-
ents. Democracy seemed fragile. The Bulgarian government had
resigned in February, but snap elections in May had failed to produce a clear winner, and now the streets of Sofia were once again
filled with protestors demanding yet another round of elections. As
if that would solve anything.[1]

After some questioning of the villagers in Litakovo, we drove up
a hill to the monument commemorating fallen communists both

The monument to those who died fighting fascism in Litakovo

during the uprising of 1923 and during World War II. The road leading out of Litakovo was unpaved, and Sincho left me at the base of a long stairway that led up to the monument and the graves that surrounded it. The sun was high as I trudged up the steps to the obelisk. The site was deserted and falling into ruin. The surrounding forest encroached in on the lonely plateau, but the view from the monument remained spectacular. The hills and valleys of the surrounding countryside could be seen for miles.

Frank Thompson's name was listed among some others on one side of the base of the obelisk. On the other side of the base were the following lines:

> PLEASE TELL OUR STORY SIMPLY
> TO THOSE WE WILL NOT SEE,
> TELL THOSE WHO SHALL REPLACE US—
> WE FOUGHT COURAGEOUSLY.[2]

From the obelisk I walked through some barren flower beds that must have once been carefully tended by members of the local Communist Party. Off to the right behind the large obelisk I saw a simple white stone statue of a partisan woman with her hands tied together. She looked out over the horizon, and it was only when I approached her that I realized that she was also looking out over a row of large graves. I trod down some decrepit steps to get close enough to read the names on the slabs of marble. Four graves were lined up below the statue of the bound woman. On the first two, the names etched in the marble had begun to fade. They were hard to read. On the third grave down from the statue, however, someone had filled in the etchings with gold paint. It was here that I read the Cyrillic words "Captain Frank Thompson, Englishman." Apparently, the tombstone had been prepared before the Bulgarians knew that Thompson had been gazetted major.

The marble tombstone was cracked, and the bottom half was crooked. Frank Thompson shared his final resting place with two named members of the Bulgarian Communist Party and nine other people simply listed as "unknown." Trees shaded this quiet place. I wiped the accumulated dirt off of the tombstone with my hands. Then, right below Thompson's name, I laid four red carnations.

As I stood over the grave on that hot August day, I allowed my mind to wander. Frank Thompson was a communist. What did this mean? For some, communism represented the democratic dream of a world in which peasants and workers could control their own fates. For others, communism celebrated our common humanity, a political program whose promised end was

Frank Thompson's final resting place in Litakovo

unity and world peace. If men and women embraced their working brothers and sisters across national, ethnic, religious, or linguistic differences, there would be no more wars. Communism was an economic program as much as a political one — for the poor and backward countries of Europe, it provided a road map to rapid modernization and catching up with the West. During the Spanish Civil War and during World War II, communism was the ideological goal that gave many men and women something to fight *for* when they fought *against* the Nazis and their fascist allies. But even more important than these geopolitical mobilizations of the communist ideal, communism had local personal meanings that shaped choices and decisions in ways that altered the course of individual human lives.

Frank Thompson joined the Communist Party of Great Britain because he believed that only the working-class movement could prevent the spread of fascism, but also because he fell hard for an Irish girl with leftist sympathies. The Lagadinov brothers embraced communism because they were poor, but perhaps because they also admired the revolutionary spirit of previous Bulgarian heroes like the poet Hristo Botev, who gave his life in the fight against oppression. To Elena Lagadinova, communism was a family inheritance. She risked her life to help her brothers because they were her brothers, but also because she believed that communism meant dolls and books for all children. Eventually she made communism her own cause and spent her life trying to realize its ideals for women and families.

To E. P. Thompson, "communism" was a word that had become tainted by Stalin and the brutal postwar aggression of the Soviet Union, a word that could be easily replaced by "socialist humanism," and a word that he did not want applied to his brother. Freeman Dyson wrote that communism was perhaps a "bad cause" made good by the generous spirit of self-sacrifice of those who fought and died for it. It wasn't communism that inspired men to action, it was men's actions that made communism such an inspiration.

For some, communism was an incentive for selflessness. Women like "Veneta" believed that the most important thing in life is to help others, to leave this world a little better than it was when you came into it. For men and women like "Anelia," communism was just politics—meetings and seminars and speeches that were boring. Communism was a system that you lived under without questioning it much. You took from it what you could; you did your work and didn't get involved. You got angry when they didn't let you have the byline for an article you wrote, but you didn't say anything. You knew about the surveillance and the secret police, but you ignored them because you believed you were not doing anything wrong. For Anelia, communism wasn't good or bad—it was just there.

Anelia lived under a communism that she never fought for. Frank Thompson and Assen Lagadinov fought for a communism that they never lived under. Had Thompson lived he may have come to abhor the crimes committed in the name of his ideals. "Anelia's" own apathy toward communism slowly faded as she came to realize that not everything she was taught about capitalism was a lie. Only after twenty years of Bulgarian democracy did she finally make the effort to read the books she was supposed to have read under communism. Only when she found herself in debt and unemployed did the critique of capitalism in those books start to make sense.

Communism could also mean the gulag, like the Siberian prison where Kostadin Lagadinov spent three years, or the labor camp, Belene, where they sent Maria Znepolska's husband. Communism meant shortages of feminine-hygiene products. It meant travel restrictions and the ubiquity of the secret police. Communism meant that magazines were censored and that people were not given all of the information they needed to be able to think for themselves.[3] Communism meant one-party rule and leaders who remained unchallenged for thirty-five years.

At the same time, communism provided support for working mothers and promoted programs to ensure the de jure and de facto equality of men and women. Communism promoted literacy and education and health care and guaranteed full employment for anyone able to work. Communism gave people jobs, homes, and daily routines that were predictable and stable, even as they were limited and constrained.

And yet the memory of communism had become one-dimensional. A few months before my trip to Thompson's grave, Bulgaria celebrated February 1 as the official Day of Homage and Gratitude to the Victims of the Communist Regime for the third time since the holiday was created in 2011. The date marks the decision of a Bulgarian People's Court on February 1, 1945, to summarily execute three regents to the young Bulgarian king, sixty-seven members of parliament, twenty-two cabinet ministers, and forty military generals and senior officers of the Bulgarian Royal Army as well as a number of other political figures.[4]

One article in an English-language newspaper in Bulgaria reported that on this day "Bulgaria's former political and military elite was liquidated at a single stroke."[5] Sending the story out on the newswire, the Associated Press reported that some Bulgarians laid wreaths at a wall inscribed with the names of many who died at the hands of the communists: "The victims memorialized on the wall include many political opponents of communism executed after September 1944, when Bulgaria's communists seized power in this tiny Balkan country."[6] Around the world the AP story was published and republished on news websites under the headline "Bulgaria Honors Victims of Communism."[7] Nowhere was it mentioned, even in passing, that Bulgaria's "political and military elite" were allied with Nazi Germany.

On February 1, 2013, Bulgarians brought their wreaths to the monument for the victims of communism. This monument, designed by the architects Atanas Todorov and Dimitar Krastev, sits near a chapel in a slightly hidden alcove in the park in front of the National Palace of Culture in Sofia. The monument was completed in 1999 for the ten-year anniversary of the collapse of Bulgarian communism.[8] An openly pro-American government funded its construction, the same government that would, in that same year, incompetently take seven days to demolish the mausoleum that Georgi Dimitrov's mourners had built in only six.

The architects of the monument etched an emotional message in Bulgarian on the monument. The following words are literally written in stone:

The monument to the victims of communism in Sofia

Bow before this wall, fellow Bulgarians! It contains the suffering of our people. This memorial has been erected for our compatriots, victims of the communist terror: those who lost their lives, those who vanished without a trace, those who were shot by the so-called "people's tribunal." It commemorates the concentration camp prisoners, the political prisoners, those who were interned, those subjected to political repression, and their ill-fated families and relatives. May the memory of the innocently shed blood burn in our hearts like an eternal flame. May the past never repeat itself!

Lord, give peace to the souls of your martyrs, grant them your justice. Accept them as our guardians, holy and immortal—now and forever. Amen.

Since the physical monument can only be visited in person, a virtual monument was also constructed. The American Research Center in Sofia (ARCS) created the VictimsofCommunism.bg website for the twentieth anniversary of 1989.[9] The website, which includes over seventeen thousand names, was an admonition to Bulgarians to never forget the evils of their communist past. The description on the project's home page stated: "The 20th century created two monsters: nazism [sic] and communism. While no educated, humane, and democratically minded person today would defend nazism [sic], many still justify communism, a regime responsible for the death of over 100 million people worldwide. In 1944 communism was forcefully introduced in Bulgaria. Terror followed overnight and lasted a very long time. Thousands were murdered or sent to prisons and concentration camps for being wealthy, educated, skilled, politically 'dangerous' or for no pretext whatsoever."[10]

Apparently, all of this "innocent" blood shed "for no pretext whatsoever" continues to haunt Bulgaria's political elites today. In 2009, a new government commissioned yet another physical monument to the victims of communism. In her emotional speech on February 1, 2013, Vice President Margarita Popova declared: "No one has the right to falsify history or to rewrite it, and no one can take away the memories of the people whose relatives were massacred."[11]

Of course, there were truly innocent victims of the communist regime in Bulgaria. There were certainly those who were persecuted and sent to labor camps for their political opinions, and certainly victims of political purges. But the February 1 Day of Homage and Gratitude specifically commemorates the deaths of 147 members of the Bulgarian "political and military elite" who were sentenced by the People's Court in 1945. Who were these men? And what does it mean that they are considered "victims of communism" today?

Many of these "victims" cut off the heads of the partisans Thompson came to help, shoved pikes up their severed necks, and mounted them in village squares. Some of these men ordered the burning of houses, the rapes, the torture, and the indiscriminate murders of peasants and anyone who questioned the absolute authority of the king. Others summarily executed uniformed British officers in blatant violation of the Geneva Convention.

As I stared at Thompson's grave, I recalled that General Kocho Stoyanov, the man responsible for the interrogation and torture of Frank Thompson, shot himself in the head before the partisans captured him. Captain Yanko Stoyanov, the man who oversaw the prison in Litakovo, was arrested after September 9, 1944, when the Bulgarian Communist Party came to power. Although the details are still unclear, it seems that the partisans arrested between five and eight men and charged them with the murder of Frank Thompson. Most of the men denied their participation in the shooting or claimed that they had shot over Thompson's head. Only two men—Boris Lukanov Stoyanov (found wearing Frank's shoes) and Ilya Tapkanov—admitted to opening fire on the partisans. Stoyanov claimed to be respon-

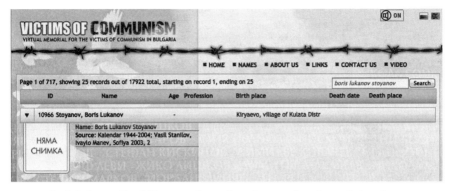

Page 1 of 717, showing 25 records out of 17922 total, starting on record 1, ending on record 25

boris lukanov stoyanov   Search

ID	Name	Age	Profession	Birth place	Death date	Death place
▼ 10966	Stoyanov, Boris Lukanov	-		Kiryaevo, village of Kulata Distr		

НЯМА СНИМКА

Name: Boris Lukanov Stoyanov
Source: Kalendar 1944-2004; Vasil Stanilov,
Ivaylo Manev, Sofiya 2003, 2

Boris Lukanov, Frank Thompson's murderer, is remembered as a victim of communism

sible for actually shooting Frank in the ditch. Docho Hristov, the minister of interior who led the gendarmes toward the end of the war and who placed the 50,000-lev bounty on the head of any dead partisan, was also arrested and accused of being an enemy of the people.

With the exception of General Kocho Stoyanov, who was already dead, the remaining men were all tried by hastily assembled People's Courts. They were found guilty of their crimes and sentenced to death by firing squad. But today they are remembered as *innocent* victims of communism.

The "victims" of communism also include major military and political figures who worked closely with Nazi Germany. Bogdan Filov was the Bulgarian prime minister from 1940 to 1943.[12] His government passed the Law for the Protection of the Nation in 1940, the law that deprived all Bulgarian Jews of their civil rights and set up the Commissariat for Jewish Affairs. Although Filov yielded to local pressure to protect the Bulgarian Jews, it was his government that decided that roughly eleven thousand Jews in the annexed territories in Macedonia and Greece would be deported to the death camps in Treblinka.[13] Filov was a passionate and committed ally of Hitler. He became one of the three regents of the young King Simeon II after the death of Boris III. He was also sentenced to death by a People's Court and executed by firing squad in February 1945.[14] Today, he is honored as an innocent victim of communism.

Petar Gabrovski served as the minister of interior under Filov and was briefly Bulgaria's prime minister in 1943.[15] He enforced the infamous Law for the Protection of the Nation. Gabrovski himself was a virulent anti-Semite. He started his political career as a Nazi, but ultimately decided to form a new

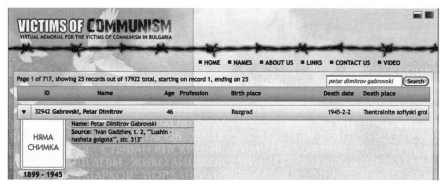

Petar Gabrovski, the man who personally signed the deportation orders for twenty thousand Jews, is listed as a victim of communism

political movement called the Ratniks for the Advancement of the Bulgarian National Spirit. Although the Ratnik movement never became a popular nationalist movement among the country's peasants, several prominent politicians openly identified as Ratniks. In his 1972 book, *The Bulgarian Jews and the Final Solution 1940–1944*, historian Frederick Chary published English translations of the actual warrants concerning the fate of the Greek and Macedonian Jews. One of these warrants states, "The Commissar for Jewish Questions is charged to deport from the borders of the country in agreement with the German authorities up to 20,000 Jews, inhabiting the recently liberated territories."[16] It is signed personally by Petar Gabrovski.

A close associate of Gabrovski was a man named Aleksandar Belev who was a cofounder of the Bulgarian Ratnik movement. Belev served as the first chairman of the Commissariat of Jewish Affairs. He had been sent to Germany to study the legal apparatus constructed to ensure the purity of the German race. He actively collaborated with the Nazis and was a good friend of Adolf Eichmann's personal representative in Bulgaria, Theodor Dannecker, the highest German officer in charge of implementing the deportation of the Jews of Macedonia and Thrace. On February 22, 1943, these two men signed the Dannecker-Belev Agreement, which outlined the details of the deportation, including the number of trains that would be used (five trains for five thousand "passengers" from Skopje, three trains for three thousand "passengers" from Bitola, etc.) Although the People's Court sentenced Belev to death for his cooperation with Dannecker in the execution of the "final solution," he was not technically a "victim" of the communist

General Nikola Zhevkov's name on the wall honoring the victims of communism in Sofia

government. After he was found guilty, Belev committed suicide before his sentence could be carried out.

Another listed victim of communism in Bulgaria who was not really a victim was General Nikola Zhekov, a personal friend of Adolf Hitler, and the head of the Bulgarian far-right Legionnaires.[17] After the Red Army entered Bulgaria in September 1944, Zhekov fled Bulgaria fearing political persecution by the new communist regime. He was already in Germany when the People's Court sentenced him to death on February 1, 1945. He died in Bavaria in 1949 at age eighty-four, far from any Bulgarian firing squad. Since his name appears on the list of the "political and military elite" who were found guilty of collaboration with the government of Bogdan Filov, however, he is still celebrated as a "victim of communism."[18]

A truly extreme case is General Hristo Lukov.[19] He was assassinated by a band of partisans allegedly led by a nineteen-year-old girl on February 13, 1943, well before the People's Courts ever had a chance to execute him by firing squad.[20] Lukov served as the Bulgarian minister of war and was an extreme right-wing politician who led the Union of Bulgarian National Legions (the Legionnaires). Lukov called for the racial and ethnic purity of the Bulgarian people during World Wars I and II. In 2013, he was still a beacon for neo-Nazi sympathizers in Bulgaria. In fact, in 2011, the European Network Against Racism (ENAR) issued a press release asking the mayor of

Thompson's tombstone. The inscription reads "Captain Frank Thompson. Englishman." He is buried with eleven other Bulgarians, nine of whom remain unidentified.

Sofia to ban an impending "Lukov March." The letter protested the annual permit granted to this march, which was organized by a coalition of nationalist forces in the name of Hristo Lukov. The letter states: "The Lukov March is the most important public event of [right-wing] groups in Bulgarian society, which have showed open or covert adherence to fascist, neo-Nazi and ultra national-populist ideas. [The] Lukov March is especially dangerous for its impact on young people, promoting authoritarian and anti-democratic ideas under the guise of patriotism and reverence for the national war heroes."[21] A European NGO against racism can protest against marches held in Lukov's name, but in Bulgaria he is listed as an innocent victim of communism.

About men such as these, the monument tells us: "Lord, give peace to the souls of your martyrs, grant them your justice. Accept them as our guardians, holy and immortal—now and forever. Amen."

The creation of monuments in Bulgaria and the celebration of the Day of Homage and Gratitude are not isolated episodes. Since the global economic crisis that began in 2008, governments and corporations are especially eager to remind the public about the evils of communism. In 2009, the European Union created a new holiday to be marked each year on August 23: the Euro-

Frank Thompson

pean Day of Remembrance for Victims of Stalinism and Nazism.[22] In that same year, the American Victims of Communism Memorial Foundation launched a virtual Global Museum on Communism, "an international portal created to honor the more than 100 million victims of communist tyranny and educate future generations about past and present communist atrocities."[23] In June 2013, a Madrid court ordered the dismantling of a monument that commemorated the sacrifices of the International Brigades who fought against Franco in the Spanish Civil War.[24]

As the anticommunist memory industry does its best to blackwash the past, to absolve the crimes of fascists by making them victims of the supposed abomination of communism, I needed to remind myself that not all who fought or found themselves on the left side of history were radical Marxist zealots bent on world domination. I wanted to recognize the nuances of what communism meant to ordinary people, how it motivated or paralyzed them, how it fueled hope or spread despair. There is the official history of communism and there is the intimate history of communism— the latter composed of individual men and women making individual decisions in a confused and sometimes chaotic world.

As I stood over the grave of a man who died at age twenty-three for something he truly believed in, I felt my own inadequacy. I could see the way the world was headed, but I was lost. I was not fighting for anything. "Objectivity" was my excuse. Better not to believe than to believe in something "wrong."

I stared down at the ground. I wondered if Frank Thompson had ever felt this way. I wondered what he would do. The answer came as soon as I had asked the question. Frank would write a poem.

I wrote a book instead.

ACKNOWLEDGMENTS

While I was writing this book, I was not the best mother, partner, friend, or colleague. There are therefore many people to whom I owe apologies as well as thanks. First and foremost, I would like to thank the members of my writing group who helped me work through many parts of the manuscript: Annie Finch, Pope Brock, and Sarah Braunstein. Their patience and generosity gave me the opportunity to talk through this manuscript, and they listened to and provided critical feedback for the early drafts of several chapters. Susan Faludi was an invaluable interlocutor; our many productive gabfests about feminism, communism, and East European history helped me sharpen my arguments and consider the wider implications of how the memory of World War II shapes contemporary politics. I also discussed this project with many colleagues and friends: Maria Bucur, Russ Rymer, Jennifer Scanlon, Page Herrlinger, Anne Clifford, Barry Logan, Olga Shevchenko, Joan W. Scott, Judy Vichniac, Barbara Weinstein, Sonya Michel, Maria Stoilkova, Josephine Sehon, Doug Rogers, Christian Filipov, and Dimitar Dimitrov. Their input and suggestions were invaluable. Miroslava Nikolova was my Bulgarian research assistant at Bowdoin College for three years between 2010 and 2013, and provided a wide variety of support for this project, especially with the initial translations of Boris Lagadinov's memoir from the Bulgarian. Other Bowdoin students inspired me in various ways, but I particularly want to acknowledge four members of the class of 2016: Caroline Martinez, Julia Mead, Sara Hamilton, and Matthew Goroff. Scott Sehon, Miroslava Nikolova, Sarah Braunstein, Andrea Simon, Anne Clifford, Vera Dellwig, and Danielle Lubin-Levy all read and gave comments on a full draft of the manuscript. For their comments and suggestions I am deeply grateful. I am also indebted to Andrea Simon for her inspirational work on Angel Wagenstein and the Bulgarian Holocaust. Finally, the blue pencil of the novelist Sarah Braunstein immeasurably enhanced the quality of my prose.

I must acknowledge the support of the Institute for Advanced Study (IAS) in Princeton, the Radcliffe Institute for Advanced Study (Radcliffe IAS) at Harvard University, the National Council for Eurasian and East European Research, Bowdoin College, and the John Simon Guggenheim Memorial Foundation. In particular, I am grateful for a summer fellowship at the Radcliffe IAS, which allowed me to spend the month of June 2013 at Harvard to complete the first full draft of the manuscript. I gave an informal lunch talk there and benefited from some great feedback. In Cambridge, Warren Goldfarb was a wonderful landlord. The apartment on the third floor on Grey Street was very auspicious (especially since it was previously occupied by Jamaica Kincaid!). Linda Cooper at the IAS deserves much gratitude for organizing my many trips back to Princeton for the Association of Members of the Institute for Advanced Study (AMIAS) board meetings. I am especially grateful to Freeman Dyson for first introducing me to Frank Thompson and for sharing his papers and recollections with me.

My deepest thanks goes out to Elena Lagadinova and the other men and women whom I interviewed in Bulgaria over the last five years. I also want to acknowledge the help of the archivists at the Central State Archives in Sofia. I want to thank George Dyson for sharing a photo of his father with me, as well as Kate Thompson for sending me all of the photos that she could find of her uncle. All of the photos of the Lagadinovs come from the personal archives of Elena Lagadinova, and I am deeply grateful to her for giving me permission to reproduce them. Hayden Sartoris was the IT wizard who helped me edit the Bulgaria map template made available through d-maps.com.

Courtney Berger at Duke University Press wins the award for the smartest, most thoughtful and generous editor; her guidance and support were essential for this project. Courtney took a raw manuscript and helped me cook it into a book. It is a glorious thing to have an editor who understands what you are trying to say and who has the passion and creative insight to help you say it. At Duke University Press, I would also like to thank Erin Hanas, Christine Riggio, Laura Sell, Helena Knox, Willa Armstrong, Jessica Ryan, and Heather Hensley. I'd also like to thank my copyeditor Jen Rappaport. I am also indebted to the two external reviewers who subsequently revealed their identities to me: Professors Elizabeth Frank and Krassimira Daskalova.

Most important of all was the personal support I received both from my partner and my daughter. I seriously abused their generosity on multiple occasions. Scott stepped up and took care of so many of the day-to-day responsibilities of home and family, allowing me to become a hermit in Falmouth, Amsterdam, and Cambridge in the summers of 2012 and 2013. Once he got over his initial incredulity that I had started writing a different book in the middle of the one I was already working on, Scott was the greatest supporter of this project: an incisive interlocutor, a brilliant editor, and a patient listener.

My daughter steadfastly supported my writing, but made sure that I took a healthy number of breaks when she was around. One of our favorite things to do together is to watch films on DVD at home. Several years ago, we watched the film version of the musical *Man of La Mancha* (1972). The late Peter O'Toole plays both Don Quixote and Miguel de Cervantes. Toward the end of the film, O'Toole has a moving monologue in which Cervantes contemplates the meaning of madness. In the end, Cervantes warns us that the maddest thing of all is "to see life as it is, and not as it should be."

It is too easy to become pessimistic about the world, to completely disengage from it, and to get caught in the mind-set that the way the world is now is the way it has always been and will always be. What the world needs more than anything is political imagination, hope, and perhaps a bit of utopianism. This book is written for all of those people who still believe that some value can come from tilting at windmills.

NOTES

PROLOGUE: COMMUNISM 2.0?

1. Ironically, the streets were full of protesters during that summer as well. These were so-called middle-class protestors who were ostensibly opposed to the return of communism, even as communist and anarchist graffiti started to pop up around the capital. The snap elections held in May 2013 failed to produce a clear winner and the Bulgarian Socialist Party (BSP) returned to power with the assistance of the Movement for Rights and Freedom and Ataka. Since the BSP is widely seen as the successor party of the old Bulgarian Communist Party, a new group of protestors took to the streets to demand this new government's resignation after the BSP tried to appoint a well-known mafioso to a high government post. The BSP is a center-left party, and the anticommunist language of the protest was a rhetorical device to discredit the government. The BSP has very few left policies and is similar in character to all other existing political parties in Bulgaria—riddled with corruption and beholden to shady economic interests. Although there were important class differences between the Bulgarians protesting in the winter against the electricity distribution monopolies and the Bulgarians protesting in the summer and fall against the BSP, both groups are fundamentally opposed to the failure of Bulgarian democracy and the reality that all elected officials put the economic interests of business communities above the interests of the Bulgarian electorate. The key difference between political parties in Bulgaria is which business interests are given priority over the Bulgarian people. For center-right parties European business interests are favored and for center-left parties, Russian and domestic Bulgarian business interests are given priority. In both cases, it is the interests of citizens that are trampled. Some Bulgarians, like those scribbling graffiti on the walls in

Sofia, were beginning to realize that changing the government through elections would not improve the lot of ordinary people. There needs to be more systemic change. For further discussion of these 2013 protests, see Georgieff, "Kristen Ghodsee."

2. Jana Micochovia and Robert Muller, "Czech Communists May Get Share of Power after Snap Elections," Reuters, August 20, 2013, www.reuters.com.

3. Indeed, the KSČM was the only party of the already-existing parties in the lower house to increase its total number of votes in comparison with the election of 2010 (by 150,000 votes, or by 3.6 percent, respectively), gaining seven new seats. But the Social Democrats suffered a terrible electoral blow by the entrance of a new political party formed by agro-food billionaire Andrej Babiš. During the course of the election campaign this brand-new party went from nothing to become the second-largest party in the Czech Republic, winning 18.65 percent of the vote. See Seán Hanley, "How the Czech Social Democrats Were Derailed by a Billionaire Populist," Policy Network, November 12, 2013, www.policy-network .net.

4. Czech News Agency, "Klaus: EU Leftist Radicals Want to Destroy Democracy," *Prague Daily Monitor*, September 9, 2013, praguemonitor.com.

5. For instance, see the Platform for European Memory and Conscience (http:// www.memoryandconscience.eu): "The project Platform of European Memory and Conscience brings together institutions and organisations from the V4 and other EU countries active in research, documentation, awareness raising and education about the totalitarian regimes which befell the Visegrad region in the 20th century."

6. See the ISRP website at http://www.minaloto.org/ and the IICCMRE website at http://www.iiccr.ro/index.html/about_iiccr/institute/?lang=en&section=about _iiccr/institute.

7. Dean, *The Communist Horizon*.

8. Ronald Radosh, "Ronald Radosh: Seeger Was a Useful Idiot for Stalin," *Providence Journal*, February 6, 2014; Mark Tooley, "Pete Seeger, Stalin and God," *American Spectator*, January 31, 2014; Michael Moynihan, "The Death of 'Stalin's Songbird,'" *Daily Beast*, January 29, 2014, www.dailybeast.com; Will Rahn, "Obama Praises Stalinist and Folk Singer Pete Seeger," *Daily Caller*, January 28, 2014, http://dailycaller.com; Ellis Washington, "Pete 'Potemkin' Seeger: Stalin's Little Minstrel," www.renewamerica.com, February 1, 2014; Moynihan, "The Death of 'Stalin's Songbird.'"

9. Seeger, *Where Have All the Flowers Gone*.

10. Paul Krugman, "Crazy Climate Economics," *New York Times*, May 11, 2014.

11. Indeed, the politics of remembering any history is contested, and I prefer not to digress into the many and extended debates about historiography that concern professional historians. On questions of social memory, see, for instance, the work of the French historian Pierre Nora: Nora, *Realms of Memory*, vols. 2

and 3. Another interesting provocation is about the nature of history as a category of nonfiction. Some scholars argue that everything is fiction. See, for instance, Ryan, "Postmodernism and the Doctrine of Panfictionality."

12. E. P. Thompson, *Beyond the Frontier*, 100.

CHAPTER 1: THE MYSTERIOUS MAJOR FRANK THOMPSON

1. Known affectionately to its fans as TNG. The episode in question was called "Relics."
2. "The Dark Side of German Reunification," Reuters, September 29, 2010.
3. See, for instance, the work of the German writer and journalist Daniela Dahn.

CHAPTER 2: A COMMUNIST BY ANY OTHER NAME . . .

1. Bergen, *War and Genocide*, 54–55.
2. Dyson, "Reflections: Disturbing the Universe—I," 58.
3. Dyson, "Reflections," 60.
4. Dyson, "Reflections," 60.
5. Dyson, "Reflections," 61.
6. Dyson, "Reflections," 61.
7. Dyson, *Disturbing the Universe*, 40–41.
8. Thompson and Thompson, *There Is a Spirit in Europe*; Thompson, *Beyond the Frontier*.
9. For biographical background on E. P. Thompson, see Palmer, *E.P. Thompson*.
10. Thompson, "Socialist Humanism: An Epistle to the Philistines," 105–143.
11. This quote is directly taken from the letters kept in Freeman Dyson's personal files on Frank Thompson.
12. Neiman, *Moral Clarity*.

CHAPTER 3: "I SIMPLY WANT TO FIGHT"

1. Thompson, *Beyond the Frontier*, 50.
2. Thompson, *Beyond the Frontier*, 50.
3. Frank Thompson's interest in Georgi Dimitrov is based on the writing of Simon Kusseff, which I found in the private papers of Freeman Dyson. Kusseff's source for this information was interviews that he conducted with "Frank's friends." "Revised Transcript of a Tribute to Frank Thompson," and "In Memoriam."
4. Dimitrov, *And Yet It Moves!*, 15.
5. Dimitrov, *And Yet It Moves!*, 16–17.
6. Bell, *Bulgarian Communist Party from Blagoev to Zhivkov*, 47.
7. Two excellent studies on the Spanish Civil War are Beever, *Battle for Spain*; and Thomas, *Spanish Civil War*.
8. Thompson and Thompson, *There Is a Spirit in Europe*, 12.
9. Kusseff, "Revised Transcript of a Tribute to Frank Thompson"; and "In Memoriam."

10. Frank Thompson, as quoted by Conradi in *Iris Murdoch: A Life*, 90.

11. Frank Thompson as quoted by Conradi in *Iris Murdoch: A Life*, 93. *State and Revolution* refers to the text by V. I. Lenin.

12. Kusseff, "Revised Transcript of a Tribute to Frank Thompson"; and "In Memoriam."

13. Frank Thompson, as quoted by Conradi in *Iris Murdoch: A Life*, 111.

14. Thompson and Thompson, *There Is a Spirit in Europe*, 37. Okay, I know I should not editorialize in the notes, but (as a consummate Cole Porter fan) I love the idea that Frank believed that one's mind could be "addled" by jazz.

15. Thompson and Thompson, *There Is a Spirit in Europe*, 38.

16. Thompson and Thompson, *There Is a Spirit in Europe*, 85.

17. Thompson and Thompson, *There Is a Spirit in Europe*, 82.

18. Thompson and Thompson, *There Is a Spirit in Europe*, 76.

19. On the unfulfilled relationship between Thompson and Murdoch, see Conradi, *Iris Murdoch: A Life*; and Conradi, *Very English Hero*.

20. Many of the letters between Iris Murdoch and Frank Thompson were published in Conradi, *Iris Murdoch: A Writer at War*.

21. A letter from Iris Murdoch to Frank Thompson dated March 20, 1943, as cited in Conradi, *Iris Murdoch: A Writer at War*, 132.

22. Barker, *British Policy in South-East Europe in the Second World War*.

23. Conradi, *Iris Murdoch: A Life*, 183.

24. Thompson and Thompson, *There Is a Spirit in Europe*, 18.

25. Thompson and Thompson, *There Is a Spirit in Europe*, 170.

CHAPTER 4: THE BROTHERS LAGADINOV

1. Bell, *Bulgarian Communist Party*, 62.

2. In Bulgarian, surnames are often feminized by adding an "a" to the masculine version of the name, for example, Lagadinov becomes Lagadinova, Znepolski becomes Znepolska, Zhivkov becomes Zhivkova, and so forth.

3. For a general reference on the history of the Communist Party in Bulgaria, see Bell, *Bulgarian Communist Party*; and Crampton, *Concise History of Bulgaria*.

4. Bell, *Bulgarian Communist Party*, 35–37; Daskalov, *Debating the Past*, 128–130.

5. Bell, *Bulgarian Communist Party*, 35–37.

6. Much of the material for this section comes from the obituary of Kostadin Lagadinov published on blitz.bg: "Krum Radonov strelyal ot upor sreshtu Kostadin Lagadinov," http://www.blitz.bg/article/27908; and Asiova, "Kostadin Lagadinov," 110–118. I also had the good fortune to make a copy of a full four-hundred-page manuscript which was an oral history of Kostadin Lagadinov, Boris Lagadinov, and Elena Lagadinova titled *S Podvodnitsa kam Varha*. This manuscript was slated to be published in 1990 by the publishing house of the Fatherland Front. Because of the changes in 1989, it never went to press. There are only a few copies of the manuscript remaining.

7. "Krum Radonov strelyal ot upor sreshtu Kostadin Lagadinov."

8. "Krum Radonov strelyal ot upor sreshtu Kostadin Lagadinov."

9. Chary, *History of Bulgaria*, 34–35.

10. For an excellent treatment of Bulgaria's World War II history, see Miller, *Bulgaria during the Second World War*.

11. "Krum Radonov strelyal ot upor sreshtu Kostadin Lagadinov."

12. "Krum Radonov strelyal ot upor sreshtu Kostadin Lagadinov."

CHAPTER 5: A FAILED PETITION

1. The biographical information on Assen Lagadinov was culled from a variety of published sources, including many Bulgarian newspaper clippings published on the anniversaries of his death between 1945 and 2004. There are also some published books from the communist era, but most of these are "historical novels" whose factual basis is difficult to determine. The one useful text was Dzhodzhov, *Asen Lagadinov*. After working my way through the published sources, I relied heavily on oral history interviews with Elena Lagadinova to fill in any gaps or to try to rectify any contradictions.

2. Miller, *Bulgaria during the Second World War*, 93–106.

3. Chary, *History of Bulgaria*, 105–109.

4. On the history of the Bulgarian Jews, see Todorov, *Fragility of Goodness*; Chary, *Bulgarian Jews and the Final Solution*; Miller, *Bulgaria during the Second World War*, 93–106; and Avramov and Danova, *Deportiraneto na Evrite ot Vardarska Makedoniya*.

5. Miller, *Bulgaria during the Second World War*.

6. Tsanev, *Bulgarski Hronikli*, 552.

7. Miller, *Bulgaria during the Second World*; Vasilev, *Istoriya na Antifashistikata Borba v Bulgaria*.

8. Brunnbauer, "Making Bulgarians Socialist," 44.

9. Transki, *Grateful Bulgaria*, 39. Here there is a translator's note that defines *yatak* as "a person who provides shelter and any other kind of assistance to the partisans and other members of the underground resistance, himself living as a 'peaceable' citizen at home, a helper."

10. Personal communication with the British historian Richard Crampton in New York City in February 2012. Crampton is the author of the book *A Concise History of Bulgaria*.

11. Avramov and Danova, *Deportiraneto na Evrite ot Vardarska Makedoniya*. Also see Daskalov, *Debating the Past*, 183.

12. For an account of World War II in Bulgaria from the perspective of a Jewish partisan fighter, see Wagenstein, *Predi Kraya na Sveta*.

13. Chary, *History of Bulgaria*, 100–101.

14. Daskalov, *Debating the Past*, 162.

15. Miller, *Bulgaria during the Second World War*, 117–118.

16. Chary, *Bulgarian Jews*, 139.

17. Todorov, *Fragility of Goodness*, 84–85.

18. Miller, *Bulgaria during the Second World War*, 195–203.

19. Bell, *Bulgarian Communist Party*, 68–69.

20. Todorov, *Fragility of Goodness*, 104–105.

21. Todorov, *Fragility of Goodness*, 108–111.

22. Conradi, *Very English Hero*, 370. See also Vasilev, *Vaorazhenata saportiva*, 606–633.

23. Inglis, *Cruel Peace*, 24–27.

24. Transki, *Grateful Bulgaria*, 61.

25. Ogden, *Through Hitler's Back Door*, 151–176.

CHAPTER 6: LAWRENCE OF BULGARIA?

1. See, for instance, Gigova, "Sofia Was Bombed?"; and Gigova, "The City and the Nation."

2. Transki, *Grateful Bulgaria*, 63.

3. Ogden, *Through Hitler's Back Door*, 151–176.

4. As quoted in Transki, *Grateful Bulgaria*, 63.

5. As quoted in Transki, *Grateful Bulgaria*, 63.

6. As quoted in Transki, *Grateful Bulgaria*, 64.

7. E. P. Thompson, *Beyond the Frontier*, 101.

8. Much of the material for this account comes from the chapter "The Short and Happy Life of Frank Thompson," in Fred Inglis's book *Cruel Peace*. For specific military details, I have used Alan Ogden's accounts of the Mulligatawny and Claridges missions in his book *Through Hitler's Back Door*.

9. Inglis, *Cruel Peace*, 19–20.

10. Ogden, *Through Hitler's Back Door*, 157–164.

11. Thompson, *Beyond the Frontier*, 89–94.

12. Barker, *British Policy in South-East Europe in the Second World War*, 148–172.

13. Groueff, *Crown of Thorns*, 362–384. Michael Bar-Zohar's book *Beyond Hitler's Grasp* is also an important chronicle, giving Boris III credit for his refusal to deport about 50,000 Bulgarian Jews. The book largely ignores, however, the 11,459 who were deported from Macedonia and Thrace.

14. Hindley, *Royal Families of Europe*, 156.

15. Thompson and Thompson, *There Is a Spirit in Europe*, 183–187.

16. Thompson and Thompson, *There Is a Spirit in Europe*, 177.

17. Vukmanović, *Struggle for the Balkans*, 315.

18. Vukmanović, *Struggle for the Balkans*, 316–319.

19. Conradi, *Iris Murdoch: Writer at War*, 162.

20. Thompson and Thompson, *There Is a Spirit in Europe*, 179.

21. Thompson and Thompson, *There Is a Spirit in Europe*, 186.

22. Thompson and Thompson, *There Is a Spirit in Europe*, 178.

23. Thompson and Thompson, *There Is a Spirit in Europe*, 190.

24. Johnson, *Agents Extraordinary*, 121–124.

25. Conradi, *A Very English Hero*, 311–313.

26. Thompson and Thompson, *There Is a Spirit in Europe*, 183–187.

27. Transki, *Grateful Bulgaria*, 65.

CHAPTER 7: AMBUSHED IN BATULIYA

1. The book was published in Bulgarian and then translated into English by Bulgaria's foreign language press. I am reproducing their translation for this quote.

2. Transki, *Grateful Bulgaria*, 56–59.

CHAPTER 8: GUERRILLAS IN THE MIST

1. These figures come from Daskalov, *Debating the Past*, 193. Also see Miller, *Bulgaria during the Second World War*, 203; and Chary, *History of Bulgaria*, 100–105.

2. See Ogden, *Through Hitler's Back Door*, 187.

3. Ogden, *Through Hitler's Back Door*, 180–181.

4. Miller, *Bulgaria during the Second World War*, 195.

5. Barker, *British Policy in South-East Europe in the Second World War*, 266–268.

6. Norman Davies, writing on March 4, 1946, in SOE HISTORY 68, "Review of SOE Activities in Bulgaria, 1939–45," National Archives HS 7/103, as cited in Conradi, *Very English Hero*, 394.

7. Thompson and Thompson, *There Is a Spirit in Europe*, 176.

8. See, for instance, Znepolski, *Totalitarizmite na XX Vek v Sravnitelna Perspektiva*.

9. For a great study of the partisans of Europe more broadly, see Macksey, *Partisans of Europe*. See also the discussion in Daskalov, *Debating the Past*, 209.

10. Hemingway, *For Whom the Bell Tolls*, 254–255.

11. In March 2013, Elena Lagadinova, the younger sister of the Lagadinov brothers, found this document among the papers in her personal archives and gave it to me along with other papers about the lives of her brothers. The entire document (or at least that which was legible) was first translated into English by my Bulgarian research assistant, Mira Nikolova. After that, I reviewed the translation and put together excerpts of the document, editing heavily for clarity and coherence.

CHAPTER 9: EVERYDAY LIFE AS A PARTISAN

1. "Bai" is a Bulgarian familiar term for an older, respected man to whom one is not related. Senior partisans were often referred to as "Bai Kole" or "Bai Dine," where the Bai is added to a diminutive of the first name.

2. This was a colloquial term for the gendarmerie.

3. Karakachans are an ethnic minority group in Bulgaria and Greece.

4. This is presumably because it was destined as supplies for the Bulgarian and/or German armies.

CHAPTER 10: BLOOD OF A POET

1. Ogden, *Through Hitler's Back Door*, 176–181.
2. I owe much of what I reconstruct here to the account produced by Stowers Johnson, *Agents Extraordinary*, 155–162. His book was apparently researched by doing interviews with Kenneth Scott, who survived the war. Although E. P. Thompson had a lot of issues with the way that Johnson portrayed his brother, subsequent scholars such as Ogden and Kiril Yanev have relied heavily on Johnson's book.
3. Johnson, *Agents Extraordinary*, 155–162.
4. Transki, *Grateful Bulgaria*, 68.
5. Transki, *Grateful Bulgaria*, 65–66.
6. Conradi, *Very English Hero*, 340.
7. Znepolska, *Da Se Znae*, 238–241.
8. Znepolska, *Da Se Znae*, 240–241.
9. Conradi, *Very English Hero*, 369 (footnote).
10. Yanev, *Chovekat ot Legendata*.
11. Yanev, *Chovekat ot Legendata*, 169–170.
12. Conradi, *Very English Hero*, 4.
13. Conradi, *Very English Hero*, 4.

CHAPTER 11: THE HEAD HUNTED

1. This history comes primarily from the author's oral history interviews with Elena Lagadinova in the summer of 2012.
2. For detailed information on the activities of the Parapunov Brigade, see Radonov, *Po Stapkite*; and Madolev, *Parapunovtsi*.
3. Radonov, *Po Stapkite*, 25–29; Vasilev, *Istoriya na Antifashistkata Borba v Bulgaria*, 187–188; Dzhodhov, *Asen Lagadinov*, 48–51.
4. There are various versions of this final scene. See, for instance, Radonov, *Po Stapkite*, 25–29; and Dzhodhov, *Asen Lagadinov*, 48–51. I have based the following account on the oral history of Elena Lagadinova. She told me the story once in her apartment in Sofia, and then a second time in the summer of 2013 when we traveled to Assen Lagadinov's grave on the outskirts of Razlog. His grave is on the spot where he was killed, so I was actually able to see the topography of the area where this final event took place.

CHAPTER 12: WORDS OF ONE BROTHER ON THE DEATH OF ANOTHER

1. Thompson and Thompson, *There Is a Spirit in Europe*, 190–191.
2. Thompson and Thompson, *There Is a Spirit in Europe*, 190–191.

CHAPTER 13: THE RETIRED PARTISAN

1. This chapter and the one that follows are based on multiple interviews that I conducted with Elena Lagadinova between 2010 and 2013. For stylistic reasons, these are composite chapters taking information from different interviews and rendering them as one long interview. I have also supplemented these interviews with information from Elena Lagadinova's personal archives and from the archives of the Committee of the Bulgarian Women's Movement in the Central State Archives (Fond 417).

2. Miller, *Bulgaria during the Second World War*, 208–215.

3. For Elena Lagadinova. Georgi Dimitrov was clearly considered a great hero and statesman, but many Bulgarians would not agree with her. As head of the Comintern, Dimitrov had very close ties with Stalin, and some believe him complicit in Stalin's many crimes. For further insight into the career of Georgi Dimitrov, see his diaries and selections of his letters to Stalin, both of which have been published by Yale University Press. Dimitrov, *Diary of Georgi Dimitrov*; and Dallin and Firsov, *Dimitrov and Stalin*.

4. For more on the life of Todor Zhivkov, see his memoir, *Memoari*.

5. Daskalov, *Debating the Past*, 198–199.

6. Author's interview with Elena Lagadinova, July 2012.

CHAPTER 14: A WOMAN'S WORK IS NEVER DONE

1. This chapter is also based on multiple interviews that I conducted with Elena Lagadinova between 2010 and 2013. For stylistic reasons, this is a composite chapter taking information from different interviews and rendering them as one long interview. I have also supplemented these interviews with information from Elena Lagadinova's personal archives and from the archives of the Committee of the Bulgarian Women's Movement in the Central State Archives (Fond 417).

2. "Zhivkov's Great Society."

3. The law for total equality of rights between the sexes in Bulgaria was among the first enacted laws of the new parliament in 1944 (Act of Equality of Rights between Sexes, decree no. 30 of October 12, 1944).

4. United Nations, *World's Women*, 101, table 7.

5. Lyutiv and Gocheva, Zhenata—*Maika*.

6. Bordrova and Anker, *Working Women in Socialist Countries*.

7. On reproductive politics in communist Romania, see Kligman, *Politics of Duplicity*.

8. I was able to obtain a copy of this survey from Lagadinova's personal archive. "Anketna Karta—Sotsiologichesko Izsledvane: Zhenata v Proizvodstvoto, Ocshtestveniya Zhivot I Semeistvoto."

9. "Madame Elena Lagadinova," in Brilliant, *Women in Power*, 86–88.

10. "Za Izdigane Rolyata na Zhenata v Izgrazhdaneto na Razvitoto Sostialictichesko Obshtestvo, Reshenie na Politbyuro na TsK na BKP ot 6 Mart 1973 G." Sofia: Partizdat, 1977.

11. The historical material on the Committee of the Bulgarian Women's Movement comes from collection no. 417 in the Central State Archives in Sofia, Bulgaria. For these sources, I use the standard form of Bulgarian citation, for example, *Tsentralen Darzhaven Arhiv* TsDa-F417–05-ae96 where F = *fond* (the archival collection), O = *opis* (a subunit within the main collection), and AE = *arkivna edinitsa* (an individual folder). For sources from the personal archives of Elena Lagadinova, I use the abbreviation "PAOEL."

12. Ghodsee, "Rethinking State Socialist Mass Women's Organizations."

13. TsDa-F417–05-ae-347: 1–5.

14. TsDa-F417–06-ae-306: 1–8; United Nations, *Yearbook*.

15. Lipman-Blumen, *Connective Leadership*, 299. See also "Madame Elena Lagadinova," in Brilliant, *Women in Power*, 77.

16. "Razvitie na Supermarketite i Hipermarketite vav Frantsiya," Nauka—Tehnika—Ikonomika: Barza Informatsia, No. 76.23.11, PAOEL.

17. People's Republic of Bulgaria, *Family Code*.

18. Chirov, *Nomenklatura*.

19. On the situation of Bulgarian Turks in the late 1980s, see Baeva and Kalinova, *Vazroditelniyat Protses*; Lipman-Blumen, *Connective Leadership*, 301.

20. Dinkova, "Strasti po Velikata Zhenska Revolyutsiya," *Vesni* 13, no. 5 (2003): 27–30.

CHAPTER 15: HISTORY IS WRITTEN BY THE VICTORS

1. An excellent study of the politics of writing history and the contested nature of archival authority can be found in Blouin and Rosenberg, *Processing the Past*.

2. All of the names in this essay have been replaced with pseudonyms as per the ethical guidelines of the American Anthropological Association.

3. Bell, *Bulgarian Communist Party*, chapters 5, 6, and 7.

4. Dallin and Firsov, *Dimitrov and Stalin*, 260–261.

5. Vukmanović, *Struggle for the Balkans*, 296–298.

6. "Bravest Democrat of All, by Dr. Georgi Dimitrov as Told to David Martin," *Saturday Evening Post* 220, no. 23 (December 6, 1947): 28–32.

7. Bell, *Bulgarian Communist Party*, 103–106.

8. Bell, *Bulgarian Communist Party*, 114–117.

9. Bell, *Bulgarian Communist Party*, 115.

10. Bell, *Bulgarian Communist Party*, 107–109.

11. "EC: Poverty Level in Bulgaria Is Alarming," March 26, 2013, www.novinite.com.

12. My previous books were *Lost in Transition*, *Muslim Lives in Eastern Europe*, and *Red Riviera*.

13. Most of the research I conducted was at the Central State Archives in Sofia on

5 Moskovska Street. I was working in Fond 417, the archival collection of the Committee of the Bulgarian Women's Movement.

CHAPTER 16: ON CENSORSHIP AND THE SECRET POLICE

1. I have changed the name here to protect the identity of my interviewee (who is not a well-known historical or public figure) as per the guidelines of the ethical code of the American Anthropological Association.

CHAPTER 18: CASSANDRA'S CURSE

1. *Public Finance Balance of Smoking in the Czech Republic*, University of South Carolina, Health Services and Policy Management website, http://hspm.sph.sc .edu/courses/Econ/Classes/cbacea/czechsmokingcost.html.
2. Sarah Boseley and Kate Connolly, "Smoking Can Seriously Aid Your Economy," July 16, 2011, www.theguardian.com.

CHAPTER 19: THE RED SAMARITAN

1. Danforth and Van Boeschoten, *Children of the Greek Civil War*.
2. *Natsionalna Konferentsiya na Balgarskite Zheni* (23 i 24 Septemvri 1968–Sofiya). Sofia: Izdatelstvo na Otechestveniya Front, 1968; *Vtora Natsionalna Konferentsiya na Balgarskite Zheni* (14–14 XIII 1973—Sofiya). Sofia: Izdatelstvo na Otechestveniya Front, 1975; *Treta Natsionalna Konferentsiya na Dvizhenieto na Balgarskite Zheni* (11–12 Mai, 1979). Sofia: Izdatelstvo na Otechestveniya Front, 1979; and "Chetvarta Natsionalna Konferentsiya na Dvizhenieto na Balgarskite Zheni (20 Oktomvri 1988)," *Byuletin na Komiteta na Balgarskite Zheni*, 10–1988.
3. Ghodsee, *Red Riviera*.
4. For a two good studies on post-socialist Bulgarian politics, see Giatzidis, *Introduction to Postcommunist Bulgaria*; and Ganev, *Preying on the State*.
5. Istridis, *Social Justice and the Welfare State in Central and Eastern Europe*, 93.

CHAPTER 20: THE PAST IS A FOREIGN COUNTRY

1. Znepolska, *Da Se Znae*.
2. Znepolska, *Dencho Znepolski*.

CONCLUSION: ON THE OUTSKIRTS OF LITAKOVO

1. For a commentary on the summer protests, see "Bulgaria: Birth of a Civil Society," *Economist*, September 21, 2013, www.economist.com.
2. This is a quote from a poem by Nikola Vapstarov called "History."
3. For a great study of how American feminist scholarship was also manipulated by Cold War rivalries, see Coogan-Gehr, *Geopolitics of the Cold War*.
4. Groueff, *Crown of Thorns*, 386–387.
5. "Bulgaria Honours Memory of Victims of Communism," *Sofia Globe*, February 1, 2013, http://sofiaglobe.com.

6. Associated Press, "Bulgaria Honors Victims of Communism," http://bigstory.ap
   .org/article/bulgaria-honors-victims-communism, February 1, 2013.

7. See for instance, "Bulgaria Honors Victims of Communism, Boston.com, February 1, 2013, and "Bulgaria Honors Victims of Communism, KyivPost.com,
   February 1, 2013.

8. Http://www.apnewsarchive.com/1999/Bulgarian-Monument-Unveiled/id-8880
   26bba4df4e583c6d7df8790a4164.

9. The original website page was http://arcsofia.org/en/page/38-Victims-of
   -Communism-Project. This page was removed by ARCS, but I have archived it
   on my personal website at http://scholar.harvard.edu/kristenghodsee/galleries
   /bulgarian-victims-communism-website.

10. Just as this book was about to go to press, and perhaps in response to a critical
    article called "Blackwashing History" that I published in *Anthropology News* on
    February 22, 2013 (www.anthropology-news.org), the original text on the website was removed, and the website was renamed, although it kept the same url:
    www.victimsofcommunism.bg. Thankfully, I had screen shots of all texts and
    the names of the Bulgarian leaders responsible for many atrocities during World
    War II. These can be found in a media gallery on my personal website: http://
    scholar.harvard.edu/kristenghodsee/galleries/bulgarian-victims-communism-
    website.

11. "Bulgaria Honours Memory of Victims of Communism," *Sofia Globe*, February 1, 2013, http://sofiaglobe.com/.

12. The United States Holocaust Memorial Museum has a collection of Bogdan
    Filov's papers (Fond 456), as well as his diary. Filov, *Dnevnik*. An English translation of Filov's diary can be found in Chary, "Diary of Bogdan Filov."

13. Avramov and Danova, *Deportiraneto na Evrite ot Vardarska Makedoniya*.

14. Chary, *History of Bulgaria*, 121–122.

15. Chary, *Bulgarian Jews and the Final Solution*, 83.

16. Chary, *Bulgarian Jews and the Final Solution*, 212–214.

17. Rees, *Biographical Dictionary*; Chary, *Bulgarian Jews*, 162; Daskalov, *Debating
    the Past*, 196.

18. Gadzhev, *Tom IV, Lushin—Nikoga Veche Komunizm*.

19. Rees, *Biographical Dictionary*, 241–242.

20. Chary, *Bulgarian Jews*, 139.

21. The press release from ENAR can be found online at http://www.enar-eu.org
    /Page_Generale.asp?DocID=15951&la=1&langue=EN. The website of ENAR is:
    www.enar-eu.org. The Lukov March in 2012 drew about a thousand Bulgarians.
    "1000 Take Part in Bulgaria's Controversial Far-Right March," *Novinite*, February 18, 2012, www.novinite.com.

22. "Declaration of the European Parliament on the Proclamation of 23 August as
    European Day of Remembrance for Victims of Stalinism and Nazism." Website
    of the European Parliament, (http://www.europarl.europa.eu/), September 23,

2008. Full text available online at http://www.europarl.europa.eu/sides/getDoc .do?reference=P6_TA(2008)0439&language=EN.

23. This text is taken from the "Museum Overview" of the Global Museum on Communism website. Available online at http://www.globalmuseumoncommunism .org/museum_overview.

24. Giles Tremlett, "Spanish Civil War Monument Must Be Pulled Down, Court Rules," *Guardian*, June 5, 2013, theguardian.com.

"Za Izdigane Rolyata na Zhenata v Izgrazhdaneto na Razvitoto Sostialictichesko Obshtestvo, Reshenie na Politbyuro na TsK na BKP ot 6 Mart 1973 G." Sofia: Partizdat, 1977.

"Zhivkov's Great Society," September 23, 1968. HU OSA 300–8-3–730; Records of Radio Free Europe/Radio Liberty Research Institute: Publications Department: Background Reports; Open Society Archives at Central European University, Budapest.

Abadjieva, Nevena. "Elena Lagadinova." *Bulgarian Woman* (1970): 18–19.

Andonov, Vladimir. *Bulgaria in the War against Nazi Germany.* Sofia: Sofia Press, 1988.

Andreev, Veselin Georgiev. *Guerrilla Stories and Poems.* Sofia: Sofia Press, 1969.

Asiova, Boyka. Da Ubiesh Stalin: Spomeni ot Kostadin Lagadinov. Sofia: Janet-45, 2014.

Asiova, Boyka. "Kostadin Lagadinov: Chovekat, koita dokaza, che komunist ne e mrasna duma." *Biograf* no. 23 (July 2013): 110–118.

Auty, Phyllis, and Richard Clogg. *British Policy towards Wartime Resistance in Yugoslavia and Greece.* London: Macmillan, 1975.

Avramov, Rumen, and Nadya Danova. *Deportiraneto na Evrite ot Vardarska Makedoniya, Belomorska Trakiya i Pirot, Mart 1943, Tom I-II (Komplekt).* Sofia: Obedineni Izdateli, 2013.

Baeva, Iskra, and Evgeniya Kalinova. *Vazroditelniyat Protses: Balgarskata Darzhava i Balgarskite Turtsi.* Sofia: Ciela, 2009.

Baeva, Iska, and Plamen Mitev. *Predizvikatelstvata na promyanata.* Sofia: Univeritetsko Izdatelstvo "Sv. Kliment Ohridski," 2006.

Barker, Elisabeth. *British Policy in South-East Europe in the Second World War.* London: Macmillan, 1976.

Bar-Zohar, Michael. *Beyond Hitler's Grasp: The Heroic Rescue of Bulgaria's Jews.* Avon, MA: Adams Media, 1998.

Basmadzhieva, Magdalena. "Te zaginakha za pobedata na velikoto komunisti-chekp dela: Prouchvane, klasov i partien analiz na zaginalite bortsi protiv fa-shizma 1923–1944 g." In *Pobeda 1941–1944.* Sofia: Godishnik na muzeya na revolyutsionoto dvizhenie v Bulgariya, 1969.

Beever, Anthony. *The Battle for Spain: The Spanish Civil War, 1936–1939.* London: Penguin, 2006.

Bell, John D. *The Bulgarian Communist Party from Blagoev to Zhivkov.* Stanford, CA: Hoover Institution Press, 1985.

Blouin, Francis, and William Rosenberg. *Processing the Past: Contesting Authority in History and the Archives.* Oxford: Oxford University Press, 2011.

Bonev, Vladimir. *For a United, Popular Fatherland Front.* Sofia: Sofia Press, 1975.

Bordrova, Valentina, and Richard Anker, eds. *Working Women in Socialist Countries: The Fertility Connection.* Geneva: The International Labour Office, 1985.

Brilliant, Fredda. *Women in Power.* Delhi: Lancer, 1991.

Brunnbauer, Ulf. "Making Bulgarians Socialist: The Fatherland Front in Communist Bulgaria, 1944–1989." *East European Politics & Societies* 22, no. 1 (Winter 2008): 44–79.

Bundzhulov, Andrei. "Bitkata za minoloto." In *Litsa na Vremeto.* Vol. 1. Sofia: Tzentar za Istoricheski i Politigicheski izsledvaniya, 1996.

Central Committee of the Bulgarian Communist Party, Political Bureau. *Enhancing the Role of Women in the Building of a Developed Socialist Society: Decision of the Politburo of the Central Committee of the Bulgarian Communist Party of March 6, 1973.* Sofia: Sofia Press, 1973.

Cervantes, Miguel de. *Don Quixote.* Trans. Samuel Putman. New York: Viking, 1949.

Chary, Frederick B. *The Bulgarian Jews and the Final Solution 1940–1944.* Pittsburgh, PA: University of Pittsburgh Press, 1972.

Chary, Frederick B. "The Diary of Bogdan Filov." *Southeastern Europe* 1, no. 1 (1974): 46–71.

Chary, Frederick B. *The History of Bulgaria.* Santa Barbara, CA: Greenwood Press, 2011.

Chirov, Aleksandar. *Nomenklatura, Demokraturata i Prehoda.* Sofia: Ciela: 2009.

Conradi, Peter. *Iris Murdoch: A Life.* New York: W.W. Norton, 2010.

Conradi, Peter. *Iris Murdoch—A Writer at War: Letters and Diaries 1938–46.* London: Short Books, 2010.

Conradi, Peter. *A Very English Hero: The Making of Frank Thompson.* London: Bloomsbury, 2012.

Coogan-Gehr, Kelly. *The Geopolitics of the Cold War and Narratives of Inclusion: Excavating a Feminist Archive.* New York: Palgrave Macmillan, 2011.

Crampton, Richard. *A Concise History of Bulgaria.* Cambridge: Cambridge University Press, 2006.

Dallin, Alexander, and F. I. Firsov. *Dimitrov and Stalin 1934–1943: Letters from the Soviet Archives*. New Haven, CT: Yale University Press, 2000.

Danforth, Loring M., and Riki Van Boeschoten. *Children of the Greek Civil War: Refugees and the Politics of Memory*. Chicago: University of Chicago Press, 2011.

Daskalov, Roumen. *Debating the Past—Modern Bulgarian History: From Stambolov to Zhivkov*. Budapest: Central European University Press, 2011.

Dean, Jodi. *The Communist Horizon*. New York: Verso, 2012.

Dimitrov, Georgi. *The Diary of Georgi Dimitrov, 1933–1949* (Introduced and edited by Ivo Banac; German part translated by Jane T. Hedges, Russian by Timothy D. Sergay, and Bulgarian by Irina Faion). New Haven, CT: Yale University Press, 2012.

Dimitrov, Georgi. *And Yet It Moves! Concluding Speech before the Leipzig Trial*. Sofia: Sofia Press, 1982.

Dimitrov, Georgi. *Georgi Dimitrov: Selected Works*. Vol. 3. Sofia: Sofia Press, 1972.

Dimitrov, Ilcho. *Mezhdu Munchen i Potsdam: Bulgarskata Politika prez Vtorata Svetovna Voina (Istoricheski Ochertsi)*. Sofia: Univerzitetsko Izdatelstvo "Sv. Kliment Ohridski," 1998.

Dinkova, Maria. "Strasti po Velikata Zhenska Revolyutsiya." *Vesni* 13, no. 5 (2003): 23–37.

Dinkova, Maria. "Strasti po Velikata Zhenska Revolyutsiya." *Vesni* 13, no. 6–7 (2003): 23–46.

Dinkova, Maria. "Strasti po Velikata Zhenska Revolyutsiya." *Vesni* 18, no. 6 (2008): 33–62.

Dyson, Freeman. *Disturbing the Universe*. New York: Basic Books, 1981.

Dyson, Freeman. "Reflections: Disturbing the Universe—I." *New Yorker*, August 6, 1979, 37–63.

Dzhodzhov, Georgi. *Asen Lagadinov: Biografichen Ocherk*. Sofia: Izdatelstvo na BKP, 1955.

Filov, Bogdan. *Dnevnik*. Ed. Ilcho Dimitrov. Sofia: Izdatelstvo na Otechestveniya Front, 1990.

Gadzhev, Ivan. *Tom IV, Lushin—Nikoga Veche Komunizm*. Sofia: IIBE Ilya Gadzhev, 2005.

Ganev, Venelin. *Preying on the State: The Transformation of Bulgaria after 1989*. Ithaca, NY: Cornell University Press, 2013.

Georgieff, Anthony. "Kristen Ghodsee: Manufacturing Mass Distraction and Conspiracy Theories." *Vagabond Magazine* 87–88 (December 2013/January 2014).

Ghodsee, Kristen. "Bulgarian Protestors Take Down Their Government." *Anthropology News*, March 15, 2013.

Ghodsee, Kristen. "Bulgarians Take to the Streets." *Anthropology News*, February 25, 2013.

Ghodsee, Kristen. *Lost in Transition: Ethnographies of Everyday Life after Communism*. Durham: Duke University Press, 2011.

Ghodsee, Kristen. *Muslim Lives in Eastern Europe: Gender, Ethnicity and the Transformation of Islam in Postsocialist Bulgaria*. Princeton, NJ: Princeton University Press, 2009.

Ghodsee, Kristen. *The Red Riviera: Gender, Tourism and Postsocialism on the Black Sea*. Durham: Duke University Press, 2005.

Ghodsee, Kristen. "Rethinking State Socialist Mass Women's Organizations: The Committee of the Bulgarian Women's Movement and the United Nations Decade for Women, 1975–1985." *Journal of Women's History* 24, no. 4 (Winter 2012): 49–73.

Giatzidis, Emile. *An Introduction to Postcommunist Bulgaria: Political, Economic and Social Transformation*. Manchester, UK: Manchester University Press, 2002.

Gigova, Irina. "The City and the Nation: Sofia's Trajectory from Glory to Rubble in WWII." *Journal of Urban History* 37, no. 2 (March 2011): 155–175.

Gigova, Irina. "Was Sofia Bombed? Bulgaria's Forgotten War with the Allies." *History and Memory* 23, no. 2 (Fall/Winter 2011): 132–171.

Groueff, Stephane. *Crown of Thorns: The Reign of King Boris III of Bulgaria, 1918–1943*. New York: Madison Books, 1998.

Gruev, Mihail, and Aleksei Kalionski. *Vazroditelniyat Protses: Myusyulmanskite Obshtesti i Komynisticheskiyat Rezhim*. Sofia: Ceila, 2009.

Gyorova, Stanka, and Slavcho Transki. *Frank Thompson*. Sofia: Voenno Isdatelstvo, 1980.

Hemingway, Ernest. *For Whom the Bell Tolls*. New York: Charles Scribner's Sons, 1940.

Hindley, Geoffrey. *Royal Families of Europe*. London: Lyric Books, 1979.

Ilieva, Nikolina. *The Bulgarian Woman*. Sofia: Sofia Press, 1970.

Inglis, Fred. *Cruel Peace: Everyday Life and the Cold War*. New York: Basic Books, 2003.

Istridis, Demetrius, ed. *Social Justice and the Welfare State in Central and Eastern Europe: The Impact of Privatization*. Westport, CT: Praeger, 2000.

Jancar, Barbara Wolfe. *Women under Communism*. Baltimore: Johns Hopkins University Press, 1978.

Johnson, Stowers. *Agents Extraordinary*. London: Robert Hale, 1975.

Kligman, Gail. *The Politics of Duplicity*. Berkeley: University of California Press, 1998.

Kosashki, Ninko K. *Bulgaria and the War against Nazi Germany*. Sofia: Sofia Press, 1985.

Kusseff, Simon. "In Memoriam: Given at the Jubilee Room of the House of Commons on Thursday, May 18, 1995." Unpublished manuscript from the personal archives of Freeman Dyson, 1995.

Kusseff, Simon. "Revised Transcript of a Tribute to Frank Thompson." Unpublished manuscript from the personal archives of Freeman Dyson, 1995.

Lagadinov, Boris, Kostadin Lagadinov, and Elena Lagadinova. *S Podvodnitsa kam*

Varha. Unpublished manuscript from the personal archives of Elena Lagadi-nova, 1990.

Lipman-Blumen, Jean. *The Connective Edge: Leading in an Interdependent World*. New York: John Wiley and Sons, 1996.

Lyutiv, Atanas, and Rositsa Gocheva. Zhenata—*Maika, Truzhenichka, Obshtestve-michka*. Sofia: Partizdat, 1974.

Macksey, Kenneth. *The Partisans of Europe*. London: Hart-Davis, 1975.

Madolev, Georgi. *Parapunovtsi*. Sofia: Voeno Izdatelstvo, 1980.

Mazower, Mark. *Inside Hitler's Greece: The Experience of Occupation, 1941–1944*. New Haven, CT: Yale University Press, 2001.

Miller, Marshall Lee. *Bulgaria during the Second World War*. Stanford, CA: Stanford University Press, 1975.

Neiman, Susan. *Moral Clarity: A Guide for Grown-Up Idealists*. New York: Harcourt, 2008.

Nora, Pierre. *Realms of Memory: The Construction of the French Past*. Vol. 2, *Traditions*. New York: Columbia University Press, 1997.

Nora, Pierre. *Realms of Memory: The Construction of the French Past*. Vol. 3, *Symbols*. New York: Columbia University Press, 1998.

Ogden, Alan. *Through Hitler's Back Door: SOE Operations in Hungary, Slovakia, Romania and Bulgaria 1939–1945*. London: Pen and Sword, 2010.

Palmer, Bryan D. *E. P. Thompson, Objections and Oppositions*. New York: Verso, 1994.

People's Republic of Bulgaria. *The Family Code: Published in the State Gazette Issue No. 41, May the 28, 1985*. Sofia: Sofia Press, 1986.

Poppetrov, Nikolai. *Fashizmat v Bulgariya: Razvitie i Proyavi*. Sofia: Kama, 2008.

Poppetrov, Nikolai, ed. *Sotsialno nalyavo, natsionalizmat—napred: Programmni I organizatsionni dokumenti na balgarski avtoritarski natsionalicheski formatsii*. Sofia: Gutenberg, 2009.

Rachev, Stoyan. *Anglo-Bulgarian Relations during the Second World War (1939–1944)*. Sofia: Sofia Press, 1981.

Rachev, Stoyan. *The Bulgarians and the Other Balkan Peoples in the Anti-Fascist Struggle, 1939–1945*. Sofia: Sofia Press, 1985.

Radonov, Krum. *Po Stapkite na Otryad "Nikola Parapunov."* Sofia: Meditsina i Fizkultura, 1981.

Rees, Phillip. *Biographical Dictionary of the Extreme Right since 1890*. New York: Simon and Schuster, 1990.

Ross, Hana. "Critique of the Philip Morris Study of the Cost of Smoking in the Czech Republic." *Nicotine and Tobacco Research* 6, no. 1 (2004): 181–189.

Ryan, Marie-Laure. "Postmodernism and the Doctrine of Panfictionality." *Narrative* 5, no. 3 (May 1997).

Seeger, Pete. *Where Have All the Flowers Gone?* Bethlehem, PA: Sing Out! Publications, 1993.

Solzhenitsyn, Aleksandr. *The Gulag Archipelago 1918–1956: An Experiment in Literary Investigation, Parts I–II.* New York: Harper & Row, 1974.

Stoichev, Krastio. *Asen Lagadinov: Biografichen Ocherk.* Sofia: Izdatelstvo na BKP, 1955.

Thomas, Hugh. *The Spanish Civil War.* Rev. ed. New York: Modern Library, 2001.

Thompson, E. P. *Beyond the Frontier — The Politics of a Failed Mission: Bulgaria 1944.* Stanford, CA: Stanford University Press, 1997.

Thompson, E. P. "Socialist Humanism: An Epistle to the Philistines." *New Reasoner*, no. 1 (Summer 1957): 105–143.

Thompson, T. J., and E. P. Thompson. *There Is a Spirit in Europe: A Memoir of Frank Thompson.* London: Victor Gollancz, 1947.

Todorov, Tzvetan. *The Fragility of Goodness: Why Bulgaria's Jews Survived the Holocaust.* Princeton, NJ: Princeton University Press, 2003.

Tourlakova, Eleonora, and Pavlina Popova. *Bulgarian Women.* Sofia: Sofia Press, 1976.

Transki, Slavcho. *From the Tactics of Partisan Warfare in Bulgaria.* Sofia: Sofia Press, 1970.

Transki, Slavcho. *Grateful Bulgaria.* Sofia: Sofia Press, 1979.

Tropolova, Yordanka. *Bulgarian Women: Prospects for Progress.* Sofia: Sofia Press, 1987.

Tsanev, Stefan. *Bulgarski Hronikli: Tom 3.* Sofia, Plovdiv: Trud, 2008.

United Nations. *Yearbook, Volume 391985.* New York: United Nations, 1986.

United Nations. *The World's Women, 1970–1990: Trends and Statistics.* New York: United Nations, 1991.

Vasilev, Kiril, ed. *Istoriya na Antifashistkata Borba v Bulgaria 1939/1944: Tom Vtori* (Mart 1943–9 Septemvri 1944). Sofia: Partizdat, 1976.

Vasilev, Orlin. *Vaorazhenata saportiva 1923–1944.* Sofia: Izdanie na BRP, 1946.

Vidova, Milanka. *Legal Status of Women in Bulgaria: A Selection of Normative Acts with Annotations.* Sofia: Sofia Press, 1981.

Vukmanović, Svetozar. *Struggle for the Balkans.* London: Merlin Press, 1990.

Wagenstein, Angel. *Predi Kraya na Sveta: Draskulki ot Neolita.* Sofia: Kolobri, 2011.

Wiesel, Elie. *The Fifth Son: A Novel.* New York: Random House, 2011.

Woodhouse, C. M., and Richard Clogg. *The Struggle for Greece, 1941–1949.* London: Ivan R. Dee, 2002.

Yanev, Kiril. *Chovekat ot Legendata.* Sofia: Hristo Botev, 2001.

Zherev, Rumen. "Krum Radonov Strelyal ot Upor Sreshtu Kostadin Lagadinov." *Blitz Nad 55*, November 11, 2011. www.blitz.bg/article/27908.

Zhivkov, Todor. *Memoari.* Sofia: Trud i Pravo, 2006.

Znepolska, Maria. *Da Se Zhae.* Sofia: DTM, 2012.

Znepolska, Mariya, ed. *Dencho Znepolski: Posmartna Izpoved.* 4th ed. Sofia: Poligrafski Kombinat "D. Blagoev" OOD, 2005.

Znepolski, Ivailo. *Totalitarizmite na XX Vek v Sravnitelna Perspektiva.* Sofia: Ciela, 2010.

INDEX

Abortion, 114–15, 119, 139

AFFC (Active Fighters against Fascism and Capitalism), 111–12

Agrarian Union, 35

Agrarians, 35, 65

Allied forces, 30–31, 44–45, 102, 108

Allies, the. *See* Allied forces

Amazon, the. *See* Elena Lagadinova

Amazon.com, 96

American Research Center in Sofia (ARCS), 193

American Victims of Communism Memorial Foundation, 199

Anarchists, xv, 26, 35, 65, 205

Anschluss [Annexation], 7

Anti-austerity, xi–xiii

Apartheid (South Africa), 140

Appeasement (Munich Pact), 26

Archives: British, 8, 18–19; Central State, xi–ii, xx, 16, 165, 177, 213n1, 214n11; Ministry of Interior, 86–88; Western researchers and, 131; Women's Committee, 122–23

Arson: by the gendarmerie, 83, 92, 106; by the partisans, 45, 78

Arthur D. Little International, 152

Ataka, xiii, 205n1

Avgarski, Dimitar, 85

Avram, Nako, 73

Axis powers, 31, 43–47, 102

Babiš, Andrej, 206n3

Balkan Federation, 111, 128

Balkan Wars, 34, 39

Bansko, 73

Banya, 80

Barker, Elisabeth, 64

Battle of Moscow, 44

Batuliya, Battle of, 50, 57–61, 84, 90–92, 111, 170

Belchov, Dragomir, 79

Belene (labor camp), 172, 191

Belev, Aleksandar, 196–97

Belitsa Station: action at, 73–74

Beria, Lavrentiy, 191

Billa (supermarket), 168

Bilyov, Penka, 72

Black Army, 46, 72, 91. *See also* Gendarmerie

Blagoevgrad [Gorna Dzhumaya], 70, 74, 76, 82

Bloomberg Hall, 4

Red Army, 22, 53, 65, 71–73, 79–85, 91–93, 108, 128, 197
Red grandmothers, 177
Regional Council (Lovech), 157
Reichstag: burning of, 23
Renaissance man, Freeman Dyson as, 6
Republicans (Spain), 24–26
Ribbentrop, 44
Rila Mountains, 79
Royal Airforce (RAF), 92
Royal Artillery, 28
Russo-Turkish War, 39

Saints Kiril and Methodius, 155–56
Samizdat, 140
Scott, Kenneth, 52, 58, 84–85, 212n2
Seeger, Pete, xvii–xviii
Second Balkan War, 34, 39
Second Front, 31
Second Sofia Brigade, 50–59, 64, 84–85, 90–93, 103, 129, 170
Self-Immolation, xii, 177
September Uprising, 35
Serbia: Bulgarian-occupied, xviii, 18, 29, 32–34, 49–54, 58, 92–94, 170
Sharova, Raina, 85–86
Siberia, 38, 71, 191
Sicilian Landings, 31, 55
Simeon II, 52, 195
Simyoni, Charles, 4
Slaveikov Square, 9
Sliven, 40, 71
Smoking: study of, 152–53
Sobolev, Arkady, 42
Sobolev campaign, 41–43, 69
Social Democrats, xv, 12, 26, 65, 206n3
Socialist humanism, 18, 191
Socialism, 7, 24, 111–14, 121, 127, 161, 165
Solzhenitsyn, Aleksandr, 38
Solidarity (Poland), xii, 6
South Africa, 140–41
Soviet Union, xvi–xviii, 15, 26–31, 37–43, 66, 90, 102–4, 108, 114–15, 128–29, 139, 191

Space Tourism, 4
Spanish Civil War, 24, 190, 199
Special Operations Executive (SOE), 16, 31–33, 49–58, 63, 194
Sredna Gora Mountains, 53, 55
Stalin, Joseph, xvi–xviii, 17–19, 24–26, 31, 38–40, 64–66, 110–11, 128–29, 191, 199, 213n3
Stamboliyski, Aleksander, 35
Staminov, Naku, 88–89
Star Trek, 3, 207n1
Stasi, 140–41
Statistics, unreliability of, 127
Staykov, Marin, 74, 79, 81, 109
Stoyanov, Boris Lukanov, 194–95
Stoyanov, Kocho, 85, 87, 194–95
Stoyanov, Yanko, 85, 87, 194
Student-town (neighborhood), 144
Submarine, the (hideout), 72–73, 80
Suicide, xi, 56, 197
Supply drops (British), xviii, 32, 49–57, 85, 92–93, 146
Syntagma Square, xi
Syria: Frank Thompson in, 21, 28, 30

Tapkanov, Ilya, 194
The Next Generation (TNG), 3, 207n1
Thompson, Edward John (E. J.), 21, 96–97
Thompson, Edward Palmer (E. P.), xx, 7, 16–20, 64–66, 96–97, 191
Thompson, Frank, ix–xx, 3, 9–10, 29–35, 37, 96; in Bulgaria, 49–59, 64–65; childhood, 20–21; and communism, xiv, xix, 11, 129, 132, 136, 191, 199; death of, 84–89; and Dencho Znepolski, 111–12, 169–75; and E. P. Thompson, 17–20, 55, 96–98; and Freeman Dyson, 7–8, 12–16; and General Tempo, 53–54, and Georgi Dimitrov, 24–26; and Iris Murdoch, 27–28, 49, 56, 109, 174; memory of, 187–200; and the Special Operations Executive, 46–48; at Winchester, 22–23
Thrace (Greece), 44, 196, 210n13
Thucydides, 97

Timiryazev Academy (Moscow), 109
Tito, Josip Broz, 31, 53, 111, 128
Titoism, 111
Todorov, Atanas, 192
Topalov, Hristo, 79
Transki, Slavcho, 9–10, 59, 88, 109
Travel restrictions, 117, 138–40, 154, 191
Treaty of Berlin, 39
Treaty of San Stefano, 39
Treblinka, 47, 195
Tripartite Pact, 43
Tsar Osvoboditel Street, 165
Tsrna Trava, 33, 49
Tupolev, Andrei, 38

Union of Bulgarian Artists, 157
Union of Bulgarian National Legions. *See* Legionnaires
Union of Democratic Forces (UDF), 162–63
Union of Legionnaires, 45, 197
United Nations Decade for Women, 121
United Nations Institute for Training Women (INSTRAW), 121
United States, xiii, xvii, 4, 11, 121, 146, 148–49, 152, 159, 183–84, 187
United States Holocaust Memorial Museum, 216n12
United States Information Service, 140
USSR, xiv–xvi, 26–31, 37–38, 44, 69–71. *See also* Soviet Union

Vaptsarov, Nikola, 215n2
Victimhood, 20
VictimsofCommunism.bg, 193, 216n3

Vuchov, Georgi, 78
Vukmanović, Svetozar (General Tempo), 53–56

Wagenstein, Angel, 209n12
Warsaw Pact, 132
Wehrmacht, 39, 45
Wellington bombers, 34
Western Desert: Frank Thompson in, 30
Winchester (school), 7, 12–13, 18, 22–23, 26, 31
Woman Today, The, 122
Women's International Democratic Federation (WIDF), 139–41
Women of the Whole World, 139
Worker's Cause, The (newspaper), 47
Worker's Youth Union (WYU), 41
World Conference on Women, 120–21
World Trade Union Congress, 14
World War I, 11, 35, 39, 56, 65

Yanev, Kiril, 87, 212n2
yatak (helper), 45–46, 63, 69, 74–76, 80, 90–94, 209n9
Youth (neighborhood), 144–45, 151
Yugoslavia, xvi, 18, 29, 31, 29, 42–45, 65, 128, 139

Zhekov, Nikola, 197
Zhelyazkov, Todor, 80
Zhivkov, Todor, 59, 112–16, 120–21, 129
Znepolska, Maria, 87, 169–74, 191, 208n2
Znepolski, Dencho, 29, 50, 55–56, 86, 92, 96, 109, 129, 170–72, 208n2